St. Louis Community College

Forest Park
Florissant Valley
Meramec

Instructional Resources
St. Louis, Missouri

The Palestinian Hamas

The Palestinian Hamas

Vision, Violence, and Coexistence

Shaul Mishal and Avraham Sela

COLUMBIA UNIVERSITY PRESS

NEW YORK

Columbia University Press
Publishers Since 1893
New York Chichester, West Sussex

Library of Congress Cataloging-in-Publication Data
Mishal, Shaul, 1945–
    The Palestinian Hamas : vision, violence, and coexistence / Shaul Mishal and
Avraham Sela.
        p.   cm.
    Includes bibliographical references and index.
    ISBN 0-231-11674-8 (cloth : alk. paper)—ISBN 0-231-11675-6 (pbk : alk. paper)
    1. Arab-Israeli conflict—1993- 2. Harakat al-Muqǎwama al-Islǎmiyya. I. Sela,
Avraham. II. Title.

DS119.76 M57 2000
956.05′3—dc21
                                                                    99–047268

∞
Casebound editions of Columbia University Press books are printed on permanent
and durable acid-free paper.
Printed in the United States of America
c 10 9 8 7 6 5 4 3 2 1
p 10 9 8 7 6 5 4 3 2 1

CONTENTS

Hamas is a movement identified with Islamic fundamentalism and murderous suicide bombings. At the top of its agenda are liberating Palestine through a holy war against Israel, establishing an Islamic state on its soil, and reforming society in the spirit of true Islam. It is this Islamic vision, combined with its nationalist claims and militancy toward Israel, that accounts for the prevailing image of Hamas as an ideologically intransigent and politically rigid movement, ready to pursue its goals at any cost, with no limits or constraints. Islamic and national zeal, bitter opposition to the Israeli-Palestinian peace process, and strategies of terror and violence against Israel have become the movement's hallmark.

A close scrutiny of Hamas's roots and its record since its establishment at the outbreak of the Palestinian uprising (Intifada) in December 1987, however, reveals that contrary to this description, it is essentially a social movement. As such, Hamas has directed its energies and resources primarily toward providing services to the community, especially responding to its immediate hardships and concerns. As a religious movement involved in a wide range of social activities, Hamas is deeply rooted in the Palestinian society in the West Bank and Gaza Strip and thus is aware of the society's anxieties, sharing its concerns, expressing its aspirations, and tending to its needs and difficulties.

Although the common people constitute its main stronghold, Hamas has been able to transcend social fragmentation and class division to ensure its presence in all walks of Palestinian life: among university graduates and the uneducated, merchants and farmers, blue- and white-collar workers, engineers, doctors, and lawyers, young and old, women and men. In its social and political opposition to the Palestinian Liberation Organization (PLO), Hamas also has won the support of some Palestinian Christians.

That Hamas is a religious movement with local roots and social awareness is reflected in its principal activities, which combine social and cultural Islamic values and are implemented through traditional institutions. The movement achieved its strong social presence by providing a wide range of social services competing with those offered by the Israeli administration (until its withdrawal from most of the West Bank and Gaza Strip) or the Palestinian Authority, which tend to be few and often corrupt, if they exist at all. Hamas runs a network of educational institutions such as kindergartens, schools, libraries, youth and sports clubs, and adult-education centers. In addition, like other Muslim Brotherhood associations in neighboring Arab countries, Hamas provides medical services and runs hospitals as well as charity and welfare organizations for the needy. Indeed, the Intifada forced Hamas to direct larger portions of its financial resources for the welfare and support of families whose members had been killed, wounded, or arrested by Israel.

Hamas is not a prisoner of its own dogmas. It does not shut itself behind absolute truths, nor does it subordinate its activities and decisions to the officially held religious doctrine. Rather, Hamas operates in a context of opportunities and constraints, being attentive to the fluctuating needs and desires of the Palestinian population and cognizant of power relations and political feasibility. Hamas is fully acquainted with and adaptable to the political world, driven by primordial sentiments, conflicting interests, and cost-benefit considerations, a world of constant bargaining and power brokering, multiple identities and fluid loyalties—in which victory is never complete and tension is never ending.

Given the hostile environment in which Hamas operates—military confrontation with Israel, political competition with the PLO, and, more recently, shaky coexistence with the Palestinian Authority—the question is not how closely Hamas adheres to its official dogma, but how and to what extent Hamas is able to justify political conduct that sometimes deviates from its declared doctrine without running the risk of discontent or internal dispute among its followers.

Overall, despite external political and military pressures and internal weaknesses and disagreements, Hamas has been able to retain its ideological coherence, political vitality, and organizational unity. Although a relatively young movement entering its second decade of existence, Hamas has become a conspicuous presence in the Israeli-Palestinian arena and maintains a strong social hold in the Palestinian community. It also enjoys increasing support from and broad legitimacy within the Arab and Muslim world. As a movement with institutions closely linked to societal needs and immediate concerns, Hamas has emerged as a political force whose social presence and communal activities cannot be ignored in the foreseeable future.

As long as negotiations between Israel and the Palestinian Authority for a permanent peace settlement are marred by rivalry and disagreement, mistrust and mutual recriminations, Hamas will be able to continue mobilizing wide popular support and to maintain its public image as a standard bearer of Palestinian national values. And as long as Yasir Arafat and the Palestinian Authority fail to translate Israeli-Palestinian peace negotiations into tangible territorial achievements and economic benefits, Hamas will be able to continue playing its role as the guardian of Islam and the champion of authentic Palestinian aspirations.

Hamas itself has adopted the idea of a transitory liberation of Palestine, willing to accept a temporary truce with Israel if it agrees to return to the 1967 borders, including East Jerusalem. Still, in light of the gap between Israel and the Palestinian Authority regarding a territorial settlement, Hamas can project an image of faithfulness to core Palestinian national goals while at the same time radiating a sense of realism. Given its ability to justify controversial political conduct in religious terms, its willingness to exist with internal contradiction and protracted tension in a hostile political environment, and its experience in maneuvering in a context of conflicting relations between hierarchical organizational order and organic structures, we cannot rule out the possibility of a significant shift in Hamas's relations with Israel to the point that what seems ideologically heretical in the present might become inevitable in the future. Although it is doubtful that Hamas will revise its ultimate goal against and its public attitude toward Israel, it may find that it can accept a workable formula of coexistence with Israel in place of armed struggle. After all, it is not unknown for individuals, political groups, and social movements to profess publicly a determination to fight the existing order while at the same time not excluding the possibility of becoming part of it. Under these circumstances, the prose of reality may overcome the poetry of dogmatic ideology.

This book seeks to portray Hamas from both discursive and practical perspectives through the prism of its worldview and to examine its conduct since its inception. It also attempts to survey the ideological trends within the movement; analyze the political considerations shaping Hamas's strategies of action; and evaluate its options in the event of a future settlement between Israel and the nascent Palestinian Authority. Taking a comparative perspective, this study explains why Hamas should be seen as a political movement that is guided by particular social and organizational structures reflecting its leadership, needs, and system of beliefs yet that has behavioral characteristics similar to those of other mainstream Islamic movements in the Middle East.

The Palestinian Hamas discusses the main issues and dilemmas that Hamas has confronted during its existence. The introduction describes the world of contradictions in which Hamas has been caught—between theory and practice, ideology and political reality, rhetoric and decision making, and commitment to its constituency versus its religious militant doctrine. Chapter 1 retraces the roots and initial circumstances that led to the founding of Hamas and the shaping of its religious and political doctrine. Chapter 2 discusses the complex problems marking the encounter of dogmas and politics within the Hamas movement. Chapter 3 focuses on the development of the movement's violent activities and on the structural implications and considerations deriving from their use. Chapter 4 addresses Hamas's relations with the Palestinian mainstream power, describing the clashes and the efforts to conciliate the parties both before and after the creation of the Palestinian Authority in June 1994. Chapter 5 examines the movement's vacillations and calculations with regard to participation in the political process and the bureaucratic apparatuses under the Palestinian Authority, including the elections to the Palestinian Council in early 1996. Finally, chapter 6 analyzes structural aspects of Hamas and prospects for changes in the movement's modes of action and political perceptions.

We have drawn on primary sources, mostly unpublished documents such as flyers, leaflets, and Hamas's internal position papers, as well as material from the Palestinian, Islamic, Arabic, and Israeli press.

This study was made possible by a research grant from the Tami Steinmetz Center for Peace Research and the Faculty of Social Sciences, both at Tel Aviv University. We wish to thank Muhammad Abu Samra, who served as our research assistant, the Truman Institute for the Advancement of Peace at the Hebrew University of Jerusalem, and especially its library staff, for their help in locating the source material in the Arabic and foreign press. We also thank Kenneth Stein for putting at our disposal a valuable collection of relevant data. Finally, good fortune provided us with the help of Ralph Mandel, who edited our initial manuscript; Yonatan Touval, who assisted us during the preparation of the final draft; and Sylvia Weinberg, who bore the burden of typing the manuscript patiently and efficiently.

A strong revisionist outcry concerning national goals and means as well as social and moral rules marked Hamas's burst onto the center stage of Palestinian politics. Hamas, an abbreviation of Harakat al-Muqawama al-Islamiyya (Islamic resistance movement), emerged as an Islamic alternative to the Palestine Liberation Organization (PLO) with the outbreak of the Intifada, the Palestinian uprising against the Israeli occupation. Hamas challenged the PLO's status as the exclusive political force and sole legitimate representative of the Palestinian people and, later on, the Palestinian Authority established in the Gaza Strip. Hamas also opposed the PLO's secular nationalism and political program for Palestinian statehood and national territory, effectively appropriating the original Palestinian national narrative, strategic goals and means, historically identified with the PLO, and placing them in an Islamic context and meaning. By invoking an Islamic-national vision and community activism, Hamas was able to combine religious doctrine with daily concerns.

Viewed in a broad perspective, Hamas is typical of the widespread phenomenon of political Islam in our time, representing an effort by social and political revisionist groups to articulate their grievances and redefine the national agenda accordingly. At the same time, however, Hamas is an exception. In addition to its fundamental commitment to reform Muslim society in accordance with true Islam, Hamas also carries the particular banner of the national liberation of historic Palestine through an armed struggle with Israel and firm opposition to the Israeli-Palestinian peace negotiations. Hamas's agenda thus plays on both the domestic and international stages, a dual act that shapes Hamas's political strategies and conduct. Much of this agenda can be described in terms of an inherent tension between the fulfillment of the Islamic duty of holy war (*jihad*) against Israel and its awareness of the boundaries and constraints of the political and social environment in which it operates.

Hamas's effort to secure a dominant public position by committing itself to promote Palestinian national interests through violence against Israel while at the same time maintaining its Islamic social institutions of education, welfare, and health has led to a predicament. The problem, present since the movement's establishment, was sharply aggravated by the signing of the September 1993 Israel-PLO Oslo accord and the creation of the Palestinian Authority (PA) in Gaza and Jericho in June 1994. Hamas's awareness of its relative weakness compared with Fatah (Yasir Arafat's faction in the PLO) and the need to secure its presence and influence in the Palestinian population, often at the price of competing with the PA, necessitated a more flexible attitude toward a settlement with Israel. Indeed, our study shows that more than a year before the 1993 accord, Hamas had been considering unofficially joining the political process by taking part, as an Islamic party, in the expected elections to Palestinian representative institutions.

By adopting such a strategy, Hamas would run the risk of losing its standing as the normative opposition to the PLO, thus heightening the danger of friction within the movement and opening itself up to manipulation by the PA. Indeed, Hamas's failure to adhere to the dogmatic vision would have produced confusion and uncertainty, whereas its conformity to its stated religious doctrine could strengthen its credibility among followers and adversaries alike. But by taking action that would bring retaliation from Israel, Hamas would risk losing the support of large segments of the Palestinian public seeking an end to social and economic hardship in the Israeli-held territories—as well as in currently PA-administered areas.

How has Hamas coped with these dilemmas? More specifically, has Hamas been able to expand its influence by political means without sacrificing its credibility and unity? How has Hamas's search for space in the political sphere affected its behavior? To what extent has Hamas been able to explain the shift from its dogmatic attitude in the conflict to an innovative approach requiring a deviation from its declared doctrine?

In this study we explore Hamas's political adjustments in its methods of controlled violence, negotiated coexistence, and strategic decision making in regard to the Intifada and the struggle with the PLO, the Oslo accords and the establishment of the PA, the general election to the PA's Legislative Council and the issue of participation in the PA's institutions, and the *jihad* against Israel or a temporary peaceful settlement. Our findings suggest that Hamas's decision-making processes have been markedly balanced, combining realistic considerations with traditional beliefs and arguments, emphasizing visionary goals but also immediate needs. They have demonstrated conformity with formal Hamas doctrine while showing signs of political flexibility. While a final peace settlement with Israel was forbidden, Hamas left open the option of an agreement, provided that it was temporary.[1] And even though Hamas rejected the PLO's right to represent the Palestinian people, it was willing to forge a political coalition "on an agreed program focused on *jihad*."[2]

Moreover, a major principle in Hamas's attitude toward the PLO—and later the PA—has been its persistent call to avoid intra-Palestinian violence and bloodshed. Being aware of its weakness versus the PA's security apparatuses, Hamas used this principle as a powerful argument to justify its resignation to undesirable realities and situations in which the movement's doctrine dictated strict action. Preached from the pulpits of the mosques and in the movement's written propaganda, this principle has helped preserve Hamas's reputation of strictly adhering to its established doctrine while at the same time reinforcing its image as a responsible Palestinian national movement.

Hamas demonstrated its flexibility by differentiating between the short-term objective of a Palestinian state in the West Bank and Gaza and the long-term goal of establishing a Palestinian Islamic state on the territory of Palestine that would replace Israel. Adopting this order of objectives, Hamas effectively subordinated the former to the latter by emphasizing the provisional status of any political settlement with Israel.

By interpreting any political agreement involving the West Bank and Gaza Strip as merely a pause on the historic road of *jihad*, Hamas achieved political flexibility without forsaking its ideological credibility. Having already adopted the principle of a temporary Israeli-Palestinian settlement, Hamas was prepared to acquiesce in the 1993 Oslo process without recognizing Israel; to support the establishment of a Palestinian state in the West Bank, Gaza Strip, and East Jerusalem without ending the state of war or renouncing its ultimate goals; and to consider restraint but not to give up the option of armed struggle. Political activity here and now was thus justified in terms of hereafter. Acceptance of a political settlement in the short run was interpreted as being complementary, not contradictory, to long-term desires.

Hamas and Other Arab Islamic Movements

The all-embracing nature of the Islamic doctrine and its prevalence in the Palestinian and other Arab societies has been reflected in the far-reaching effort of political Islamic groups to impose their values and norms on all spheres of life, from education and the economy to law and social behavior.[3] Islam has been argued as being the sole organic culture existing in the Arab world and the only cultural tradition whose symbols and values substantiate and give meaning to collective action. Accordingly, spokesmen of Arab nationalism or socialism have attempted to incorporate Islamic terms and symbols into their secular doctrines, which might explain the relatively easy shift of public discourse back to Islamism that marked the decline of the secular ideologies since the late 1960s and early 1970s. Indeed, there is broad agreement among students of the Middle East and political Islam that since the late 1980s, the dominant interpreters of the region's cultural symbols have been Islamists.

The return of Islam to the center of international attention has carried a distinctly political overtone, manifested by the appearance of political organizations and movements (labeled in the West as "Islamists") based on Islamic convictions (labeled in the West as "Islamism"). These Islamic movements have been defined as political because they have adopted Islamic symbols and values as a means of popular mobilization and political influence, with the ultimate aim of obtaining access to power. The Islamists' political behavior is not necessarily dictated by Islamic zeal, however, even though their activities and goals are defined and phrased in Islamic terms. Islam does, however, serve as a normative system by which the designers of public opinion and agents of interpretation give meaning to changing social and political realities and redefine goals and means in accordance with time and place.[4] The common goal of these movements is to apply Islamic law (*shari'a*) to all spheres of life and to make it the sole source of legislation by islamizing the society from the bottom up or by gaining, if not seizing, power for the sake of reforming the society "from above."

Much of the West's attention to political Islam has derived from the violence accompanying this religious fervor and the fanaticism marking some Islamic groups and regimes, raising fears of "a clash of civilizations" and "a threat" to Western liberal democratic values and social order. Nonetheless, Iran's Shiʻi revolutionary fervor has remained confined to Shiʻi communities in the Persian Gulf and Lebanon and has gradually diminished since the late 1980s. And since 1989, Sudan has been the only state in the Muslim Sunni world to become dominated by a radical Islamic regime. Nonetheless, the international dimension of the Islamic radical trend has had an important impact on Islamic movements in the Middle East. Veterans of the Afghan resistance against Soviet occupation form the core of armed Islamic groups in Egypt, Algeria, and Yemen, and some of their leading figures have become role models for Islamic groups, including those in Palestine.[5]

In Algeria, the civil war since 1992 between the government and some murderous Islamist groups, and the armed attacks of Islamist groups against tourists, public figures, and Coptic sites and peoples in Egypt underlie these concerns about an Islamist takeover of other states' power, perceived as detrimental to Western economic and security interests. The violent nature of the Islamist wave has also been nurtured by the suicide bombings conducted by the Shiʻi Lebanese Islamist group of Hizballah against the multinational force in Lebanon in 1983 and its continued armed struggle against Israel's military presence in south Lebanon. More recently, the threat of political Islam has been represented by the suicide bombings conducted by Palestinian fundamentalist groups, such as Hamas and Islamic Jihad, against Israeli civilians in an attempt to undermine the Oslo agreement signed by Israel and the PLO in September 1993.

Yet despite the horrifying toll claimed by Islamic violence in Algeria, violence has been relatively marginal in the conduct of mainstream Islamic movements in the Arab world, embodied primarily by the Muslim Brothers since the organization's emergence in the late 1920s. Their activities and interests have focused on religious guidance and education, communal services, and, since the early 1980s, increasingly on political participation. Indeed, the continuous repression of political activity in most Muslim Middle East states has left the Islamic "party" as the only viable option. As these movements grow more popular, they tend to adopt nonviolent, modern strategies, including a willingness to participate in the political process under non-Islamic regimes. These strategies include the founding of political institutions, the participation and takeover of existing public and voluntary associations, and the coalition with non-Islamic parties in elections. The ability of Islamic movements to legitimize such nonconformist strategies, including the principle of political pluralism, has necessitated religious interpretation, facilitated by charismatic leadership, organizational coherence, and strong popular support.

Hamas is not unlike other political and social movements, secular or religious, whose fundamental principles and ultimate goals have been translated into practical decisions and workable objectives. Although political parties and movements tend to adhere to their worldview when in opposition, they often are reluctant to insist on their principles when in power, recognizing the responsibility of governing as well as of economic constraints, legal limitations, and international rules. Furthermore, even in nondemocratic regimes, opposition parties and movements may lean toward a strategy of coexistence with the ruling power, thereby avoiding confrontation that could expand into social upheaval and mass uprising. This inclination and ability to acquiesce in contradictions are characteristic of groups aware of the vulnerability of their vital interests and high potential loss if they adopt strategies of direct confrontation. As a result, the ideological discrepancies and competing beliefs between the national camp and the Islamic element in the Palestinian society might appear to an outsider as a key element that both shapes Palestinian relations internally and dictates Palestinian behavior externally. Yet a careful examination reveals that close-to-home issues—such as family ties, personal acquaintances, interpersonal affiliations, and intragroup rules of conduct, as well as deeply rooted norms, communal customs, and local traditions—are no less significant than normative perceptions and ideological preferences.

A fruitful and constructive investigation, therefore, should not search so much for areas of ideological dispute and normative disagreement but instead should identify strategies that enable individuals, organizations, and movements to successfully handle potential splits and internal contradictions. Rather than assuming fixed boundaries between organizations and groups, our investigation should focus on the dynamic process of negotiation between and within social entities over shifting boundaries shaped by the meaning of political identity and the interpretation of social values. Accordingly, unsettled tension and unresolved contradiction are intrinsic to societies undergoing national cohesion and rapid social change; it is the search for ways to mitigate conflicts and minimize tensions between opposing forces that is critical to their political survival and social well-being. Indeed, a comparative overview of religious movements affiliated with political Islam in Arab countries reveals the extent to which these movements have been reluctant to adhere to their religious dogma at any price and so have tended to adopt political strategies that minimize the danger of rigidly adhering to principle, doctrine, or ideology. And as in Hamas's case, they have moved away from dogmatic positions in a quest for innovative and pliable modes of conduct, the opposite of doctrinaire rigidity, ready to respond or adjust to fluid conditions without losing sight of their ultimate objectives.[6]

True, Islam is a religion that does not separate "mosque" from "state," and the interpretation of Islamic law (*shari'a*) is strictly the domain of the religious scholars (*'ulama'*). In addition to being a system of religious beliefs and decrees, Islam is also a juridical system that determines rules of conduct for both individuals and the community and defines internal relations among Muslims and between Muslims and non-Muslims. Still, there is a difference between laws regarding religious duties and moral codes of individual behavior, for which there is relatively little leeway for interpretation, and the wide spectrum of issues concerning the public and political domains. Here the *shari'a* leaves ample room for interpretation based on historical precedents and equivocal oral traditions that Islamic leaders can use to address current political and social issues.[7] Indeed, the popularity of contemporary Islamic movements has aggravated the problems deriving from the absence of an authoritative religious leadership, for no Muslim scholar is considered an absolute authority, particularly on public affairs. "Every Muslim who is capable and qualified to give a sound opinion on matters of Islamic law, is entitled to interpret the law of God when such interpretation becomes necessary."[8] Implicitly challenging any central authority, religious or secular, this statement reflects a traditional thrust of the *'ulama'* in Islam to speak in the name of society as a whole in an attempt to strike a balance in state-society relations and even to bring about society's domination of the state. More specifically, we find the development by contemporary Islamic movements of autonomous social activities in areas of welfare, health, and education to be filling a governmental void, which in some respects resembles the Western notion of civil society.[9]

Nowhere is this proliferation of religious authority and the quest for a workable formula of what might be termed *flexible rigidity* or *pliant conformity* more vividly expressed than in the policy adopted by many current Islamic movements to cooperate with the existing political order, even under non-Islamic regimes. Islamic thinkers discern four main strategies that mark Islamic movements: reformist, educational, didactic, and guiding; communal, providing social services; political, exerting pressure on the rulers to implement Islamic law, namely, the *shari'a;* and combatant-political, using military force or violence against the ruling elites.[10] In practice, Islamic movements have been adaptable, taking various elements from these four strategies for different social and political conditions.[11]

Islamic movements tend to be reformist rather than revolutionary, generally preferring to operate overtly and legally unless forced to go underground and use subversive or violent methods in response to severe repression. Islamic political movements operating in Arab regimes in which they are tolerated have been willing to accept the rules of the political game and to refrain from violence, as in the case of the Muslim Brotherhood groups in Jordan and Sudan.[12] Indeed, during the 1980s and 1990s, the novel phenomenon has been the growing inclination of Islamic movements to participate in their respective political systems, even under non-Islamic regimes. Moreover, this pattern has prevailed despite restrictions, or prevention, imposed by various regimes on the participation of Islamic movements in elections, as in the case of al-Nahda in Tunisia, FIS in Algeria, and the Muslim Brotherhood in Egypt.[13]

Hasan al-Turabi, leader of the Islamic National Front in Sudan, and Rashed Ghanouchi, leader of the Nahda movement of Tunisia, have been the most conspicuous advocates of this increasingly dominant trend in the Arab world. Its aim is active participation in the political process, including the formation of coalitions with non-Islamic movements. Such political activities, it is thought, will help Islamic movements seize power and impose Islamization "from above."[14] True, both leaders stress the importance of ideological guidance as a necessary stage for creating a wide base of cadres for the Islamic movement.[15] Still, they call for employing strategies of mass mobilization rather than elitist seclusion.

According to their perception, the use of violence is legitimate to counter repression by the regime. But they do not recommend violence because of the overwhelming power of the state and the danger of giving the ruling elite a pretext to wage all-out war against the Islamic movement. Reflecting on his successful experience and road to power in Sudan, Turabi emphasizes the importance of gradual penetration into the armed forces and bureaucratic apparatuses, parallel to participation in the political system.[16]

Shaped by social and economic conditions, external constraints, collective values, and common beliefs, the phenomenon of Islamists' political participation became apparent in the 1990s across the Arab world, from Algeria and Sudan through Yemen,[17] Lebanon, and Jordan. Even in Israel, defined as a Jewish state, a group from the Islamic movement decided—at the cost of a split—to take part in the 1996 general elections and even won two seats in the Knesset.[18] This inclination reflects first and foremost the Islamists' willingness to accept the rules of the game determined by the regimes in the context of controlled democratization, offering new opportunities for political participation. Although neither side would accept the other fully, both the Islamic movements and the Arab regimes have equally refrained from adopting a position of total rejection.

True, Islamic movements have been reluctant to publicly compromise their ultimate objectives, officially modify their positions, make reciprocal concessions, avoid criticizing the regime, admit to understanding the viewpoint of others, or accept mutually rewarding solutions to joint problems. But at the same time, they have hesitated to pursue their dogma at the price of all-out confrontation. Even though the goals and activities of these movements are justified in Islamic terms, the religious drive does not always guide the political conduct of these movements. Moreover, it is this Islamic value system that allows these movements to interpret unorthodox political moves in normative terms, thus enabling them to adjust to the rapid changes in social and political life and to redefine their strategic goals to fit the exigencies of time and place.[19]

Neither Fixed Identity nor Distinct Boundaries

The willingness of Islamic movements to take part in varying levels of state-controlled, limited democratic rule demonstrates the Islamists' conviction that they can gain influence and promote their objectives by operating within the existing political order. In this respect, Hamas and other Islamic movements in the Arab world escaped a binary perception regarding their relations with their ideological rivals and political opponents. They took care not to depict their social and political reality as a cluster of mutually exclusive, diametrically opposed categories, characterized by "either-or" relations. And they refrained from portraying themselves in terms of fixed identities, distinct boundaries, and stable, well-established preferences. In short, they recognized the limits beyond which they could not go in pursuing an "all or nothing" policy to advance their ultimate political goals. Given the deteriorating social and economic conditions in the Arab states in the 1980s and 1990s and the political constraints in which Hamas and other Islamic movements operated, the price for attempting to remove the other side from the political stage was seen as intolerable. Underlying this pattern of relations was the realization by the Islamic movements that making a clear decision in their ideological and political conflict with the Arab regimes would always remain mere wishful thinking and, crucially, that a straightforward conflict and a mode of action based on a zero-sum game could threaten their very existence.

It is here that we should look in order to understand the Islamic movements' inclination to consolidate their position and to enhance their bargaining ability vis-à-vis their opponents by formulating an eclectic formula and finding a workable compromise between doctrinal considerations and practical calculations: religious norms and material interests, social obligations and sectoral preferences, a broad national solidarity and a narrow communal loyalty. Indeed, Islamic political movements deal with "cultural issues of restoring familial and patriarchal authority, regulation of gender relations and sexual mores, cultural authenticity, and the restructuring of the political community according to religious norms. But at the same time, practices associated with these movements are colored by more profane, material concerns."[20]

The preference of Hamas and other Islamic movements for composite strategies and compromise tactics over an "all or nothing" policy and binary perspectives is not exceptional in the history of Islam and the politics of the Middle East. As Eickelman and Piscatori argue, the boundaries between social, political, and religious duties and preferences are constantly shifting. Thus, political power, religious symbols, and social interests are always located in a particular context and in a nexus of social and cultural relationships. "Doctrinal prescriptions," claim Eickelman and Piscatori,

> are but one factor in motivating social action. As traditional Muslim theorists maintain, ideas such as *zakat* [alms imposed by the Qur'an] and *jihad* play a role in inspiring social and political conduct. However, considerations such as family, ethnicity, class, gender, and bureaucratic access can be equally important. Doctrine enjoins the pilgrimage to Mecca on all believers able to do so, but believers are just as likely to fulfill this obligation because of the opportunity to improve their social status, commercial possibilities or . . . political influence.[21]

The process of finding a workable compromise between the doctrine and practice, ideas and interests that we have been describing, applies with equal force to Middle Eastern tribal settings:

> When one examines the ethnographic record to determine what it is that Middle Eastern tribesmen are doing in political acts, one finds

that they are talking to each other probably more than they are fighting . . . with the consequent or attendant belief that the basis of power is *persuasion* rather than the exercise of force.[22] (emphasis in original)

For Hamas and other Islamic movements, the utility and advantages of nonbinary policy devices such as composite strategies, workable compromise, flexible rigidity, and pliant conformity are quite clear. In religious fundamentalist movements, support is usually gained at the price of conformity, by publicly renouncing any tactic that could offset the group's normative values. Our study shows, however, that the many policy devices, described earlier, that Hamas uses, have enabled its leaders to manipulate normative rules in a pragmatic fashion. Indeed, Hamas leaders have been able to move publicly from an "unrealistic" posture of conflict—of total moral commitment to a principle, whatever the cost—toward a more pragmatic bargaining posture, which recognizes that certain norms and interests are shared with the other side and can be used as a basis for a workable compromise.[23]

The need of Hamas to adjust to a changing of political and social environment and its leaders' ability to justify its deviation from official doctrine and from public commitments have reduced the risk of intraorganizational disorder and enhanced the prospects of maintaining public support and gaining the rank and file's compliance.

How has Hamas combined religious dogma with practice? What were the roots of flexibility enabling Hamas to escape the pressure to translate its normative rigidity into an "all or nothing" practice?

To understand how and to what extent Hamas has been able to transform hybrid strategies and policies founded on the principle of flexible rigidity from tactical episodes into strategic patterns, we must turn from formal dimensions, like strategies of control and command, to issues that are critical and relevant, such as interrelationships and mechanisms of cooperation and conflict regulation. We need to go beyond the binary perspective and escape the linear boxes of political thought in order to home in on interconnectedness.

To follow Hamas's modes of thinking and conduct, we have to think in terms other than the political commonsense issues of stability, legitimacy, control, and hierarchy that have occupied many students of religious movements, states, and societies in the Middle East as well as in developing countries in Africa, Asia, or Latin America. The flexible organizational perspective turns these concepts on their head. The question thus becomes how a movement, state, or community can forge and encourage a political reality based on perceptions of bounded instability, negotiated coexistence, blurred boundaries, and conflicting, competing, and overlapping preferences instead of secure and prolonged stability, fixed boundaries, and consistent preferences.

The flexible, informal approach also provides an apt metaphor for the world order today. Our world is characterized more by instability than stability, by flux and not stasis, by boundaries that are ambiguous and shifting rather than distinct and static, by multiple identities and fluid loyalties. Analytical perspectives based on linear metaphors and binary modes of thinking cannot capture these uncertainties and complexities. In the Arab world, in which "defeat is never total, victory never complete, tension never ending, and all gains and losses are merely marginal and temporary as winners fall out and losers regroup,"[24] a departure from binary perception provides a novel way to comprehend the intricacies of Hamas's policy, which has enabled the movement to maneuver within the prose of political reality while never ceasing to recite the poetry of ideology.

CHAPTER ONE

Social Roots and Institutional Development

Much of the politics of Hamas can be explained in terms of the tension between the movement's dogmatic ideology and its pragmatic approach to political and institutional survival. This tension is between Hamas's adherence to the Islamic vision of holy war (*jihad*) against Israel as the most effective instrument of mass mobilization and its awareness of the necessity of reckoning with political considerations without abandoning the armed struggle. The origins of this tension and its impact on Hamas's political behavior are intimately bound up with the historical development of the Palestinian national movement.

Palestinian nationalism emerged as a construction of British colonialism, its ideology and strategy shaped by its confrontation with the Zionist movement and the state of Israel, as well as by its interaction with the surrounding Arab states. As in similar cases of constructed nationalism, the Palestinian national movement sanctified territorial boundaries—in this case, those demarcated by the British Mandate from the Jordan River to the Mediterranean Sea—and gave them the symbolic political status of a historic homeland. And like other national movements in which a religion based on scriptures and universal ends played a role, Islam was an instrument, not a key factor, in constructing the Palestinian national identity, both before 1948 and afterward.[1]

Since the early 1920s, the legitimacy of any political leadership in the Arab-Palestinian community has been conditioned on its adherence to an unequivocal rejection of the Zionist enterprise and a commitment to the just cause of Palestinian Arabs. This approach characterizes the Arab-Palestinian national movement and its political institutions, of which the most conspicuous has been the PLO from its advent in 1964 but mainly after 1967. In addition to its demand for the total reversal of the outcomes of the 1948 war—reclamation of the lost land of Palestine from which Israel was created and repatriation of the Arab refugees—the PLO also articulated essential values and symbols underpinning Palestinian nationalism. In its National Charter, the PLO defined the Palestinian people, asserted its inalienable links to the national homeland within its Mandatory borders, and sanctioned "armed struggle" as the only way to its liberation.

After the Arab-Israeli war of 1967, the PLO was known for its popular mobilization for a military struggle against Israel and its uncompromising political goals. Indeed, the PLO's National Charter of 1968 defined these goals as the liberation of all of Palestine by armed struggle and the establishment of an independent Palestinian state with a negligible minority of Jewish citizens. However, years of frustrated hope of total Arab mobilization for the sake of Palestine, military debacles suffered at the hands of Arab regimes and Israel, political constraints, and growing involvement in international diplomacy induced the PLO to retreat from its goal of a Palestinian state in all Palestine. Instead, the PLO has been forced to acquiesce in the political reality by adopting a two-state solution—Israel within its 1967 borders and a Palestinian state in the West Bank and Gaza Strip. By the late 1970s, the two-state solution had won the support of the Palestinian leadership in the occupied territories as well as that of most Arab states and other members of the international community.

The PLO's loss of its autonomous territorial base in Lebanon as a result of the Israeli incursion into that country in 1982 generated mounting ideological and structural crises within the organization, which had effectively been deprived of its military option and had its political options severely curtailed by being forced out of Lebanon. A deep sense of hopelessness gripped the Palestinians, who perceived a widening gap between their expectations for the imminent removal of the Israeli occupation and the PLO's state of fragmentation and political weakness.[2] It was under these circumstances that the national discourse began to change, prompted by marginal Islamic groups. By presenting an alternative orientation and strategy that seemed to address the needs of the people, these groups were able to break through to the center stage of the Palestinian political community. Deriving their political thought, terminology, and values from radical Islam, the upstart groups offered a different perspective on the collective reality and a redefinition of the Palestinians' national goals and means to achieve them. At the same time, they identified themselves with the history of Palestinian struggle and its symbols and myths, appropriating them from the national-secular stream led by the PLO.[3]

One such group was Hamas, a product of the Intifada, the Palestinian uprising in the Israeli-occupied territories that erupted at the end of 1987. At the time and place of its emergence, Hamas appeared to address more authentically and appropriately the expectations of many, if not most, Palestinians in the West Bank and the Gaza Strip, thereby supplementing the usual Islamic interpretation of essential elements of Palestinian nationalism, such as "people," "territory," "history," and "interrelations with the Arab-Muslim world." At a time when the PLO appeared to have abandoned the armed struggle and to be willing to accept a territorial compromise that would leave the Palestinians only a small fragment of Mandatory Palestine, Hamas clung to established national values, which were encapsulated in the notion of relentless armed struggle until the complete liberation of Palestine. Moreover, Hamas conferred an Islamic meaning on its version of Palestinian nationalism. That is, the Palestinian state envisioned by Hamas would come into being through a holy war (*jihad*), encompass all of Palestine, and implement the Islamic law (*shari'a*).

Hamas thus confronted the PLO's secular nationalism with an Islamic-national concept, which needed no alteration of the PLO's original goals or its strategies for achieving them, but merely their Islamization. Thus, in its religious vision, political goals, and communal concerns, Hamas challenged the PLO's claim to be the exclusive political center of the Palestinian people. Hamas infused religion with nationalism, thus implying a claim for the Islamization of the Palestinian society and state. This entailed a new interpretation, anchored in Muslim history, of the parameters of the struggle against Israel.

Whereas the doctrine of Arab nationalism had initially incorporated Islamic values and symbols into its secular viewpoint, mainly in order to appeal to the masses, Hamas reappropriated the secular elements and symbols of Palestinian nationalism as already defined by the PLO. Indeed, Hamas offers the Palestinian masses an alternative religious narrative whose powerful message is embedded in its religious authenticity, clarity, and familiarity. Hamas thus sanctions its doctrine regarding both the means of struggle (*jihad*) and its strategic goals—an Islamic Palestinian state and society—by means of Islamic law and tradition, thereby clearly differentiating itself from the PLO's political goal of a secular state-to-be.

Origins

Hamas's origins are rooted in the Muslim Brothers movement (MB) and, more specifically in its main institutional embodiment since the late 1970s, the Islamic Center (al-Mujamma' al-islami) in the Gaza Strip. Islamic political activity in Mandatory Palestine appeared as early as the late 1920s in the form of local branches of the Egypt-based Young Muslim Men's Association (Jam'iyyat al-shubban al-muslimin). The Haifa branch was headed by Sheikh 'Izz al-Din al-Qassam, who in the early 1930s led a group that assassinated Jews and British officials. These actions were portrayed as a *jihad* for the liberation of the land of Palestine. In 1935, al-Qassam was killed in an armed clash with a British force in northern Samaria, in what he had intended to be the beginning of a guerrilla war. His religious status and his fall in battle against the British turned Qassam into a national symbol and role model of self-sacrifice and dedication to the duty of war against foreign intruders in the land of Islam. Some of his companions (*qassamiyyun*) later became the hard core of the 1936–1939 Arab Revolt in Palestine.[4]

In 1945, the first Palestinian branch of the MB was opened in Jerusalem as an extension of the movement in Egypt. Soon, with the assistance of the latter and close affiliation with the mufti al-Haj Amin al-Husseini, other branches were established in most of the major Palestinian towns and villages, and by 1947, there were thirty-eight branches with more than ten thousand registered members. The MB in Palestine generally focused on social and cultural activities and, unlike their colleagues in Egypt, refrained from active involvement in politics or violence.[5] Indeed, during the first Arab-Israeli war, in 1948, the Islamic movement in Palestine had little impact on the fighting, apart from the mufti's "sacred *jihad*" (*al-jihad al-muqaddas*), a popular militia that operated in Jerusalem, Ramla, Lydda, and Jaffa. By the end of the war, the MB as an organized movement had disappeared, caught up in the social and political collapse and territorial fragmentation of the Arab-Palestinian community.

Between 1948 and 1967, Jordan and Egypt ruled the West Bank and the Gaza Strip, respectively, and shaped the development of the MB movement in accordance with their attitudes toward pan-Arab nationalism, the Palestinian issue, and the Arab-Israeli conflict. During the Jordanian rule of the West Bank, the MB renewed its activities as an organized political movement. The official annexation of the West Bank into Jordan in April

1950 and the regime's relatively tolerant policy toward opposition parties enabled the MB to become established as an open but moderate opposition group. During the 1950s, the MB maintained a policy of "loyal opposition" to the Hashemite regime, which was manifested in the MB's participation in all parliamentary elections and facilitated the development of the movement's modest social infrastructure. The political truce with the Hashemite regime derived from common values and shared interests, primarily their adherence to social traditionalism and rejection of revolutionary Arab nationalism led by President Gamal Abdel Nasser of Egypt. It was the MB's tacit alliance with the Hashemite regime of Jordan that led to the split in 1952 that created a militant group with strong anti-Western and revolutionary inclinations and headed by Sheikh Taqi al-Din al-Nabhani, who established the Islamic Liberation Party (Hizb al-tahrir al-islami).[6]

Unlike Jordan, Egypt refrained from annexing the Gaza Strip and preserved the military administration established during the 1948 war. Under this military administration, the MB's activity in the Gaza Strip was either tolerated or repressed, in line with Egypt's policy toward the MB's mother movement in Egypt itself. Thus, when the MB was banned in Egypt in early 1949, the MB's branch in Gaza was reorganized by its local leadership and turned into a religious-educational center entitled Unification [of God] Association (Jam'iyyat al-tawhid). During the short-lived honeymoon, from 1952 to 1954, between the Free Officers' regime and the Muslim Brothers, the latter's branch in the Gaza Strip flourished, attracting many young Palestinians from the refugee camps as well as Palestinian students in Egyptian universities. But a new ban on the MB in Egypt in 1954, following its attempt on Nasser's life, began a long period of brutal repression, which created the hostile relationship between the Nasserist regime and the MB in Egypt and the Gaza Strip. This ban forced the MB in Gaza to conduct its activities secretly until finally, under the joint pressures of the Nasserist regime and the wave of Arab nationalism in the early 1960s, the movement was forced to go underground and significantly limit its public presence. Nasser's harsh policy against the MB reached a peak in the aftermath of the alleged coup attempt in 1965, which led to the arrest of thousands of the movement's activists in Egypt and the execution of their leading figures. Most important of the executed leaders was Sayyid Qutb, whose writings and school of thought were adopted by many Islamic groups advocating violence against non-Islamic regimes.[7] In 1965, one of the MB members arrested was Ahmad Yasin, who later became the founder and spiritual leader of Hamas.[8]

The differences between the West Bank and the Gaza Strip in terms of opportunities for political action—reflecting the better economic and social conditions in the former—left their imprint on the nature and structure of the MB in each region. In the West Bank, its activities were open and moderate but in the Gaza Strip, they assumed a clandestine, militant form.

With Israel's conquest of the West Bank and Gaza Strip in 1967, a new era began for the MB movement in these areas. Israel was more permissive regarding social and cultural Islamic activity, and the very fact that the West Bank and Gaza Strip were now under one government enabled a renewed encounter between Islamic activists of both regions. This in turn paved the way to the development of joint organizational endeavors, backed by mutual coordination and support, which allowed the West Bankers to learn from their Gaza colleagues' experience with clandestine activities and apply it to the West Bank. In the late 1960s, a joint organization of Islamic activity for the Gaza Strip and the West Bank—the United Palestinian [Muslim] Brotherhood Organization—was founded. Israel's policy of "open bridges" across the Jordan River facilitated the establishment of organizational links and close cooperation between the MB movements under Israeli occupation and in Jordan, where Palestinians constituted a large portion, if not a majority, of the population. Jordan, too, benefited from this situation, as its interest was to secure its political status in the West Bank and counteract the influence of the PLO. The 1970s witnessed growing links between the MB in the Israeli-occupied territories and Israel's Arab citizens. Thus, leading MB figures from the West Bank and Gaza Strip, like Sheikh Yasin, visited Israeli Muslim communities from the Galilee to the Negev to preach and lead Friday prayers.[9]

Hamas's semiofficial history points to 1967 as the date of the movement's genesis. According to its own historical narrative, Hamas evolved through four main stages:

1. 1967–1976: Construction of the "hard core" of the MB in the Gaza Strip in the face of oppressive Israeli rule.
2. 1976–1981: Geographical expansion through participation in professional associations in the Gaza Strip and the West Bank, and institution building, notably al-Mujamma' al-islami, al-Jam'iyya al-islamiyya, and the Islamic University in Gaza.
3. 1981–1987: Political influence through establishment of the mechanisms of action and preparation for armed struggle.
4. 1987: Founding of Hamas as the combatant arm of the MB in Palestine and the launching of a continuing *jihad*.[10]

In fact, these stages, as will be explained later, reflect the development of the MB movement in the Gaza Strip, but not in the West Bank. Moreover, it describes the development of the mainstream MB and ignores other Islamic groups that were active in the Gaza Strip from the late 1970s. The first period, 1967–1976, was indeed marked by the meticulous construction of the MB's institutional and social infrastructure under the leadership of Sheikh Ahmad Yasin. Yasin was recognized as the preeminent MB figure in the Gaza Strip in 1968, following the departure from Gaza of Isma'il al-Khalidi, the movement's leader until then. Yasin now became the driving force behind the rapid rise of the MB movement in the Gaza Strip, which was spearheaded by his institutionally based efforts to imbue the society with *da'wa*, that is, religious preaching and education.[11]

The young sheikh's charisma, Islamic scholarship, and organizational mastery proved particularly influential among the youth of the refugee camps. His focus on *da'wa* was the result of a major lesson the MB had learned from its experience in Egypt: as long as it confined its activity to education and preaching, the regime would leave it alone. Operating out of his home in the Shati' refugee camp, Yasin embarked on a systematic penetration of the society by creating cells of three members each throughout the Strip, reaching even the neighborhood level. With the expansion of the movement, the Gaza Strip was divided into five subdistricts under the responsibility of Yasin's close aides or disciples.[12]

The movement's inroads were made possible largely by the depressed socioeconomic conditions of the local population, more than half of whom lived in refugee camps. These teeming camps in the Gaza Strip, which housed the world's highest population density, provided fertile soil for communal activism informed by radicalized religiosity. This striking social reality welcomed the Islamic option as an alternative way to challenge poverty and life under Israel's military occupation.

As the Islamic movement grew in the Gaza Strip, it sought to establish formally registered associations that would accord legal status to the MB's religious and social activities. However, beginning in 1970, repeated requests by Yasin and his companions to the Israeli military administration were rejected, not least because of the opposition of traditional Islamic elements, especially the Associations for the Learning [by heart] of the Qur'an (Jam'iyyat tahfiz al-qur'an) led by Sheikh Muhammad 'Awwad.

The crucial act in the MB's institutionalization in the Gaza Strip occurred in 1973 with the founding of the Islamic Center (al-Mujamma' al-islami) as a voluntary association, which was formally legalized in 1978. The Mujamma' became the base for the development, administration, and control of religious and educational Islamic institutions in the Gaza Strip, under Yasin's supervision. One of its major instruments was the Islamic Association (al-Jamʿiyya al-islamiyya), established in 1976 as a framework for religious and communal activities, with branches in various parts of Gaza Strip. In 1981 the Mujammaʿ created the Young Women's Islamic Association (Jamʿiyyat al-shabbat al-muslimat) as another association for social action and mobilization. The Mujammaʿ was composed of seven committees: preaching and guidance, welfare, education, charity, health, sport, and conciliation. Because the activities conducted by the Mujammaʿ did not encompass all MB groups in the Gaza Strip, power struggles emerged over resources and social influence. Nonetheless, by the late 1970s, the scope and organizational efficiency of the Mujammaʿ made it the spearhead of the MB's mainstream in the Gaza Strip.[13]

Social Orientation

The Mujammaʿ's activities were directed inward, focusing on the long-term goal of reshaping the Muslim community. Its project rested on a large-scale social program to create a network of schools and Qur'anic classes to preach the message of Allah (tabligh wa-daʿwa). The Mujammaʿ leaders encouraged social activities at both the individual and communal levels conducted in accordance with traditional and Islamic norms. Adherence to the Islamic way of life applied mainly to the family, women, and education. On a wider scale, an intensive effort was undertaken to eradicate "immoral" behavior, such as the dissemination of pornographic material, the drinking of alcohol, prostitution, drug abuse, and joint activities of young men and young women.

The "return to Islam" was envisioned as an evolutionary process to be achieved by means of comprehensive education aimed at everyone, from infants to the uneducated elderly. The Mujammaʿ followed the MB's traditional practice of applying the Islamic duty of charity (zakat) to the poor as a central avenue for social infiltration and expansion of its public support among the needy. The movement set up kindergartens and schools, a blood bank, medical clinics, vocal education centers for women, and youth and sports clubs. All these activities revolved around the mosque, combining worship, education, and social welfare with subsidized services such as medical treatment, children's day care, free meals, and sports clubs. A striking illustration of the Mujammaʿ's indispensable social role occurred in 1981 when it extended financial and technical assistance to help rehabilitate more than a thousand homes, mostly in refugee camps, that were severely damaged by a winter storm.[14]

The focus of the Mujamma' on developing a civil society by forming voluntary associations did not clash with the hierarchical and secret structure of the MB, whose main units were the "family" (*'usra*) and "chapter" (*shu'ba*). In fact, the open communal activities of the Mujamma' acted as a kind of security valve in relation to the Israeli authorities. This dual structure may explain the movement's ability to turn to violence in due course. The most effective means of expanding the Mujamma"s influence was the mosque. With Israel's tacit consent, mosques proliferated in Gaza. As sanctuaries, they were an ideal venue for various public activities, safe from Israeli interference. From this point of view, the MB enjoyed a clear advantage over the nationalist forces represented by the PLO. That is, mosques afforded the MB not only a relatively secure space within which the Islamic movement could flourish, shielded from the Israeli intelligence apparatus, but also an invaluable stage for propagating its message and mobilizing public support.

From 1967 to 1986, with Israel's consent, the number of mosques in the Gaza Strip doubled—from 77 to 150, and rapidly rose to 200 by 1989. Most of the new mosques were private, independent of the religious *waqf* establishment in the Strip.[15]

Another social sphere in which the Mujamma' made inroads, through its conciliation committee, was mediation and conflict resolution between clans involved in feuds. In Palestinian society, based on kinship relations with almost no history of civil law and courts, the customary law of mediation and arbitration serves as the principal mechanism of conflict resolution. Given the social prestige of mediators in this society, the tendency of customary law to favor the stronger clan enabled the Mujamma"s conciliation committee to inject greater equity into this process and thus gain the support of the deprived and the indigent.[16]

The Mujamma' leaders did not confine themselves to the local arena. Their ties with the MB in Jordan were instrumental in enabling them to forge close relations with Islamic institutions in Saudi Arabia, which in the 1970s and 1980s provided generous financial aid to Islamic associations and communities in the Middle East and elsewhere. These relations enabled the Mujamma' leadership to select and foster cadres among young Palestinians in the Gaza Strip who planned to attend school in the Arab states. Like the Palestinian resistance organizations, which received stipends and fellowships for Palestinian students from East European Communist states, the Mujamma' cultivated its future leadership and provided for its higher education by means of financial aid, ideological guidance, and scholarships for study in Saudi Arabia and the West.

These international connections abetted the Mujamma"'s fund-raising efforts in the neighboring countries and in the late 1980s contributed to the restructuring of Hamas based on "inside" and "outside" leadership and institutions and facilitated the movement's activism in the context of Middle Eastern regional politics. During the Intifada, this pattern of relations was consolidated, with the center of gravity moving out of the occupied territories, reflecting the movement's marked financial dependence on the outside supporting bases, especially those in Jordan.

The early 1980s witnessed a rapid growth of the Islamic movement in the Israeli-occupied territories, the causes of which were both external and internal. The 1979 Shi'i revolution in Iran helped stir the potent brew of militant Islam, especially in the Middle East. The plunge of oil prices caused a recession in the Gulf states and, concomitantly, a significant decrease in the demand for labor migrants, many of whom were Palestinians from the West Bank and Gaza. In addition, the unstable Israeli economy, battered by a stock market crisis in 1983, soaring inflation, and constraints imposed by the Israeli government or by free-market forces on the Palestinian economy, brought about a grave deterioration in social and economic conditions in the West Bank and Gaza.

Spurred by these developments and encouraged by its growing popularity, the Mujamma' leadership moved to penetrate the public sphere, hitherto dominated by the PLO. The Mujamma' stepped up its communal activities, particularly its attempts to take over mosques from the Department of Islamic Endowments (Da'irat al-awqaf al-islamiyya) and gain a foothold in voluntary and public institutions. The Mujamma' young leaders displayed their assertiveness by their willingness to use violence in confrontations with the nationalist Palestinian organizations, including Fatah. The Mujamma' appointed its own confidants as clergy, turning the mosques into political pulpits. Yet the repeated efforts, often accompanied by threats or sheer force, to take over the mosques officially controlled by the Department of Islamic Endowments and install Mujamma' clergy in key positions were only partially successful. The Islamic Endowment Department continued to finance the maintenance and pay the wages of employees in mosques that were now under Mujamma' control. However, the Mujamma' was unable to gain control of the Department of the Islamic Endowments of the Gaza Strip, which, given the volume of assets and personnel under its control, would have given the former incomparable economic and social leverage over all other institutions in the area.[17]

Although so far abstaining from the armed struggle against Israel, the Mujamma' did not rule out violence as a means to impose the "true path" for the Palestinian Muslim community. Violence was built into the movement's worldview from its very inception. Like other Islamic movements, the Mujamma' employed violence to impose Islamic norms on the population, particularly to prevent the consumption of alcohol and to ensure women's modesty. Moreover, with the Mujamma' enjoying extensive popularity and undeniable presence in the Gaza Strip by the late 1970s, Yasin and his lieutenants, in their efforts to dominate the public sphere, encouraged the MB followers to join professional associations, labor unions, and other public institutions. Especially targeted for penetration were professional associations of physicians, lawyers, and engineers, in which the Mujamma' achieved rapid influence, reflecting the state of frustration and disillusionment among university graduates.

Most important still was the shaping of the Palestinian public agenda in the Gaza Strip by calling strikes, first on specific sectors and afterward also on trade and services. In January 1980, members of the MB who were identified with the Mujamma' set fire to the Palestinian Red Crescent office in Gaza, which was recognized as the stronghold of the leftist groups. In November 1981, Islamic figures who were identified with the Mujamma' and led by Mahmud al-Zahar imposed a general strike on the doctors' association in the Gaza Strip to protest Israel's introduction of a value-added tax into the occupied territories. In 1983, sporadic violent clashes erupted between Mujamma' members and PLO adherents over control of the Islamic University in Gaza, and such clashes became routine in the following years. By the mid-1980s, the Mujamma' and its offshoots had become increasingly involved in a political struggle with the nationalist mainstream. Relations between the Mujamma' and the Popular Front for the Liberation of Palestine (PFLP), which represented an ultraleftist viewpoint, were particularly volatile.[18]

The Struggle over the Universities

The Mujamma''s efforts to deepen its influence through lawful institutionalization peaked with its successful takeover of the Islamic University in Gaza. The university was established in 1978 following Egypt's decision to deny Palestinian students access to its universities owing to a crisis in its relations with the PLO generated by President Anwar Sadat's visit to Jerusalem. Its student body grew rapidly.[19] The takeover of the university was brought about by the decline in the funds raised by the PLO for its budget, a shortfall that was made up by the Mujamma'. Until 1985, the PLO had contributed the lion's share of the university's budget, utilizing financial aid it received from the Gulf oil monarchies thanks to a decision by the Baghdad Arab summit conference in November 1978. However, the constant decrease in Arab financial aid to the PLO meant that a growing share of university funding had to come from abroad, primarily from the Islamic movement in Jordan, the Saudi-sponsored Muslim World's League, and the Islamic Conference Organization. The fact that much of this funding was funneled to the university by the Islamic movement in Jordan through the Mujamma' underscored the movement's developing international reach, albeit mainly in the context of fund-raising. By the early 1980s, representatives of the Islamic movement in Jordan constituted a majority on the university's board of trustees, and in 1983 the MB-PLO power struggle in the university was decided in favor of the Islamists, leading to the appointment of Muhammad Saqr, a member of the MB in Jordan, as president. Saqr's expulsion by the Israeli authorities a year later did nothing to diminish Islamic control of the university, which became a bastion of Islamic activity in the Gaza Strip. Parallel to the Islamic takeover at the management level, the Islamic students won a similar victory when in January 1983, the "Islamic bloc," linked to the Mujamma', won 51 percent of the votes in the elections to the student union. In 1986, the Islamic bloc obtained 61 percent of the votes, defeating a unified list of candidates linked to the PLO factions.

By the early 1990s, with more than five thousand students, mostly identified as Islamists, the Mujamma' became intensively involved in every facet of the university, from setting the budget to setting the curriculum and appointing the faculty. The university also became a legitimate instrument for channeling financial aid from external organizations and private donors to the Mujamma'. The Mujamma''s central role in the university was strikingly demonstrated by the fact that more than 10 percent of the 415 members of Hamas and Islamic Jihad deported by Israel to Lebanon in December 1992 were students and employees of the institution.[20]

The Mujamma''s growing presence and ideological influence at the Islamic University led to an escalation of the struggle with Fatah and the leftist factions on campus, which by 1985 had assumed an increasingly violent character. The campus clashes between the Mujamma' activists and the nationalist factions were a microcosm of the mounting tension and political struggle between the two currents. The growing violence employed by the Islamists against rival factions reflected their burgeoning self-confidence and their boldness in implementing an "internal *jihad*" to impose the rules of Islam on the society. This inclination toward violence, later directed also against the Israeli occupation, might have been influenced by the Egyptian MB's experience and practices, in addition to the extremely poor social and economic conditions of the Gaza Strip: the incomparable density of population, the scarcity of economic resources, and the reality of refugee camps as the single dominant social factor.

Unlike the MB in the Gaza Strip, their colleagues in the West Bank engaged in more moderate and traditional public activities and their attempt at social penetration by institutional means came relatively late. The MB movement in the West Bank constituted an integral part of the Jordanian Islamic movement, which for many years had been aligned with the Hashemite regime. Furthermore, compared with their counterparts in the Gaza Strip, the MB in the West Bank represented a higher socioeconomic profile—merchants, landowners, and middle-class officials and professionals. The alignment with the Hashemite regime facilitated the MB's penetration of the religious establishment in the West Bank, which even after 1967 remained administratively and financially linked to Jordan. By the mid-1980s, a significant portion of the positions in West Bank religious institutions were held by MB.

Similar to, and possibly at the behest of the MB in the Gaza Strip, in 1974 a Young Men's Muslim Association was established in East Jerusalem. The association sponsored various social activities in the fields of culture, education, youth and sports, in accordance with Islamic tradition. In the following years, the association opened branches in West Bank cities, villages, and refugee camps. A sharp shift occurred in the activities of the MB in the West Bank in the late 1970s, caused by the growing influx of students from the Gaza Strip, who were no longer able to pursue a higher education in Egypt, to the universities of Bir Zeit, Nablus, and Hebron. At the same time, increasing numbers of students from the West Bank's rural periphery entered the higher educational system. By the mid-1980s, the vast majority of university students in the West Bank and Gaza came from rural families, representing a more militant political approach, which converged with the rising tide of radical Islam as an overall ideological system.[21]

The widening Islamization of the West Bank society was seen in the growing presence of Islamic students on university campuses, including the reputable nationalist-leftist university of Bir Zeit. In the early 1980s, the Islamic groups were equal rivals of the nationalist factions identified with the PLO in elections for student councils. The trend toward Islamization in the West Bank was more broadly apparent in the intensive construction of new mosques, the closure of film theaters, and a general return to Islam as manifested in greater religious observance by individuals and the modest deportment of women in public.[22]

The turn to Islam in the West Bank was probably also boosted by the ascendancy to power in 1977 of a nationalist-religious coalition in Israel. The new right-wing government embarked on a large-scale Jewish settlement effort in the West Bank, in which Gush Emunim (Bloc of the faithful), a religious-nationalist messianic group, played a central role. An intensified struggle by ultraradical Jewish messianic groups over shrines sacred to both Judaism and Islam—the Temple Mount (al-Haram al-sharif—the Noble sanctuary—site of the al-Aqsa and Dome of the Rock mosques) broke out in the early 1980s in Jerusalem, and the Tomb of the Patriarchs (al-Haram al-ibrahimi—the Sanctuary of Abraham) in Hebron—thereby increasingly identifying the Israeli-Palestinian conflict as a religious one. A series of violent events linked to sacred sites heightened the image of a religious conflict, including the murder by a Jewish zealot of two Muslims in the Temple Mount compound in 1982, the attempt by a Jewish underground group to blow up the Temple Mount mosques in 1984, and another attempt by Jewish zealots to bomb the Muslim shrines, together with the murder of two Palestinian students at the Islamic University of Hebron. Although the merger of Islam and Palestinian nationalism was fully effected only after the eruption of the Intifada, Islamic verses and motifs appeared more and more often on maps of Palestine, and motifs of violent struggle adorned the logos of students' Islamic groups.[23]

Manifestations of internal violence by the MB in the West Bank were widespread by late 1986. As in the Gaza Strip, this violence was initially directed against individuals suspected of immoral conduct and against rival leftist factions. Yet despite voices in the MB calling for a *jihad* against Israel, the Israeli authorities continued to categorize the movement as nonviolent, even after the eruption of the Intifada.[24] As in other Arab-Muslim societies, then, the rise of radical Islam in the Gaza Strip and the West Bank soon exceeded its original cultural and social boundaries, spilling over into the political sphere, with a growing impact on the public discourse.

CHAPTER TWO

Dogmas and Dilemmas

The "return of Islam" in the Middle East was the result of a host of un-derlying processes, beginning with the searing Arab defeat in the 1967 war, which demonstrated the failure of the dominant nationalist and socialist ideologies to address the social and political problems in the Arab states. The perceived success with which the Arabs emerged from the 1973 war and the consequent rising expectations for political and economic gains deriving from the unprecedented flow of Arab oil wealth paradoxically led to a deepening sense of alienation toward the ruling elites among grow-ing segments of the Arab public.

The failure of the Arab states to make the social and economic progress their people yearned for, the widening socioeconomic gap between rich and poor, and the growing phenomenon of social and moral anomie iden-tified with Western culture especially affected the urban, educated, lower middle-class Muslims. Their disillusion with modernity and revolutionary secularism heightened their inclination to seek refuge in religious tradi-tions as a cure for the current social malaise and as a source of individual and collective hope. The growing trend of Islamization and institutional-ization in the cultural and social spheres soon assumed a political, some-times violent, form.

The revival of Islam as a collective cultural and political force and its return to the center of the public stage were relatively rapid, not least because the secular political discourse itself had drawn heavily on Islamic symbols and terminology, reflecting Islam's primacy in the social and cultural life of the Arab Muslim peoples.[1] The new Islamic discourse became the primary means of preserving collective identity and unity, as well as for legitimizing political movements and regimes. Its spokesmen portrayed Islam as the sole normative option capable of guiding public conduct and individual behavior in the face of internal and external challenges to the Islamic society.

The Islamic trend was significantly encouraged by the permissive policy of Egypt's President Anwar Sadat toward the Muslim Brothers (MB) in Egypt, which allowed the movement to renew its public activity, as well as by Saudi financial aid to establish and institutionalize communal Islamic activities in both the Middle East and the West. Since the 1920s, advocates of a return to Islam had urged the adoption of the ideals of the Prophet's community of believers as the proper response to moral disorientation, social disintegration, and the political weakness of Islam vis-à-vis the West. The call for a return to basics thus became the guiding tenet for modern Islamic movements. The early Muslim faithful—the "Righteous Ancestors" (al-Salaf al-salih)—were portrayed as an exemplary religious and political community in which Islamic law (*shari'a*) prevailed as the sole source of guidance and in which the community of believers (*umma*) determined the boundaries of the Islamic state, cutting across ethnicity and national identities. Even though this universal approach has marked many of the more extreme Islamic groups, mainstream Islamic movements have increasingly assumed a national character, acquiescing in the emerging international order of independent and sovereign states and confining their activity in state boundaries.[2]

Indeed, contemporary political Islam has displayed diversity not only between but also within states, in the form of diverse political groups, social movements, and parties that differ in their platforms, priorities, attitudes, and relations with the ruling elites. Students of contemporary Islamic movements have discerned two poles of Islamic thought in the twentieth century. One is revolutionary, holding that society should be "Islamized" through the seizure of power, legally or violently, after which the state machinery is used to re-Islamize the society from above, as happened in Iran and Sudan. The other pole is reformist, for which the advent of the Islamic state is the result of a long-term, continuous, incremental process of Islamization, achieved primarily by education and social action from the bottom up (neofundamentalism).[3]

Reformist Islam was espoused by the founder of the MB movement, Hasan al-Banna, following the Indian example of associations for Islamic education and missionary activity (*tabligh wa-daʿwa*). Al-Banna assumed a comprehensive approach to society and politics, envisioning a gradual change from the bottom of the pyramid up to the state's power base. He did not restrict himself to education and preaching, however, and in the late 1930s when his movement began to assume mass dimensions, he also tried to enter the political arena. Although he failed as a candidate for the Egyptian parliament in the 1945 elections, his approach until his assassination in 1948 reflected an attempt to combine reformist missionary activity with revolutionary methods, including penetration of the military, the use of political violence, and the creation of an armed force, leading to a clash with the regime. Al-Banna's combined strategy of *daʿwa* and militancy for creating an ideal Islamic society may explain the sharp fluctuations in relations between the MB and the Egyptian regime since the 1940s. With some variation—avoiding the use of armed force—al-Banna's reformist-political strategy was adopted by Islamic movements in other Arab countries where political conditions allowed, as in, for example, the Jordanian MB's lengthy record of coexistence and cooperation with the Hashemite regime, and the movement's similar pattern in Sudan.

Revolutionary, violent Islam has been identified primarily with Sayyid Qutb's militant doctrine, which viewed non-Islamic rule as *jahiliyya* (the pre-Islamic era, portrayed by Muslims as a period of ignorance and darkness). This sort of regime, which contradicts the principle of "the sovereignty of God" (*al-hakimiyya li-llah*), is inherently heretical and therefore must be fought through a holy war. At the same time, the true believers must separate themselves from the contaminated society by means of migration (*hijra*) and create their own Islamic space, protected from the omnipotent state machinery.[4] Qutb's views, shaped during the mid-1950s, the worst years of persecution and violent repression of the MB by the Nasserist regime in Egypt, had by the mid-1970s become a beacon for extremist Islamic groups in Egypt and afterward in Syria and Algeria. These militant groups adopted the idea of a violent "internal *jihad*" in the Muslim community, making it a cardinal element of their theory and practice.[5]

The idea of violent revolution as a means of imposing Islamization from above and restoring the Islamic caliphate has been preached by the Palestinian "Islamic Liberation Party" since the early 1950s, and an offshoot of this group staged a violent coup attempt in Egypt in 1974. But it was the 1979 Shi'i Islamic revolution in Iran that seemed to seal the triumph of the revolutionary approach in political Islam, inducing previously reformist-minded groups to shift to revolutionary Islamism. The revolutionary approach also was adopted by Islamic groups, including Palestinians, in the Arab countries as the operative model against regimes that refused to implement Islamic law.[6]

The use of violence by Muslims against other Muslims has remained generally unacceptable to the mainstream of radical Islam. In fact, such violence has been repeatedly depicted as civil strife (*fitna*), a loaded term evoking the recurrent civil wars in Islamic history, which are considered to have caused the decline of Islam's political power. But the use of violence by Muslims against non-Muslims in military confrontations, notably in the Arab-Israeli conflict, is viewed in an entirely different light. In the early 1980s, the ethos of Islamic mobilization for a defensive war against Islam's enemies was invoked in the wake of the Soviet invasion of Afghanistan and Israel's 1982 incursion into Lebanon. The effective elimination of the Palestinian armed struggle as a result of the expulsion of the PLO and its armed forces from Lebanon, and Israel's continued presence in southern Lebanon, paved the way for the emergence of Lebanese radical Shi'i resistance to the Israeli occupation. The continued armed struggle against Israel in southern Lebanon, conducted primarily by the Iranian-backed Hizballah, affirmed the militant Shi'i movement as the true carrier of the Islamic ethos of defiance of foreign invaders by holy war.[7]

The perception that Islam was under political attack by non-Muslims, coupled with the rise of radical Islam in the Arab world, rekindled the debate over the use of *jihad*. Though theological in character and taking as its point of departure the Islamic perception of *jihad* as a fundamental duty, the new discourse reflected a struggle between rival social and political viewpoints that might be explained in the context of state-society relations. Clearly, for militant Islamic groups, *jihad* in defense of Islamic lands was a useful rallying myth and a potential instrument of political mobilization. Hence, they adopted the classical interpretation of defensive holy war, elevating it to a primary precept—second only to the Islamic credo (*shahada*)—of the individual Muslim. The definition of *jihad* as an individual duty (*fard 'ain*) clashed head-on with the traditional perception of holy war as a collective duty of the Islamic community (*fard kifaya*) or as the prerogative of the political authority.[8] To support this militant interpretation, exemplary Islamic figures were evoked, such as 'Izz al-Din al-Qassam, whose individual *jihad* against the British Mandate authorities and the Jewish community in Palestine in the early 1930s became a role model for the current Islamic generation.[9]

Between Revolution and Reform: Palestinian Militant Islam

It might have been thought that the Jewish domination of historic Palestine and the Israeli occupation of the West Bank and Gaza Strip would decisively turn Palestinian Islamists toward the revolutionary version of Islam. In fact, the MB in the occupied territories oscillated between two main attitudes and strategies: revolutionary versus reformist.

The interpretation of a defensive *jihad* as the principal religious duty of a Muslim became increasingly popular among Palestinian Islamists during the 1980s, along with the MB's growing presence and influence among the people. Palestinian Islamic radicals, however, took conflicting approaches toward the implementation of a defensive *jihad*, between a universal Islamic view, represented by Sheikh ʿAbdallah ʿAzzam, and an ultranationalist trend, embodied by the group called Islamic Jihad (al-Jihad al-islami).

Defending Islamic lands in the face of the infidels' invasion was deemed tantamount to defending the Islamic community as a whole, since any political or military success by the infidels might sow doubts about Islam itself. The most conspicuous spokesman of this approach was Sheikh ʿAbdallah ʿAzzam, who issued a scholarly religious opinion (*fatwa*) to this effect, supported by highly respected scholars in Muslim countries. Individuals were thus enjoined to undertake the duty of *jihad* on their own, in disregard of basic social norms and commitments—the child without permission from his father, the wife without her husband, and the slave without his master.[10] ʿAzzam, who represented the young militant leadership in the MB movement in Jordan, had spearheaded their military activities against Israel in the late 1960s.[11] In view of the Soviet invasion of Afghanistan, he fulfilled his own *fatwa* by leading a group of Jordanian and Palestinian volunteers as *mujahidun* in the guerrilla war against the Soviet invaders, where he was killed in 1989. ʿAzzam's explanation why the duty of *jihad* in Afghanistan should take precedence was circumstantial, namely, the Muslim rebels' commitment to establish an Islamic state and geographic and social conditions favorable to guerrilla warfare.[12]

ʿAzzam's all-Islamic approach to the fulfillment of a defensive *jihad*, however, has remained marginal among Palestinian militant Islamists. Rather, the mainstream of Palestinian adherents of *jihad* has given clear priority to the armed struggle against Israel, a preference that carries a clear nationalist imprint. In the early 1980s, the Palestinian Islamist spectrum was mainly inspired, at the revolutionary pole, by Jihad groups in Egypt and the Iranian Shi'i revolution. The leading figures in this current emerged from the ranks of the Islamic Liberation Party, which since 1974 had been active against the Egyptian regime. The usual spokesman of this activist stream among Palestinian Islamists was Fathi Shiqaqi, a physician who in the mid-1980s became the leader of Islamic Jihad.

Shiqaqi called for the unification of Sunni and Shi'i Islam and the mobilization of all Muslims for the liberation of Palestine through *jihad*. Other Islamic figures who subscribed to an Islamic type of Palestinian nationalism were Sheikh As'ad Bayyud al-Tamimi (aka "the commander of Jihad"), the leader of Al-Jihad al-Islami—Bait al-Maqdis (the Islamic Jihad—Jerusalem), and Sheikh 'Abd al-'Aziz 'Awda, who, like Shiqaqi, was influenced by Egyptian *jihad* groups. These spokesmen of holy war against Israel, however, were fully aware of the division in the Muslim world and so were impatient to turn to arms "here and now." It was this motivation that underlay the new agenda they offered to Palestinian Islamists, as well as to MB worldwide: *jihad* for the liberation of Palestine should precede any other defensive holy war. Indeed, the spokesmen of Islamic Jihad perceived the idea of Islamic revolution as a means to promote the armed struggle against Israel rather than to pave the way to the Islamization of society.[13]

Contrary to the Islamic Jihad, which prescribed a revolutionary holy war without delay, the mainstream of MB in the Gaza Strip identified with al-Mujamma' al-Islami, adhered to the reformist concept and refrained from violent activity against Israel. Al-Mujamma' leaders in Gaza envisioned a transformation of the society from below through the creation of an Islamic space. That the Mujamma' continued to focus on a reformist approach to Islamic action was due mainly to Israel's tacit consent to Islamic education and preaching and the establishment of a social and religious infrastructure in the occupied territories. Apparently the Israeli authorities considered this brand of Islamic activity harmless and able to offset the nationalist militant movements operating under the PLO's umbrella.[14] Thus, whereas al-Jihad al-Islami adopted an unequivocal Palestinian national identity, the Mujamma' claimed allegiance to an imagined Islamic community. And contrary to the Islamic Jihad, the Mujamma' blurred the boundaries between a narrow territorial state (*dawla qutriyya*) and a broad Islamic nation (*umma*), following instead the "great religion" (*al-din al-'azim*) and its written law, the Qur'an.[15]

Before the Intifada, the Mujamma' gave priority to an "internal *jihad*" in the Muslim community over an "external *jihad*" against Israel and the West. The Mujamma' founders believed that the external *jihad* should be postponed until the advent of the Islamic state, which would assume responsibility for it. Moreover, since Israel's very existence was the result of the abandonment of Islamic norms, only when the Islamization of society was completed and the *shari'a* fully implemented would the Muslims be capable of defeating Israel.[16] Thus, although the Mujamma' identified Israel as a religious and political enemy, the military option seemed premature as long as the Islamic state had not been established and preparations for a prolonged armed struggle remained inadequate. The MB's passive approach to the armed struggle against Israel drew fire from the nationalist Palestinian factions, which accused the MB of collaborating with Israel. This criticism, combined with the violence launched by Islamic Jihad against Israel and the growing number of young Islamic activists imprisoned by Israel, caused the young militants of the Mujamma' to press the veteran leaders to take up arms against Israel.[17]

The PLO's expulsion from Lebanon in 1982 effectively nullified the Palestinians' military option and weakened the PLO politically in the Arab world. More specifically, the first three years after the Lebanon debacle witnessed a deepening rift between the PLO and Syria, a Syrian-backed revolt in Fatah against the PLO leadership, the disintegration of the PLO on grounds of ideological differences, and a prolonged siege imposed by the Shi'i Amal militia on Palestinian refugee camps in Lebanon. At the same time, the Palestinians in the Israeli-occupied West Bank and Gaza Strip, although living under stressful economic and psychological conditions, were trying to build institutions and strengthen the civilian society, which, particularly in view of the PLO's situation, was demonstrating greater self-reliance and motivation for collective political action. Indeed, after the Lebanon war, the center of gravity in the Palestinian national movement shifted from the neighboring countries into the occupied territories, which were now perceived as a crucial political asset and the only one that could reactivate international interest in the Palestine national cause.[18]

The implications of the PLO's situation after its expulsion from Lebanon and the developments in the Palestinian society in the West Bank and Gaza were clearly reflected in the MB's thought and practice. The perception that the PLO was militarily and politically bankrupt apparently induced the Mujamma' leadership to contemplate the possibility that it could become a political alternative. Such a radical transformation in the

Mujamma' strategy necessitated conceptual and structural changes, expressed particularly in actions of a national nature, which meant, in practice, armed struggle against Israel. Already in 1983, Sheikh Ahmad Yasin, the founder and first president of al-Mujamma', ordered members of the organization to secretly gather firearms, which were then distributed among selected operatives. In 1984, this effort was discovered by the Israeli military authorities, who also found weapons in the home of Sheikh Yasin himself. Yasin claimed that the weapons were intended for defense against rival Palestinian groups and not against Israel. Nonetheless, he was sentenced to thirteen years in prison but was released after less than a year as part of a prisoner exchange between Israel and the Popular Front for the Liberation of Palestine—General Command.[19]

It was probably Israel's exposure of the Mujamma''s new policy that led to Yasin's decision in 1986 to establish a security apparatus that would collect information about collaborators with Israeli intelligence. Once established, the security unit also became involved in the "internal *jihad*," which had the aim of imposing Islamic rules on the society and punishing drug dealers, prostitutes, and purveyors of pornographic videos. The main lessons the Mujamma' drew from the arms-gathering fiasco were to ensure strict compartmentalization and to entrust such activities to junior, less familiar activists, who would be unlikely to attract the attention of Israeli intelligence. The new apparatus was entitled the Organization of Jihad and Da'wa (Munazzamat al-jihad wal-da'wa), abbreviated Majd (literally, glory). This unit carried out violent activities, including arson, kidnapping, and rough interrogations and—with Yasin's permission, apparently rendered in the form of a *fatwa*—also executed suspected collaborators with Israel. In 1987, Majd was headed by Salah Shihadah, a well-known preacher, who was in charge of student affairs at the Islamic University in Gaza.[20]

The growing tendency of Islamic youth to undertake violent activities against Israel was reflected in the establishment in 1986/87 of the Movement of the Islamic Resistance (Harakat al-muqawama al-islamiyya), the Frontier Guards on the Land of the Travel (al-Murabitun 'ala ard al-isra'),[21] the Islamic Holy Warriors Organization (Munazzamat al-jihadiyyin al-islamiyyin), and, as already noted, the Islamic Jihad. Even before the outbreak of the Intifada, then, nascent Islamic military organizations had been formed, presaging the full-blown involvement of the Islamic movement in violence and mass protests.[22]

The spontaneous riots that erupted on December 9, 1987, in the Jabalia refugee camp in Gaza and rapidly swelled into a popular uprising, soon to be called the Intifada, underscored both the power of the ethos of armed struggle against Israel and the social and political conditions, which were ripe for its fulfillment in the occupied territories. The volcanic eruption of violence took the Mujamma' leaders by surprise and presented them with a dilemma in view of their previous official abstention from armed struggle against the Israeli occupation and their focus on communal and educational activities. The Mujamma' leaders were also concerned that the PLO would capitalize on the riots to restore its status, which had declined since 1982. Furthermore, the riots offered the potential for mass mobilization; any other course would provoke the defection of young activists. A keen competitor was the Islamic Jihad, which had played a leading role in the armed struggle against Israel in 1986/87.

Faced with this situation, the Mujamma' leaders felt constrained to submit to the pressure of their young militants and adopt an actively combatant posture, consistent with the Palestinians' public mood and expectations. The young leaders of the Mujamma' consisted of students and professionals who had taken part in confrontations with their nationalist counterparts over the control of voluntary and public institutions, in which they acquired experience in mobilizing, organizing, and leading violent protests. Many of them had also spent time in Israeli prisons, where veteran Palestinian prisoners trained them in clandestine activities. Thus, as the Intifada erupted, these young Mujamma' activists were psychologically and organizationally keyed up for armed struggle against Israel.[23]

The Mujamma''s decision to adopt a "*jihad* now" policy against "the enemies of Allah" was thus largely a matter of survival. But it also sparked an internal debate revolving around personal rivalries, interests, and worldviews, which eventually resulted in a compromise between the communal-educational reformist approach and the combatant activist approach of defensive *jihad*. In the early days of the Intifada, the compromise led to the formation of Hamas as a separate body.[24] Ostensibly independent of the MB mother movement, Hamas would presumably ensure the Mujamma''s immunity from Israeli reprisal and enable it to continue its activities. It was not until February 1988, however, after the Intifada had swept through the Palestinian population in the occupied territories and demonstrated the new popular role played by the Islamic movement, that the name Hamas (an acronym for Harakat al-muqawama al-islamiyya—literally, enthusiasm) was formally adopted. In May 1988 Hamas took another step toward consolidating its image as a combatant movement and an inseparable part of the MB, by defining itself as the "strong arm" of the Muslim Brothers. And in its charter, published that August, Hamas styled itself as a "wing" of the MB.[25]

Hamas's entry into the political arena was announced in a leaflet it published—the first of many—on December 14, five days after the serious rioting had begun. This leaflet reflected an interweaving of Islamic ideology, social institutions, and Palestinian nationalism, which injected a new militancy into the idea of Palestinian national liberation and accorded the new movement an image of authenticity and strong appeal to the masses. By launching Hamas, the founding fathers of the Mujammaʿ had effectively adopted *jihad* as a means for achieving national and religious redemption, recognizing the primacy of armed struggle to mobilize the masses, and taking the initiative in guiding the popular uprising. That the advent of Hamas was indeed spontaneous, caused by the riots, is confirmed by the absence of a similar response by the MB in the West Bank. It was not until January 1988 that at Yasin's direction, an organizational infrastructure began to be formed in the West Bank and Jerusalem. This mission, beginning with the delivery of Hamas leaflets from Gaza and their distribution in the West Bank and Jerusalem, was entrusted to Jamil Hamami, a clerk in the Waqf office in Nablus.[26]

It is noteworthy that in retrospect, Hamas invoked its prestige as a *jihad*ist-nationalist movement to embellish its pre-Intifada history and refute the claim that it had been dragged unwillingly into the uprising. To accomplish this, Hamas traced its roots in pre-PLO history, from Sheikh ʿIzz al-Din al-Qassam in the early 1930s through the MB's adherence since 1967 to the principle of *jihad* for the liberation of Palestine. The Mujammaʿ's passive approach to the Israeli occupation was now presented as a necessary period of preparation for the Islamic armed struggle, which eventually sparked the uprising. The rewriting of the MB's pre-Intifada history in a Palestinian nationalist context was a symptom of the intensifying political competition with the PLO over the shaping of the Palestinian agenda. Above all, it epitomized the primacy of the Palestinian nationalist discourse in the West Bank and Gaza Strip as an integral element of the Intifada.[27]

Hamas's active participation in the Intifada threatened the PLO's hegemony and political domination of the Palestinian arena. Concerned that Hamas might fragment and weaken the Intifada effort, the PLO argued repeatedly that it was Israel that had brought about the establishment of Hamas in order to split the forces of the Intifada and degrade the PLO's status in the Palestinian population. An escalation of the tension between Hamas and Fatah was inevitable once Hamas began to compete with the United National Command (the PLO-based Intifada leadership) over the day-to-day agenda of the uprising, employing similar means of public communication, such as leaflets, and identical strategies of struggle against Israel, including armed resistance.[28]

The transition to politics and armed struggle represented by Hamas was intended to complement, not replace, the social activities identified with the Mujammaʿ. Nonetheless, Hamas also represented a shift of emphasis in the Islamic movement's strategy from reformist and communal to political and from the spiritual life of the individual to national action. Whereas it had previously been focused almost exclusively on education, welfare, and community life, the Mujammaʿ's core now assumed a bifocal form, combining the previous activity with organized political protest and violence against Israel, which posed a challenge to the mainstream Fatah organization. Initially intended to be an autonomous organization within the MB movement, Hamas practically turned into the hard core of the Islamic movement, with its own ideological and political stature, which soon overshadowed and in fact co-opted the MB mother movement.

The founders of Hamas, headed by Sheikh Ahmad Yasin, were essentially the senior figures of the Mujammaʿ in the Gaza Strip, hence the latter's significance for understanding Hamas's conduct and the interplay between the civilian and the military spheres of action and between the reformist and the nationalist-activist approaches of Islamic action. The hard core of Islamic activists in both wings of the MB was composed of young men in their thirties, who were residents of refugee camps, mostly professionals, some of whom were preachers, and the leadership was composed of predominantly white-collar professionals with a secular academic background and, to a lesser extent, of religious scholars.[29]

A Pan-Vision and National Perceptions

By adopting the defensive *jihad* as a pivotal principle in the liberation of Palestine, the Islamic Jihad and Hamas effectively followed Fatah and other Palestinian activist groups, which in the late 1950s and early 1960s formulated the Palestinian revolutionary strategy of a "popular armed struggle" against Israel. This strategy represented not only a Palestinian outcry in reaction to the Arab states' delay in undertaking the necessary military effort to liberate Palestine. It also embodied the nucleus of Palestinian nationalism, asserting the role of the Palestinians in this effort, though without exempting the Arab states from their overall responsibility to liberate Palestine.

The new strategy was an effort to reorder the strategic pan-Arab priorities that had been set by Egypt's President Gamal Abdel Nasser, namely,

Arab unity as a prerequisite for the liberation of Palestine. Thus, with the establishment of the PLO in May 1964, Fatah and other Palestinian guerrilla groups criticized its founder and first chairman, Ahmad al-Shuqairi, for subordinating the Palestine cause to Nasser's agenda. Fatah claimed that adherence to a distant vision of Arab unity as a panacea for the Palestine problem effectively meant indefinitely procrastinating the war against Israel, thus perpetuating Israel's existence and wiping out the Palestinian identity and cause. Fatah suggested that an immediate popular armed struggle for the liberation of Palestine would serve the cause of Arab unity, since it was bound to deepen solidarity among the Arab peoples through their joint military effort on behalf of Palestine. Fatah went still further, declaring that the very fate of the Arab world depended on the liberation of Palestine and the elimination of the "Zionist entity."[30]

Fatah's revisionist approach intensified the intrinsic contradiction between the *raison d'état* of particular Arab ruling elites and the *raison de la révolution* of the Palestinian militants. Fatah did not balk at deliberately embroiling the Arab states in a war with Israel against their will. Rather, by undertaking the role of the vanguard of the Arab world in its struggle to liberate Palestine, Fatah challenged Nasser's status as the standard bearer of pan-Arab nationalism and the collective strategy in the conflict with Israel.[31] The organization's revolutionary style did not question the underlying premises of pan-Arab nationalism. On the contrary, it took into account the indispensable role of the Arab world as the mainstay of the material and moral resources needed for the liberation of Palestine. In fact, Fatah strove to subordinate pan-Arab interests and capabilities to the Palestinian cause and, more specifically, to the Palestinian armed struggle, which was meant to be a primary mechanism of mass mobilization and Palestinian nation building. Thus, apart from dragging the Arab world into the fray, the armed struggle was meant to be a rallying ideological and practical force that would unify all Palestinians, regardless of their ideological and political differences or geographical disconnection.[32]

This shift among the Palestinians from a visionary pan-Arabism to a territorial-national perception was most vividly expressed in the years after the 1967 war. Following the Arabs' military defeat and the Israelis' occupation of the West Bank and Gaza, Palestinian nationalism underwent radical changes, especially in its operational strategy, institutions, and leadership. It is here, therefore, that one should look to understand how the PLO became more aware of the need for autonomous Palestinian decision making rather than for all-Arab calculations and why the liberation of all of Palestine, through a strategy of armed struggle, became the common goal of all PLO factions.

In retrospect, however, it was this grand PLO strategy that accelerated the thrust toward territorialization and the adjustment of policy to the new circumstances and to "here and now" considerations. In the post-1973 war era, the PLO adopted the "phased strategy," namely, the establishment of a Palestinian state in a recovered West Bank and Gaza Strip as a "temporary" solution, deferring the realization of the ultimate goal of a state in all of Palestine to an indefinite future. Justification for the process was the PLO's recognition of its limits and, more concretely, of its diminishing resources and opportunities. Apart from the developing peace process between Israel and its neighboring Arab states following the 1973 war, it was the quest for the "independence of Palestinian decision making" that reshaped the PLO's preferences and strategies. By the same token, it was this process of accommodation to changing circumstances that led the PLO to gradually forsake its association with the grand Arab vision, which indeed no longer had the support of the Arab states themselves.

This redefinition of aspirations in narrow territorial terms has been a major source of the Palestinians' national debate, cutting across nationalist and religious groups. Nonetheless, forced by regional developments, the PLO's focus on the Israeli-occupied territories steadily widened in the 1970s, and its competition with Jordan intensified over representation of the Palestinians in the post-1973 war peace process and the Israelis' parallel efforts at settling these areas. Seeking to build its political position in these territories as the exclusive Palestinian national authority, the PLO embarked on a process of institution building, in addition to accelerating its dispersal of financial aid. This process was further heightened by the PLO's expulsion from Lebanon in 1982/83 by Israel and then Syria, leaving it at a political and military nadir and forcing it more than ever before to rely on the Palestinian territorial and communal base of the occupied territories. From the mid-1970s through the uprising in the late 1980s, the significance of the occupied territories as a primary asset for the Palestinian national movement had already been manifested by the PLO's increasing political involvement and presence through social and political institutionalization in the West Bank and Gaza. Hence, in addition to the diminishing opportunities and resources at the regional level, the PLO was constrained to fulfill its responsibility as the national representative of the Palestinian people by paying more attention to the hardships and needs of the Palestinian population in the West Bank and Gaza Strip.[33]

The Palestinian shift from a pan-Arab vision toward a more particularist perception dovetailed with the larger processes of the nationalization and territorialization of "pan" movements in the Arab Middle East after 1967. This trend was spawned mainly by a conspicuous strengthening of

Arab states due to the emergence of military-authoritarian regimes, the expansion of state bureaucracies, and centralized economies. Once they consolidated their power and stability, the Arab ruling elites were better able to reinterpret pan-Arab symbols in accordance with their specific interests and to promote a sense of nation-state at the expense of suprastate identities. Both pan-Arab radical groups and Palestinian organizations were repressed or co-opted into the political system by the ruling elites. Nonetheless, suprastate symbols and values remained a powerful attraction among the masses, spawned by a deep sense of Arab-Islamic solidarity. The restrictions on civilian groups and associations in most Arab states until the late 1980s left the arena free for the Islamic movements to flourish, thanks to their network of mosques and other religious institutions, and access to the media for Islamic preaching.[34] Islamic activism also stepped into the vacuum caused by the ruling elites' failure to provide appropriate solutions to social and economic distress. As in the case of Egypt in the late 1970s, the strengthening popular power of the Islamic movements and mounting socioeconomic difficulties in the 1980s forced the ruling elites in Tunisia, Jordan, Algeria, and Yemen to adopt a strategy of controlled and limited democratization. Despite its shortcomings, this process enabled the Islamic movements to further penetrate the society through voluntary associations, to establish political organizations, to participate in general elections, to gain a presence in representative institutions, and, for insignificant periods, even to share executive power.

On the whole, the greater the opportunities were for the Islamic movements to engage in legal political activities, the more they were inclined to use this channel to gain access to power, legitimacy, and public influence. In the process, the Islamic movements adopted the concept of a state and territorial boundaries to mark their arena of political action. They also tended to define their goals less in terms of changing the regime and more in terms of a comprehensive implementation of Islamic law in society and state (on the issue of political participation, see chapter 5). The road was thus clear for the emergence of a narrowly defined nationalism based on the territorial state (al-Dawla al-qutriyya) and the rapid Islamization of society. Nonetheless, tension between secular nationalism and Islamic religiosity still prevailed, nurturing ideological as well as political competition.

In the microcosm of the Israeli-occupied territories, these developments took a very localized form. Thus, it was against the backdrop of a PLO-dominated political arena that the emergence of al-Mujamma' al-islami in the Gaza Strip, with its efforts at social penetration and mobilization and also competition over existing institutions and public power bases in the

Palestinian society, challenged the established Palestinian leadership. Indeed, by the mid-1980s, the competition between the Mujamma' and Fatah became the hallmark of Palestinian communal politics, especially in the Gaza Strip.

From the outset, the Mujamma' focused on communal activity, which underlay its local nature and link to the specific needs of the population under Israeli occupation. Al-Mujamma' provided civil services that constituted an effective network combining a social infrastructure, political protection, and a popular basis. This network functioned as a parallel system to the absent, or meager, Israeli occupation services, which had been particularly lacking in the Gaza Strip's refugee camps, whose population comprised more than half the population in this territory. The necessity for such civil services was doubly acute because since the late 1970s, the Israeli military government had gradually reduced its social and economic investments in the Palestinian infrastructure in the occupied territories. Moreover, the very existence of a military occupier encouraged local Palestinian individuals and groups to establish voluntary organizations, mainly with the aim of extending social services, which were generally identified with PLO factions.[35] In retrospect, the image of the Mujamma' as an institution focusing on religious and social activities apparently well served the Islamic trend in the Gaza Strip, which could gather public support without appearing to threaten the PLO's hegemonic position among the Palestinians.

Hamas and the PLO

As in the case of Fatah, the genesis of Hamas represented a shift from the Mujamma''s universal Islamic vision to a focus on the Palestinian national agenda and a strategy of armed struggle. In retrospect, this shift was more gradual than it may seem, evolving gradually in the mid-1980s following the PLO's expulsion from Lebanon and the growing awareness among Palestinians that armed struggle was no longer a viable option. For the refugees especially, their sense of despair at the PLO's performance was compounded by the organization's effective abandonment of its national charter, a development manifested in its adoption of a two-state solution. Indeed, the results of the 1982 war in Lebanon, seen in the flagrant discrepancy between the PLO's conduct and the principles of the Palestinian National Charter, brought about the virtual disintegration of the organization and undercut the charter's moral force as a rallying call for all the Palestinian factions in the PLO. Particularly crucial were the PLO's political dialogue with Jordan over the acceptance of the 1967 United Nations Security Council resolution 242 and its consent to participate in an international peace conference with Israel. This perception was apparently one reason for Sheikh Ahmad Yasin's decision to establish an armed body to resume the military struggle against Israel.[36] Indeed, as mentioned earlier, the emergence of Hamas was preceded by several attempts to combine the nationalist and Islamic visions in a combative *jihad* movement.

The adoption of a combative *jihad* by the Mujamma' leaders represented a revolt against the conventional agenda and strategic priorities that was similar to Fatah's revolt against the Nasserist agenda of "unity first." Just as Fatah's "popular armed struggle" had challenged Nasser's insistence on long-term preparations for the decisive war against Israel, the principle of individual *jihad* defied the PLO's authority as the exclusive national force, not least because the PLO seemed no longer involved in an armed struggle against Israel. Furthermore, Hamas espoused political as well as religious fundamentalism, adhering to the basic Palestinian national premises and strategic values at a time when the PLO seemed to have compromised them.

The emergence of Hamas as a full-fledged Islamic-nationalist liberation movement only after the uprising had been perceived as durable reflected an acute internal debate in the Islamic movement. The essential problem was how to combine an Islamic vision with a nationalist one in a "*jihad*ist" movement. At first, the Mujamma' leaders pressed for full involvement in the struggle for Palestinian national liberation. But they had to test the public's response before finally committing themselves to the new movement and its mélange of Palestinian Islamic nationalism. And as in the case of Fatah, the Mujamma''s decision to adopt a "nationalist *jihad*" was meant to serve as an instrument of mobilization and to build a national society driven by a high combative spirit rather than as a means to liberate Palestine physically from Israeli occupation.[37]

Essentially, the establishment of Hamas by the Mujamma' sought to bridge the gap between Palestinian nationalism and Islamism, on the theory that a thrust in the direction of one would hasten the realization of the other. Hamas thus adopted both ideas, of a national territory and an armed struggle, in their religious meaning: "To raise the banner of Allah over every inch of Palestine." Aware, though, of its inability to liberate Palestine, Hamas also injected an all-Arab and all-Islamic dimension into its goals: it would serve as an exemplary vanguard in the resurgence of the Arab and Muslim world against Zionism and imperialism in order to rescue it from its state of servile inaction. Like Fatah, then, Hamas presented the liberation of Palestine and the Arab-Islamic resurrection (*nahda*) as a dialectic in which the success of either depended on the advancement of the other.[38]

With the outbreak of the Intifada, the advent of Hamas with a discourse fusing Palestinian nationalism and Islamism clashed head-on with the PLO's claim to exclusive national authority. According to the Islamic movement, this situation was what prompted the secular-nationalist groups to join forces under the Unified National Command (UNC) in January 1988 and impede the rise of Hamas.[39] In a few months, the UNC and Hamas found themselves taking very different paths as the Intifada began to yield concrete results. In June 1988, an Arab summit conference in Algiers allocated funds to the PLO to fuel the Intifada. In late July, King Hussein declared Jordan's administrative disengagement from the West Bank, paving the way for the publication of a political program to establish a government in exile and bring about an independent Palestinian state, worked out by a Jerusalem-based group of Fatah activists led by Faisal al-Husseini.

The UNC announced its full support for Husseini's program. It urged the Palestinian National Council (PNC), which was due to convene its nineteenth session in Algiers in November, to adopt decisions that would expedite the end of the Israeli occupation and establish a Palestinian state on the basis of Husseini's plan. Hamas, however, denounced the plan as "a stab in the back of the children of the stones,"[40] namely, the youngsters who played an active role in the Intifada. Moreover, Hamas protested King Hussein's disengagement from the West Bank, perceiving it a threat to the unity of the Islamic movement on both banks of the Jordan River.[41] Sheikh Ahmad Yasin came out publicly against the proclamation of a Palestinian state, arguing that such a state would divide the Palestinian people between "within" and "without."[42] Hamas's principal response, however, was its formulation of a normative and political alternative to the PLO's political program in the form of its Charter of the Islamic Resistance Movement.

In August 1988, more than eight months after its founding, Hamas presented an Islamic platform that blatantly appropriated the PLO's national values, as set forth in its charter, cast in Islamic terminology and the Islamic belief system.[43] Hamas effectively proclaimed the PLO's charter as null and void, asserting its replacement by a true covenant that was uncompromisingly faithful to both Palestinian national principles and Islamic beliefs and values. The Hamas document reiterated the MB's slogan of "Allah is its goal, the Prophet is the model, the Qur'an its constitution, *jihad* its path, and death for the sake of Allah its most sublime belief" (article 8). In addition to Hamas's universal objectives to establish the rule of Islam and combat injustice and falsehood, the charter articulated the movement's political goals, which were identical to those of the PLO's charter and boiled down to an armed struggle to retrieve the entire Palestinian homeland. The land of Palestine was held to be whole and indivisible and defined as an Islamic *waqf* (endowment) "consecrated for future Muslim generations until Judgment Day" (article 11). Consequently, any relinquishment of the land was unlawful and forbidden by Islamic law, under any circumstances or authority: "Neither a single Arab country nor all Arab countries, neither any king or president nor all the kings and presidents, be they Palestinian or Arab" (article 11). Indeed, this article epitomized the Islamic movement's ripening process of territorialization, shifting from a pan-Islamic to a national-Palestinian movement.[44]

Hamas resolved the contradiction between the national idea, with its sacrosanct principle of state sovereignty, and the divine law, with its sanctification of the "sovereignty of Allah," by defining the national struggle in religious terms. Hence, nationalism became an indivisible element in the Islamic creed itself, and the territorial objective and the strategy for its realization were defined as integral to Islamic duties and beliefs. According to its charter, Hamas is a "universal movement" and "one of the branches of the MB in Palestine" (article 2); at the same time, however, Hamas is defined as a "distinctive Palestinian movement" that regards nationalism (*wataniyya*) as "part of the religious creed." Unlike other nationalisms, Hamas claims uniqueness because in addition to material, human, or territorial sources, it is also linked to divinity and faith. Hence, "nothing in nationalism is more significant or deeper than [waging *jihad* against the enemy and confronting it] in the case when an enemy should tread on Muslim land" (article 12). Hamas "strives to raise the banner of Allah over every inch of Palestine" (article 6).

Since Palestine is an Islamic problem, Hamas's nationalism intertwines with the religious creed, and fighting the enemy that threatens a Muslim land is the most sacred duty of every individual Muslim (*fard 'ayn*) man, woman, or slave (articles 12 and 15). Any exclusive political solution to the Palestinian conflict is rejected as an act against Islam, and so it follows that the only solution to the Israeli-Palestinian dispute is *jihad*.

The liberation of Palestine is perceived as the responsibility of three concentric groups: the Palestinian people, the Arab nations, and the Islamic world. Hamas thus adopted both concepts of nationalism current in the Arab world, namely, the territorial-state nationalism (*wataniyya*) and pan-Arabism (*qawmiyya*), which in the Palestinian case is clearly equivalent to Islamism. Both are indispensable to Hamas's ideology. The revisionist nature of Hamas's nationalist viewpoint is succinctly reflected in the perception that the Palestinian problem is an Arab-Islamic cause, which enables Hamas to deplore the PLO's secular, narrow nationalism as a departure from the Arab and Muslim worlds (article 15).[45]

Despite the similarity of the PLO's and Hamas's charters concerning national goals and strategies for their realization, they assume different natures. The PLO's charter was clearly formulated in national, civil, and legal terms, and one of its articles (33) stipulates that the document can be amended by two-thirds of the Palestinian National Council. By contrast, Hamas's charter is anchored in religious principles of holiness, divinity, and eternity, with no option for amendment. Moreover, it has the characteristics of a comprehensive cultural, social, and moral charter, encompassing issues such as the role and status of women in society and the national struggle, the importance of educating the younger generation in regard to religious values, and the roles of culture, literature, and art and their contribution to the liberation campaign. The charter also speaks of social and economic solidarity, support for the poor and needy, human rights in an Islamic society, and the correct attitude toward members of the other monotheistic religions. The Hamas charter is saturated with historic examples of the continued clash of Western and Islamic civilizations and the central role of Judaism and Zionism in the West's offensive against the Islamic world in modern times. Hamas hardened the conventional tone among Arab nationalists toward the Jews, adopting anti-Semitic charges based on *The Protocols of the Elders of Zion* concerning a Jewish conspiracy for world domination.

Despite its rivalry with the national-secular factions, its militant attitudes, and its opposition to the PLO's policies, Hamas stated its willingness to subordinate itself fully to the PLO if that body were to adopt Islam as its way of life (article 27). Yet even without the fulfillment of this condition, Hamas affirmed the kinship and national bonds linking members of the two rival movements, emphasizing their shared goal and common enemy. Coexistence with the PLO was also mandated by the disastrous consequences of internal strife (*fitna*) in Islamic history.

Hamas's drive to become an all-Palestinian political and moral center able to challenge the PLO was manifested also by the immediate concrete goals it set for itself, which were linked to the situation of the Palestinian political community and especially to its struggle for liberation from Israeli occupation. These aims included resistance to Israeli settlement in the occupied territories and to the Israeli occupation policy, that is, the expulsion and administrative detention (arrest without trial) of Palestinians, their brutal daily treatment, prevention of family reunification, the refusal to release prisoners, and the heavy taxes levied on the Palestinian populace.[46]

Hamas's Dilemmas

Hamas's adoption of Palestinian national values was compatible with its leaders goal of becoming a political alternative to the PLO, although they tried to play down this goal for tactical reasons (see chapter 4). Any other course of action would have been tantamount to accepting marginalization and risking demise. Furthermore, Hamas's tacit claim to all-Palestinian leadership encouraged the new movement to address a wide range of issues relevant to its constituency. By doing so, Hamas showed that it was attending to the basic needs of the people and was willing to deal with day-to-day issues as well as with national questions significant to the Palestinians' political future.

The Islamic movement's shifting focus from building an Islamic society from below to engaging in a program of political action with specific national aims to be achieved by armed struggle is a familiar phenomenon in the social and political life of ideological movements elsewhere. The more that such movements concentrate on territory and community, the more that they must attend to a concrete agenda based on practical problems; and the more that they are involved in practical decision making, the more that they are held responsible for the consequences of those decisions. In the case of al-Mujamma', and later on of Hamas, the pattern of communal action served as a pillar for building a local political power base. Furthermore, the Islamic movement's leaders repeatedly announced their recognition of the community as a crucial determinant in defining their strategy and building an infrastructure of civil society. This approach not only remained valid following the advent of Hamas but also became doubly significant for the Islamic movement as a whole in view of the Oslo accords and the establishment of the Palestinian Authority (PA).

Yet Hamas's attempt to assume the trappings of a national movement in terms of institution building and mass mobilization has been problematic. In general, Sunny Islamic movements have always had difficulty generating an institutional hierarchy, probably because it would contradict the principle of an open and equitable interpretation of Islamic law by the religious scholars (*'ulama'*). A formal structure, then, might threaten the logic of religious authority based on scholarship and the informal collective acceptance (*ijma'*) by the community of the faithful Muslims (*umma*), one of the four bases (*usul*) of medieval Islamic legislation.[47] This has been even more complicated with regard to ongoing public and political issues that are not clearly decided by Islamic jurisprudence. Without a separation of state and religion, such issues are effectively left to personal and group interpretation, with endless opportunities to legitimize or delegitimize political authority by employing classic Islamic arguments, oral traditions, and historic precedents to support their views.

The effort to secure a dominant public position through a commitment to advance particular Palestinian national interests and, at the same time, maintain an adherence to Islamic dogma caused Hamas many problems. Although these quandaries had troubled Hamas from its inception at the beginning of the Intifada, they had become grave by the September 1993 Israel-PLO accord and the establishment of the PA in Gaza and Jericho in May 1994. Hamas's interest in securing its presence and consolidating its influence on the Palestinian people amid competition with the PLO and, later, with the PA necessitated a measure of flexibility, despite its intransigent attitude, toward a settlement with Israel—that is, a willingness to consider measures implying acquiescence and some form of participation in building the PA. Such an approach may serve Hamas's interest in protecting and continuing its communal activity, thus strengthening its position in the Palestinian society. However, by adopting such a strategy, Hamas also risks losing its authenticity and uniqueness as a normative opposition to the PLO and increasing friction in the movement and subjecting it to manipulation by the PLO and the PA.

By the same token, adherence to the dogmatic vision would also sow confusion and uncertainty. Conformity to Hamas's stated religious doctrine would certainly signal consistency and adherence to the "great tradition" of Islam and thereby strengthen the organization's credibility among its followers and adversaries alike. But conformity to the doctrine might undermine the support and sympathy of many Palestinians, particularly those in the Gaza Strip, who hope that the peace process will end their social and economic hardships. Conformity to its doctrine, therefore, might have kept Hamas's ship afloat for a time but offered little prospect of finding a safe harbor. Political flexibility might enhance the prospect, but only at great risk.

Hamas's dilemmas over adopting national trappings have been aggravated by the blurring of the social and ideological boundaries separating it from Fatah, the PLO's principal arm, and, in practice, the ruling party under the PA. Even though both movements appeal to wide and diverse Palestinian public groups, they derive their support mainly from the majority whose social values and collective identity are characterized by a lack of formal political affiliation and who tend to be strongly associated with the Islamic-Arab "great tradition." Owing to the broad interpretation of reality by both Hamas and Fatah, social boundaries that are supposed to clarify the differences between them seem fluid. An indication of these blurred boundaries can be found in the establishment of the "Islamic Jihad Units" (Saraya al-jihad al-islami) in Fatah's ranks in the late 1980s. Moreover, it is these blurred boundaries that gave rise to the popular view of Hamas and Fatah as being more complementary than competitive.[48]

How did Hamas cope with these dilemmas? More specifically, how could Hamas promote its interests by political means without sacrificing its credibility and unity? How did Hamas's search for a transition to the political route affect its policy? To what extent was Hamas able to justify shifting from its "unrealistic" attitude in the conflict—from a total commitment to the vision of an Islamic state in the territory of Mandatory Palestine and a rigid rejection of any territorial compromise—to a new pragmatic approach that would not preclude an Israeli-Palestinian settlement, even a temporary one, which entailed a calculated deviation from its stated doctrine? The principle that guided Hamas's response to these dilemmas was based on the assumption that the more the need for political dialogue, tacit understanding, or cooperation with the PLO (and the PA) could be justified in normative terms—that is, as the right and just thing to do—the less likely that it would be accused by its members and followers of deviating from its ultimate vision and hence the less danger there would be of organizational disintegration.

Hamas's discursive and political maneuvers to escape being defeated by these dilemmas are best analyzed in the context of a triangular sphere of interrelations since the outbreak of the Intifada in late 1987. This refers to the relations between Hamas and the Palestinian arena, with the PLO and the PA as the central actors, on the one hand, and with Israel, on the other. In maneuvering between these two poles, of a rival at home and an enemy outside, Hamas has combined current political interpretation with established norms and beliefs, differentiating between long-range goals and short-term requirements, showing signs of political flexibility while at the same time demonstrating its conformity with formal Hamas doctrine. Political adjustment in terms of controlled violence, negotiated coexistence, and calculated participation in the PA's system of power and institutions have become the main features of Hamas's political conduct. To determine the intensity and the effectiveness of these patterns, it is necessary to examine the ideological trends, social circumstances, and political considerations that shaped Hamas's strategies and to evaluate its options in the shifting political environment of mutual recognition and peace negotiations between Israel and the Palestinian national leadership.

CHAPTER THREE

Controlled Violence

Hamas was a product of the new circumstances imposed on al-Mujamma'
al-islami by the Palestinian civil uprising. This quandary was further compounded by the PLO's endeavor to reap political fruits through international diplomacy and a propaganda campaign, both of which the Islamic
movement and Hamas had been lacking. A visit by U.S. Secretary of State
George Shultz to the region in early 1988, the November 1988 PNC proclamation of an independent Palestinian state (based on the November 29,
1947, UN resolution 181 on the partition of Palestine into two states, one
Jewish and one Arab), and the beginning of a U.S.-PLO dialogue in December of 1988 all indicated that the PLO was rapidly attaining the status it had long craved, that of an equal partner in the Middle East peace
process. Thus, in addition to Hamas's daily competition with the UNC
over shaping the agenda for the Intifada, the PLO's possible inclusion in
renewed peacemaking efforts threatened Hamas's political future and compelled it to address this issue immediately.

It was against this background that Hamas embarked on an intensive
propaganda campaign against the PNC's resolutions, invoking deep-rooted
Islamic symbols and beliefs to delegitimize the PLO's diplomatic efforts
to achieve a settlement in the West Bank and the Gaza Strip. More effectively, Hamas challenged the PLO by reviving the ethos of the armed
struggle against Israel, combined with continued civil revolt in the occu-

pied territories, as a vehicle of political mobilization that would avert any serious Israeli-Palestinian peacemaking. Whereas Israel was a target to fight, Hamas condemned the PLO—and, later, the PA—for their willingness to recognize Israel at the price of abandoning most of the Palestinian territories. Nonetheless, Hamas was aware of the limits of its power on both the intra-Palestinian and regional levels and therefore calculated its strategy on the basis of cost-benefit considerations. *Jihad*, as we will show, was subordinated to political calculations. A policy of controlled violence became a key component in Hamas's political strategy and daily conduct.

The Jihad Ethos

A primary aim of Hamas was to establish an Islamic state in the territory of Palestine whose liberation was to be achieved by holy war. As we saw, the emphasis on this term was congruent with the Islamic symbols and beliefs that constituted Hamas's political doctrine. Defined as an Islamic endowment (*waqf*) of the Muslim world as a whole, *jihad* was adduced not only as a duty that devolved on individual Muslims but also as the sole legitimate way to retrieve Palestine in its entirety. Hamas thus adopted the principle contained in the PLO's National Charter of 1968, which defined armed struggle as "a strategy and not a tactic," in order to preclude the possibility of a negotiated settlement, which by definition would entail a territorial compromise. To establish the legitimacy and historic significance of an armed struggle in its Islamic meaning (*jihad*), Hamas presented itself as a link in the chain of holy war against Zionism and Israel in the defense of Palestine. The inevitability of *jihad* was strictly linked to religious faith. Because to forgo parts of Palestine was tantamount to forgoing part of Islam, Palestine as a whole could be liberated only by armed struggle. However, *jihad*, as explained earlier, also had another meaning, namely, the internal *jihad* that entailed the enforcement of Islamic social and moral norms. Interpreted in Islamic terminology, such a mission provided Hamas with a legitimate avenue by which to impose its authority among the Palestinians.

Another similarity between Hamas and Fatah in its early years was the revisionist, antiestablishment nature denoted by their respective concepts of individual *jihad* and "popular armed struggle." Fatah's concept of guerrilla warfare for the liberation of Palestine challenged Nasser's doctrine of Arab unity as a prerequisite for a decisive war against Israel and sought a shortcut to the liberation of Palestine. By the same token, Hamas's concept of *jihad* challenged the PLO and its main arm (Fatah), which by the mid-1980s had virtually abandoned guerrilla warfare against Israel and drifted toward a peaceful settlement of the conflict. Both Fatah and Hamas in turn represented a revolt against the current military inaction toward Israel, underpinned by *raison d'état*—equivalent to the Islamic concept of *jihad* as a collective, or state, responsibility (*fard kifaya*). And both movements suggested instead an alternative concept, which meant not only to subordinate the "reason of state" to the revolution but also to legitimize autonomous action by peripheral social and political groups.

Hamas's adherence to the principle of "not [ceding] one inch" and its emphatic claim to all of Palestine found frequent expression in its leaflets. Leaflet no. 28 (August 18, 1988), entitled "Islamic Palestine from the [Mediterranean] Sea to the [Jordan] River," asserted:

> The Muslims have had a full—not a partial—right to Palestine for generations, in the past, present, and future. . . . No Palestinian generation has the right to concede the land, steeped in martyrs' blood. . . . You must continue the uprising and stand up against the usurpers wherever they may be, until the complete liberation of every grain of the soil of . . . Palestine, all Palestine, with God's help.

Leaflet no. 22 (June 2, 1988) declared: "For our war is a holy war for the sake of Allah unto victory or death."

In Hamas's eyes, the Muslims' right to establish an Islamic state in the territory of Palestine leaves no opening for a dialogue or a political settlement with Israel. Hamas believes that the *jihad* against Israel articulates the true aspirations and needs of the Palestinian people, expressing the real meaning of the Palestinian national ethos. The following quotations from Hamas leaflets exemplify this approach:

> Let any hand be cut off that signs [away] a grain of sand in Palestine in favor of the enemies of God . . . who have seized . . . the blessed land. (March 13, 1988)

> Every negotiation with the enemy is a regression from the [Palestinian] cause, concession of a principle, and recognition of the usurping murderers' false claim to a land in which they were not born. (August 18, 1988)

> Arab rulers, who invest efforts for the false peace . . . and who
> entreat Israel to agree to a "just" peace. . . . We hope you will fight
> at least once [in order to prove] that you partake of Arab boldness or
> Muslim strength. (leaflets of January 1988)

And in a rhetorical appeal to Israel: "Get your hands off our people, our cities, our camps, and our villages. Our struggle with you is a contest of faith, existence, and life" (undated leaflet).

Hamas also used political arguments to reject any attempt to achieve a political settlement with Israel. Thus, in leaflet no. 28: "Israel understands only the language of force and believes in neither negotiations nor peace. It will persist in its evasiveness and in building a military entity, in exploiting the opportunity for attack, and in breaking the Arabs' nose." And in the same leaflet: "The Arab world is not so weak as to run after peace, and the Jews are not so strong as to be able to impose their will. . . . How long can Israel withstand all the forces?"

Furthermore, Hamas ascribed to Israel and the Jews demonic traits that justified its refusal to hold a dialogue: Israel is a "cancer that is spreading . . . and is threatening the entire Islamic world" (May 3, 1988). The Jews, according to another leaflet, are "brothers of the apes, assassins of the prophets, bloodsuckers, warmongers. . . . Only Islam can break the Jews and destroy their dream" (January 1988).

Hamas often drew on images and events from the history of Islam to underscore the religious character of its conflict with Israel and also to substantiate its claim for perseverance (*thabat, sumud, tamassuk*) and faith (*iman*) in the final victory of Islam, no matter what the current difficulties of the Arab and Muslim community (*umma*) were. To validate its argument that Israel was bound to be defeated by Islam, the leaflets of Hamas frequently rehearsed Islam's great victories over its enemies in Palestine, upholding the names of Muslim military heroes: Ja'far Ibn Abi Talib, who fought Byzantium in the Battle of Mu'tah (629 C.E.); Khalid Ibn al-Walid, who commanded the Battle of Yarmuk (636 C.E.) and was called by Muhammad "the sword of Allah"; Salah al-Din, who vanquished the Crusaders at the Battle of Hittin (1187 C.E.); and the Mamluk sultan, Baybars, who defeated the Mongols in the Battle of 'Ayn Jalut (1260 C.E.).

The Khaybar affair also attracted Hamas's attention. Many Hamas leaflets concluded with the call "Allah akbar [Allah is great]—the hour of Khaybar has arrived, Allah akbar—death to the occupiers." Khaybar was a wealthy Jewish community in the Arabian Peninsula. According to a Muslim tradition, the Jews of Khaybar betrayed Muhammad by serving him poisoned meat that eventually killed him. The Prophet and his followers had conquered Khaybar in 628 C.E., allowing "the Jews their land in return for binding themselves to turn over half their harvests."[1] For Muslims, Khaybar became a symbol of Jewish treason. Similarly, the Muslims who reside in the territories are looked upon as *mujahidun*—the warriors of the holy war—or as *murabitun,* inhabitants of the frontier (*ribat*). These were Muslims who settled in the countryside during the period of the Muslim conquests to defend the borders; they were considered to be fulfilling a religious precept. By emphasizing the Muslim nature of Palestine in the past and present and advocating a Muslim state throughout Palestine that would ameliorate the ills of the Muslim community, Hamas ignored the Palestinian Christians while demonstrating closer links to Muslims outside Palestine.

Whereas the PLO perceived the conflict with Israel in national-secular and realistic terms, Hamas regarded any possibility of a political settlement based on compromise as a violation of Palestine's status as an Islamic endowment (*waqf*) as well as the Islamic precept of holy war against the Zionist invasion. Hamas maintained that the peace process intended to legitimize the "Zionist entity" and clear the way to further usurpation of the Muslim and Arab wealth by the foreign invaders.

The conflicting stands of Hamas and the UNC regarding a Palestinian state and the political process often created friction between the two contenders. The disagreements grew worse as the UNC began to express support for a peaceful solution, and the PLO intensified its diplomatic activity. When Hamas drew up its charter in August 1988, it demonstrated an inclination toward autonomy in its political activity, ceasing its coordination with the UNC. Thus, in leaflet no. 25 (September 6, 1988), the UNC assailed Hamas's decision to call a two-day general strike on a date different from that set by the UNC. The UNC termed this a blow to the unity of the Palestinian ranks and a boost for Israel. The UNC also decried acts of violence against those who did not respond to Hamas's call for a strike. Hamas was quick to retaliate and in its leaflet no. 30 (October 5, 1988) absolved itself of all blame:

> The Jews and their supporters are striving to split our ranks and
> generate disputes by spreading rumors that Hamas is competing
> [with other movements] or seeking to replace them. In reaction to
> these virulent rumors, we call on the people to peruse the charter
> of the Islamic resistance movement [of August 1988] in order to
> acquaint themselves with it and learn its goals. The competition will

consist of confrontation against the [Israeli] enemy and inflicting grave damage on his camp. We reiterate that we are for unity of ranks, against schism, and for everyone who works faithfully for the liberation of Palestine—all of Palestine. We are against conceding so much as an inch of our land, which is steeped in the blood of the Companions of the Prophet and their followers.

Tension between Hamas and the UNC mounted in the wake of the events at the PNC meeting held in Algiers in mid-November 1988. At this meeting, the PNC declared the establishment of a Palestinian state on the basis of the UN General Assembly resolution 181 of November 1947 calling for the partition of Palestine into two states, one Jewish and one Arab. In leaflet no. 29 (November 20, 1988), entitled "The Joy of the Palestinian State," the UNC issued

> [an appeal to] a number of fundamentalist elements to favor the general national interests, our people's national interest, away from their basic assumptions and factional interests . . . and to cease presenting negative stands and manifestations. For they serve the enemy, whether they wish to or not. They must draw the conclusions from the mass celebrations . . . marking the declaration of the [Palestinian] state, reflecting the deep roots of our legitimate leadership and sole representative [the PLO]. It is still not too late to fuse all the loyal forces in the melting pot of the uprising and its United National Command.

In reaction, Hamas declared, in leaflet no. 31 (November 27, 1988), that it opposed splitting the Palestinian ranks but that this might result from "leaflets being planted in the name of Hamas that the [Israeli] occupier circulated in order to split the ranks and cast aspersions on the [various] currents." And above all, Hamas believed, they should "preserve the unity of the people. Pay no heed to the enemy's attempts to cause a rift in families, clans, currents of thought, and ideas."

Hamas's response to the UNC's charges attest to its complex attitude toward the national camp. On the one hand, Hamas was not eager to aggravate its disagreements with the UNC to the point of a head-on clash, as that would be counterproductive in the struggle against Israel. On the other hand, Hamas did not back away from a confrontation in the future should the UNC, together with the PLO, assent to a political settlement that jettisoned the principle of liberating all of Palestine. Its military weakness might have influenced Hamas's approach, explained by its desire to refrain from civil strife (*fitna*), a notorious recurrent phenomenon in Islam's history. Yet while repeating its determination to prevent *fitna* and its menace to the Palestinian people, from the early days of the Intifada Hamas also maintained that preserving the national unity must not be at the expense of its independence and distinctiveness.[2]

The Intifada as a Controlled Revolt

Hamas's Intifada activities were conducted under the direct guidance and control of Ahmad Yasin, who was behind the contents of the movement's leaflets, in consultation with his close aides. Like their UNC counterparts, Hamas's leaflets also included directives for social conduct. On the anti-Israeli front, Yasin directed his followers from the outset to use firearms against the "occupation troops," though such actions must not be identified with Hamas, he told his followers, fearing a backlash that could paralyze the nascent movement. At the same time, "strike groups" (*al-sawaʿid al-ramiya*, "the shooting arms") were founded, similar to Fatah's "strike committees," to carry out most of the daily Intifada activities, such as blocking roads, throwing stones, writing slogans and directives on walls, and enforcing Intifada directives on the population, including work strikes and not working in Israel.

Yasin also maintained Hamas's links with the Islamic movement in Jordan. According to his testimony to the Israeli authorities, he received financial aid from the "general guide" of the movement in Jordan, ʿAbd al-Rahman Khalifa, totaling until August 1988, about half a million dollars, brought in by money changers and emissaries. At the same time, Yasin built up the movement, appointing his close aides to key positions. He gave his aides considerable operational and organizational freedom, reflected in the timing and character of the violence perpetrated by Hamas activists, which originated at the local, grassroots level and at times was the work of unorganized supporters. Indeed, from the beginning Hamas was organized into a small number of hard-core activists who coordinated and activated a wide network of supporters through the mosques whose preachers were often members of the movement or had close acquaintances in the Islamic students' associations and communal services.[3]

In the early months of the Intifada, Hamas did not call for mass demonstrations, fearing that this might lead to a direct confrontation with the Israeli security forces and jeopardize the movement's fragile existence before it took root among the Palestinian public. Another concern was that

Hamas's public weakness and its limited support—compared with that of the UNC—would be exposed; indeed, there might even be a violent collision with the UNC in which Hamas would emerge as the loser. Hamas therefore directed its followers to take only those actions that had religious overtones and thus would be easily understood as integral to Islamic ritual—such as fasting, praying, and exploiting dates of religious significance in order to escalate the Intifada under its leadership. This perhaps was the reason for the relatively tolerant attitude displayed by the Israeli government toward Hamas during the first year of the Intifada, as compared with that toward other Palestinian organizations, reflecting its perception of the PLO and its factions as Israel's most dangerous enemies. It was not until June 1989, fully eighteen months after the outbreak of the Intifada, that the Israeli government declared Hamas to be a terrorist group, along with the Islamic Jihad, outlawing both and imposing tight control over them. A year later, in the summer of 1990, the Israeli security authorities began to raid and search mosques in the Gaza Strip and the West Bank, even closing some of them for short periods.[4]

Hamas's establishment involved a functional division between the internal security apparatus and the Islamic Holy Warriors Organization (Munazzamat al-jihadiyyin al-islamiyyin), the movement's military units.[5] From the beginning, Hamas's organization had a clandestine, decentralized character. To ensure compartmentalization and secrecy, recruitment was based on personal acquaintance, and communication was through messages, directives, leaflets, and weapons left in apparently innocuous places, often in or around mosques. Hamas's focus never wavered from maintaining a horizontal separation between active members, in an effort to slow the arrests of leading figures. Still, imprisoned Hamas leaders managed to maintain contact with the movement and smuggle out operational orders even from prison. Hamas's organic nature, rooted in its social institutions and communal infrastructure, with its network of mosques and large following of believers, offered the movement a better chance of survival in the face of repeated Israeli repression. Hamas's existence was secured by the steady stream of followers from which new activists were enlisted or emerged spontaneously, becoming spearheads of the movement's violent and political activities.

Despite Hamas's efforts to stay underground, its military and political leadership was repeatedly jolted by the large numbers of arrests and expulsions after September 1988. In response, Hamas tightened its horizontal compartmentalization and turned to vertical hierarchy between local activists and affiliated headquarters abroad. Such contacts, through which organizational and operational orders were issued and financial aid was transferred, were maintained by phone and fax, written messages, and direct meetings outside the country. The result was greater fragmentation of authority and blurred hierarchical links between the political-religious leaders and the military activists.

Hamas's turn to violence was a matter of necessity in view of its competition with the nationalist Palestinian groups—including the Islamic Jihad—which had led the armed struggle against Israel. In its first year, Hamas's military activity was relatively limited (ten operations), including shooting at Israeli military patrols and civilian transportation in the Gaza Strip and the use of "roadside charges" against Israeli vehicles. At this stage, Hamas still lacked a solid operational infrastructure and gave priority to acquiring arms, mobilizing cadres, and training its forces in the use of arms and explosives. By the second year of the Intifada, the scope, sophistication, and daring of Hamas's violent activity (thirty-two actions) had risen sharply. The most conspicuous of these operations were the kidnapping and murder of Israeli soldiers (in January and May 1989) inside Israel, by the same squad (as revealed later). It is noteworthy that following the first kidnapping, Yasin refused to allow the perpetrators to bargain with the Israeli authorities for a trade for Palestinian prisoners. The reason was that Yasin continued to fear that identification of the movement with that action might induce Israel to retaliate against Hamas's social institutions, particularly the Mujamma'. In the second year of the Intifada, Hamas extended its military activity to the West Bank, notably Hebron, and this was followed by actions inside Israel proper, including knife attacks on civilians and the burning of forests.[6]

Despite these activities, Hamas still lagged behind the Palestinian national organizations in terms of its impact on the Palestinian public. Nonetheless, Hamas's message of holy war turned out to be a particularly powerful answer to Israel's violence against Palestinians, for it had the effect of substantiating the meaning of *jihad* and investing it with a specific, immediate significance. Thus, after the Israeli police killed seventeen Palestinians during a violent clash in the Temple Mount compound on October 8, 1990,[7] Hamas called for a *jihad* "against the Zionist enemy everywhere, in all fronts and every means." The most tangible result was a sharp rise in spontaneous knifing attacks committed by Palestinian individuals against Israeli civilians, police, and soldiers. The perpetrators of these attacks had no organizational connection with Hamas, though many were clearly susceptible to the Islamic message. In any event, Hamas presented these attacks post factum as a manifestation of Islamic devotion and self-sacrifice. In five months after the Temple Mount massacre, thirteen Israelis were killed in such actions.[8]

A roundup by Israel of Hamas's senior leaders in the Gaza Strip in September 1988 forced Ahmad Yasin, who remained free, to compartmentalize the movement even more tightly. For example, he appointed Isma'il Abu Shanab as the general commander of Hamas in the Strip and Nizar 'Awadallah as the commander of the military organization. He also divided the Gaza Strip into five separate districts, each under the command of new figures that he appointed. But the kidnapping and murder of the second Israeli soldier, in May 1989, resulted in the arrest of Yasin himself and a number of senior figures of the military branch who were later convicted for their role in the action. The arrests effectively paralyzed Hamas and created a vacuum at the top level of leadership. The result was the working visit to Gaza of a group of Hamas activists from the United States, led by Musa Abu Marzuq, to rehabilitate the movement. The decision to take this action was made following consultations with Hamas leaders in Jordan. Marzuq and his aides introduced a strict hierarchy. They divided the West Bank and Gaza Strip into seven and five subdistricts, respectively, headed by separate headquarters that included four apparatuses—security, religious indoctrination (*da'wa*), political activity, and coordination—the heads of which constituted each subdistrict's command. The West Bank and Gaza Strip were linked by a coordinating committee under the movement's higher leadership, which consisted of three major committees: political, military, and indoctrination.

With the restructuring of the movement, Yasin's status as the one supreme authority came to an end. For the first time since its establishment, Hamas was controlled from outside the occupied territories—from Springfield, Virginia, where Abu Marzuq resided, and from Amman. The Jordanian headquarters of Hamas served as a vital link to the "inside" leadership of the movement in the Israeli-occupied territories and determined its social policies and its military activities (in 1992/93, Hamas's military command was located in London). In 1993, after the United States named Hamas as a terrorist organization, Amman became Hamas's political and military headquarters, where the movement enjoyed a semilegitimate status and could operate openly. This status, which Hamas retained well after Israel and Jordan signed their peace treaty (October 1994), was supported by the widespread presence of the MB in Jordan[9]—in which Palestinians were a significant and the more radical part—and the Hashemite rivalry with the PLO and, later, with the PA.

The new structure stressed the supremacy of the "outside" over the "inside" leadership, determined primarily by the former's control of financial resources and their flow into the territories. The external financial aid was necessary not only to maintain Hamas's civic, political, and military activities and to support the families of the "martyrs" and prisoners, but the inside leadership badly needed the funds also to enhance the movement's political stature and enable it to compete better with the national-secular groups prevailing in the West Bank and Gaza Strip, by expanding its social services and civic penetration. Hamas thus became structurally similar to the PLO, with political representation and supportive groups based in various Muslim and Western countries. The external apparatus played the principal role in the movement's political decision making, control of propaganda and publications, and activation of the military units. Still, compared with the status and authority of Fatah and its PLO partners vis-à-vis their followers in the occupied territories, the "outside" leadership of Hamas, given its communal character, ultimately enjoyed less power over the "inside" and its social institutions.[10]

The power struggle between Hamas and the PLO-based UNC created a potentially irreparable rift between the two camps. Nonetheless, despite their conflicting ideological interests, both groups had common practical interests, namely, the day-to-day struggle against the Israeli authorities. In appeals to the PNC members, Hamas stated that

> the Islamic resistance movement, Hamas, has already made it clear
> that it posits [as a goal] an all-embracing *jihad* until the liberation of
> Palestine . . . for the people chose the way . . . the way of *jihad*,
> honor, and sacrifice, finding that for the sake of Allah and the
> liberation of Palestine, whatever is more precious and more valuable
> than money, than a son and a soul, is cheap. . . . Our struggle with
> the Zionists is not a campaign for partition of borders, and it is not
> a dispute over the division of land; it is a campaign over existence
> and destiny. In this position, we see the hope and aspiration of our
> people everywhere to arouse in you the spirit of the struggle, the
> spirit of the outbreak of the revolution of 1965 [the beginning of
> Fatah's guerrilla war against Israel]. We call on you to take under
> your wing the spirit of the children of the stones and the
> continuation of the armed struggle, no matter what the cost. Our
> people have often confronted plots and have made many sacrifices to
> thwart them. Our people still possess the same readiness to make

sacrifice after sacrifice, and they express this blessed uprising that has been recorded as a phenomenon unparalleled in history.[11]

Hamas's concern about the population's daily hardships and immediate needs, however, increased its awareness and hesitation to translate its dogmatic vision into actual practice. Hamas thus combined a calculated policy of confrontations with Israeli soldiers—including military actions—with elevated religious rhetoric laced with symbols of *jihad*, Qur'an-based hatred of the Jews, and calls for mass confrontations with the Israeli occupation forces. This was reflected in Hamas's directives to the Palestinian public about its role in the uprising, which were almost identical to those issued by the UNC.

Like the UNC, Hamas called on the population to cooperate in both violent and nonviolent actions. The former included throwing stones and firebombs, building barriers, burning tires, wielding knives and axes, clashing with the Israeli forces, and attacking collaborators. In regard to non-violent activities, the people were asked (1) to sever their economic ties with Israel and develop local institutions that would provide the same public services; (2) to engage in civil disobedience, that is, disobey laws and regulations; and (3) to carry out activities promoting intra-Palestinian solidarity.

The directive to sever ties with Israel included refusing to work in Israel and in Jewish settlements in the occupied territories; boycotting Israeli products; withdrawing deposits from Israeli banks; resigning from the Civil Administration; developing a home-based economy, including growing vegetables and raising domestic animals; setting up and expanding committees on education, information, guard duty, and agriculture; and establishing and cultivating local bodies for "popular education"—a directive calling on parents, teachers, and students to uphold the routine of classes despite the protracted closure of educational institutions by the Israeli authorities. On this issue Hamas challenged the UNC, refusing to turn the schools and higher educational institutions into a battleground of protest and civil disobedience and repeatedly calling for the resumption of studies, inside or outside school. Hamas finally prevailed, and after the summer of 1989 the schools ceased to be an arena of demonstrations and riots.[12]

Directives regarding civil disobedience included not paying taxes and fines; staging partial commercial strikes, and holding general strikes on specified days. In order to build solidarity, the people, or sometimes certain groups, were called on to stage day-long strikes of solidarity with prisoners and with families of victims; hold memorials for traumatic events such as the civil war in Jordan that broke out in September 1970; help lawyers deal with prisoners; schedule press conferences to expose conditions in the detention camps; stage sit-in strikes by students, teachers, and parents in front of foreign missions and closed schools; volunteer to help farmers with the olive harvest; offer assistance to needy families; refrain from raising rent; reduce doctors' and hospitals' fees; and write slogans on walls and raise flags.

In table 3.1, the analysis of the first 30 leaflets issued by Hamas shows that of 139 violent and nonviolent directives, 36 (about 26 percent of the total) appeared in the first 10 leaflets, 40 (29 percent) in leaflets 11 through 20, and 63 (more than 45 percent) in leaflets 21 through 30. The increase in the number of directives was accompanied by a significant change over time in the proportion of instructions calling for violent or nonviolent activities.

Table 3.2 shows that even though Hamas's level of violence was consistently high from the start of the Intifada that is, 30.5 percent of the 36 instructions in the first 10 leaflets, 40 percent of 40 instructions in leaflets 11 through 20, and 39.7 percent of the 63 instructions in leaflets 21 through 30, the number of instructions for severing economic and public service ties with Israel drastically decreased. From nearly 25 percent in the first 20 leaflets, the calls to break economic ties with Israel fell to less than 5 percent in leaflets 21 through 30.

TABLE 3.1 Types of Directives in Hamas Leaflets by Periodic Distribution[14]
(absolute numbers)

Type of Directive	Period 1 (Nos. 1–10)	2 (Nos. 11–20)	3 (Nos. 21–30)	Total
Violent	11	16	25	52
Nonviolent:				
Severance of contact	10	11	3	24
Disobedience	7	2	19	28
Acts of solidarity	8	11	16	35
Total	36	40	63	139
Percentage	25.9	28.8	45.3	

TABLE 3.2 Types of Directives Contained in Hamas Leaflets by Periodic Distribution[15] *(in percentage)*

Type of Directive	Period		
	1 (Nos. 1–10)	2 (Nos. 11–20)	3 (Nos. 21–30)
Violent	30.5	40.0	39.7
Nonviolent:			
Severance of contact	27.8	27.5	4.8
Disobedience	19.4	5.0	30.2
Acts of solidarity	22.2	27.5	25.4
Total	100 (36)	100 (40)	100 (63)

These trends reflect the contradictory considerations that guided Hamas's behavior. On the one hand, Hamas, like the UNC and the PLO, was aware of the vital role of violence in propelling the Intifada and securing political prestige. Violence also served as an outlet for the younger generation's ideological fervor and political frustrations. The demographic weight of the younger Palestinians and their level of education and political awareness, together with the organizational frameworks at their disposal, made them the leading participants in the uprising. Moreover, as the violence grew and claimed more Palestinian casualties, the Intifada's political gains rose accordingly. The daily skirmishes between the population and Israeli troops, widely covered in the media, thrust the Palestinian problem back into international consciousness. Even public figures, politicians, and the press in countries friendly to Israel were sharply critical of the latter's policy, and governments and international organizations condemned the methods it used to suppress the uprising, leading to a conviction in Israel of the necessity of finding a political solution to the ongoing violence.

The violence also deeply affected Israel itself. Many Israelis perceived their country's occupation as morally indefensible, socially deleterious, economically ruinous, and politically and militarily harmful. Israel's political leadership faced mounting pressure from broad segments of the public to stop trying to quell the uprising by force and instead to propose political solutions. In short, it was the Palestinians' growing awareness of the role played by violence in promoting the Intifada and producing political gains that accounted for the large number of violent directives in Hamas and UNC leaflets.

On the other hand, the Intifada's endurance depended on the Palestinian people's economic health. Without a self-sustaining economy, the Palestinians were dependent on Israel, thereby neutralizing the pressure to sever their economic contact with Israel. Consequently, to intensify the economic boycott against Israel and disengage from its economy would mean economic hardship for more than 100,000 workers who earned their living in Israel and a huge loss of revenue for many local merchants and factory owners who maintained commercial ties with Israeli firms. In turn, a severe economic downturn in these sectors could weaken the influence of Hamas and the UNC, lead to disobedience, and encourage anarchy. If the Intifada's strength lay in its ability to obtain the cooperation of all social strata and age groups, it is readily understandable how the ideologically heretical suddenly became the economically inevitable.

The inability or unwillingness of merchants, factory owners, and workers to break off economic relations with Israel forced Hamas to adapt to the prevailing conditions. Hence, the number of directives urging an economic break with Israel gradually fell as the Intifada turned into a way of life for the Palestinian population. Instructions in this spirit continued to appear, but more selectively, as in regard to work in Israel and the boycott of Israeli products. Later, Hamas's leaflets announced that the prohibition on working in Israel was confined to general strikes or to persons employed in sectors that competed with products of the territories, such as the citrus industry. In the same vein, Hamas called for a boycott of products for which local substitutes were available, principally milk products, agricultural produce, cigarettes, and soft drinks.

The decline in the number of directives calling for a total economic break with Israel indicates a reassessment by Hamas concerning the limits of the Intifada. This awareness also explains why Hamas decided not to declare a general civil revolt but instead to hammer home the idea that the uprising was a transitory stage toward general revolt. This change of position is illustrated in the following examples from Hamas leaflets:

> Know that victory demands patience [*sabr*] and God is on the side of the righteous (January 1988).
> Know that the road [of struggle] with the Jews is long and will not end soon (April 1, 1988).
> Spare no efforts [to fan] the fire of the uprising until God gives the sign to be extricated from the distress. Invoke God's name often, for with hardship comes ease (January 1988).

This controlled civil revolt, like the continuing decline in the number of directives calling for breaking economic ties with Israel, indicated that from the very beginning of the Intifada, Hamas had calculated its strategy on a cost-benefit basis and so now was trying to avoid a slide into absurdity in its effort to realize its objectives. Hamas recognized the limits of its power and was careful not to cross the line and fall into an all-out confrontation with Israel. *Jihad* turned out to be not an ultimate goal but a political instrument wielded by political considerations.

Hamas's ability to differentiate between an all-out struggle and pragmatic considerations depended to a large extent on its leadership's prestige and authority to justify the deviation from the movement's doctrine. It is in this context that the religious concept of *sabr* (self-restraint, patience) proved useful in justifying current policies by adjusting to the change of political environment. *Sabr* was enlisted to avoid confronting realities without acquiescing to them. It has been explained and justified by the assumption that the true believers will eventually prevail, no matter how desperate the present. The future will reward the believer, but he must be patient ("Allah is with the patient").[13] *Sabr*, therefore, was meant to justify the temporary acceptance of, and adaptation to, reality. This principle has been presented in Islamic writings in the context of Islam's ultimate victory regardless of its weakness at the present. It might also be used to legitimize the current reinterpretation and temporary deviation from hitherto sacrosanct Islamic norms. *Sabr* thus helped explain that the struggle against Israel should be based on cost-benefit considerations, even though Israel was the enemy of Allah and the Prophet.

Controlled Violence, the Oslo Agreement, and the Palestinian Authority

Despite Hamas's efforts at reorganization during the second half of 1989, a new Israeli crackdown in late 1990 and early 1991 led to another crisis. These developments underlined its failure to survive as a clandestine movement despite horizontal compartmentalization and separation between its military and civilian apparatuses. Hence, in 1991 the "battalions of 'Izz al-Din al-Qassam" (*kata'ib 'izz al-din al-qassam*) were formed and became Hamas's official military apparatus. The creation of this organization was one of several local initiatives taken by senior military activists, and their recognition by the movement's leadership as its official military apparatus was due to their success and attractive name.

The battalions were given their name by Walid 'Aql, a senior activist of Hamas in the Gaza Strip who was their founder and first commander. In late 1991, squads of 'Izz al-Din al-Qassam carried out most of their activities in the Gaza Strip, executing suspected collaborators with the Israeli intelligence agencies and announcing their responsibility for the executions in leaflets and on wall graffiti. The 'Izz al-Din al-Qassam apparatus attracted attention in early 1992 when one of its groups assassinated an Israeli settler in the Gaza Strip. Following the assassination, the organization attacked more Israeli civilians, also by using car bombs. As its prestige gained by killing Jews grew, many Islamic adherents previously active in the Intifada began to emulate the militants. Some of them embarked on daring independent military initiatives without the coordination or knowledge of the regional or outside military command but under the name 'Izz al-Din al-Qassam, as in the case of the kidnapping and assassination of an Israeli border guard in December 1992.[14]

In 1992, similar branches of 'Izz al-Din al-Qassam were founded in the West Bank, first in Hebron and later also in Nablus (where Hamas had not been very active). In July 1992, Hamas's headquarters in the United States sent an emissary to the occupied territories with a large sum of money, the names of activists to contact, and directions for coordinating military activities in the West Bank with those in the Gaza Strip. He was arrested by the Israeli authorities, and his interrogation revealed that the military squads were to be separated into districts and operate under the direct command of the outside headquarters that would coordinate the various districts and supply funds for purchasing arms and cars, renting safe apartments, and training, mostly in Jordan.[15]

It is not clear how much the escalation in Hamas's military activity was affected by Israel's policies toward the movement or by the international peace conference held in Madrid in late 1991, the first formal public negotiations between Israel and a Palestinian delegation from the West Bank and Gaza Strip. Although the conference resulted in a stalemate, the prospects for a breakthrough seemed to grow after the June 1992 general elections in Israel brought to power a Labor government headed by Yitzhak Rabin. In any event, the increase in Hamas's military activity, indicated by an abortive attempt to explode a car bomb in a neighborhood near Tel Aviv five months later and followed by suicide attacks, was apparently based on Hamas's closer relations with Iran and consequent beginning of military cooperation with Hizballah. As in its decision on armed struggle, here too Hamas lagged behind the Islamic Jihad, which already in 1991 had begun cooperating with Hizballah against Israeli forces in south Lebanon.

The deportation of 415 Islamic activists by Israel to Lebanon in December 1992 was a milestone in Hamas's decision to use car bombs and suicide attacks as a major modus operandi against Israel. Shortly after-ward, Hamas's leaders in Amman instructed its military activists to carry out two attacks, one by a car bomb, as a gesture to the deportees.[16] Hamas's escalated military activity was an indirect result of the presence of the de-portees for almost a year in south Lebanon, which provided the Palestin-ian Islamists an opportunity to learn about Hizballah's experience in fight-ing the Israelis, the effect of suicide attacks, and the construction of car bombs. Indeed, it was Hizballah's spectacular attacks since 1983 on the multinational force in Beirut and the Israeli forces in Lebanon that ended the American presence in Lebanon and forced Israel to withdraw in 1985, except from a self-defined "security zone" along the Lebanese border. Thus it was no coincidence that Hamas's first suicide operation was carried out shortly after the deportees had returned to the occupied territories.[17] More-over, Hamas and the Islamic Jihad adopted the same procedure of find-ing a candidate for a suicide operation, training and preparing him psy-chologically, writing a farewell letter, and making a videotape before his mission.[18]

In April 1993, the battalions of 'Izz al-Din al-Qassam scored another victory when a booby-trapped car driven by a Hamas activist exploded in the Jordan Rift Valley between two parked Israeli buses, whose passen-gers had, by chance, gotten off. It soon became clear that the West Bank was taking the lead in military activity against Israel following the move there from Gaza of senior Hamas figures sought by Israel. The most con-spicuous of them was 'Imad 'Aql, who staged many of the attacks on Is-raeli targets around Hebron. His killing by Israeli forces in November 1993 triggered a wave of riots in the occupied territories, the declaration of a three-day mourning period by Hamas and Fatah, and his colleagues' an-nouncement that they would "punish" Israel with five actions to avenge 'Aql's death.[19] Such announcements by Hamas's military apparatus became the expected response to the killing of senior Palestinian military figures or civilians by Israel. Hamas's quasi-apologetic approach indicated its con-tinuing need to secure legitimacy from the Palestinian people for its armed struggle against Israel, by presenting this approach as legitimate self-defense, thus absolving Hamas of responsibility for the repercussions of its actions, such as collective punishment by Israel's total closure of the territories.

The conclusion of the Oslo agreement and the signing of the Decla-ration of Principles (DOP) between Israel and the PLO in September 1993 dramatically changed Hamas's strategic situation. Indeed, as a movement whose military activity against Israel now outweighed that of Fatah and the other Palestinian national organizations, the PLO-Israel agreement confronted Hamas with nothing less than an existential problem. To begin with, the agreement put an end to the Intifada, which had provided Hamas with ideal conditions to become a genuine political alternative to the PLO. In addition, the PLO's agreement to desist from hostile actions against Israel, a commitment to be imposed by the future self-governing Palestinian Authority (PA) in the occupied territories, clearly threatened to curtail Hamas's freedom of military action and provoke a head-on confrontation with the PA, which would be fully supported by both Israel and the international community.

The stunning effect of the Oslo agreement on Hamas also was reflected in the internal discourse among its activists. Internal documents circulated among the movement's senior members in the initial period after the DOP was signed conveyed a sense of despair, stemming from the awareness of Hamas's political weakness in the face of Palestinian and international support for the agreement. Hamas's deepest concern was for the future of *jihad* against Israel. Its conclusion was to continue the strategy of *jihad*, still perceived as the ultimate source of legitimacy and as a shield against any attempt by the PA to restrict the movement's activities or eliminate them altogether. At the same time, however, Hamas called on its members to preserve the "unity of Palestinian ranks" and to work to bring together all opponents of the Oslo agreement, Islamists and secular alike.[20]

Indeed, in the first few months after the Oslo agreement was signed, Hamas escalated its armed struggle against Israeli soldiers and civilians alike. Overall, though, Hamas's policy of controlled violence against Israel persisted well after the signing of the DOP. Thus Hamas continued to maintain that its policy was based on pragmatic cost-benefit calculations and was not captive to dogma. Expressing the pragmatic policy on violent attacks against Israel in the wake of the Oslo accord, the head of Hamas's political bureau, Musa Abu Marzuq, said that "the military activity is a permanent strategy that will not change. The modus operandi, tactics, means, and timing are based on their benefit. They will change from time to time in order to cause the heaviest damage to the occupation."[21]

Given Hamas's insistence on continuing its violence against Israel, the implementation of the DOP became dependent on the PA's capability and willingness to prevent Hamas and the Islamic Jihad from committing violence against Israel. Clearly, attacks by Hamas against Israeli targets risked halting the peace process or at least slowing it down. This prospect would portray Hamas among the Palestinians in the occupied territories as an obstacle to further retreat by the Israelis and thus would erode the movement's popular support.[22] Hamas sought to bridge this gap by walking a thin line between maintaining its political autonomy and coexisting with the PA. Its goal was a policy combining continued violence against Israel, a propaganda campaign designed to expose the DOP's weaknesses and thus bring about its abolition, and the avoidance, at almost any price, of violent confrontation with the PA and mutual bloodshed (*taqtil*). To achieve this, Hamas intensified its armed struggle against Israel preceding the founding of the Palestinian Authority in Gaza and Jericho and tried by this means to enhance its public prestige and thereby immunize itself from the PA's attempts to suppress the Islamic opposition.[23]

The DOP's threat to Hamas was indicated by the latter's willingness— even before Oslo accord was signed, when rumors spread about a possible unilateral Israeli withdrawal from the Gaza Strip—to seek agreement with the PLO. Through such an agreement Hamas apparently was trying to prevent the use of force against its members. by the Fatah Hawks in the occupied territories. This attempt became urgent after the Oslo accord and the anticipated establishment of Palestinian self-government in the Gaza Strip. Shortly before the Cairo agreement concerning the implementation of the Gaza-Jericho phase was signed in May 1994, a joint statement by Hamas's battalions of 'Izz al-Din al-Qassam and the Fatah Hawks was published in the Gaza Strip announcing a six-point agreement that the two rival factions had reached. This tenuous collaboration was aimed at enhancing Palestinian national unity and preventing internal war. Under the six-point agreement, the two sides would refrain from both verbal and violent disputes, commence a "constructive dialogue," and establish joint conciliation committees to resolve conflicts, suspend execution of collaborators for one month, decrease the number of strike days, and lift the prohibition on school attendance. This agreement also served as a model for resolving other tensions between local Hamas and Fatah activists.[24]

Peaceful coexistence with the PA at the price of abandoning the armed struggle against Israel, however, would risk the loss of Hamas's distinctiveness as the leading movement for the liberation of Palestine and the establishment of an Islamic Palestinian state. Without the legitimating shield of *jihad*, Hamas would be exposed to a process of containment that could eventually destroy it as a political power. Indeed, as one internal document asserted shortly after the establishment of the PA, Hamas was in a "turbulence of contradictions" without a clear policy to meet its specific needs.[25]

Indeed, even though Hamas advocated armed struggle against Israel, its leaders were forced to anticipate the expected responses of Israel and the PA and, given the wide public support for the peacemaking process, also of the Palestinian population in the West Bank and Gaza Strip. Yet Hamas's controlled violence may also have been based on the assumption that selective attacks against Israel might be desirable to the PA, to hasten Israel's withdrawal from the occupied territories. At the same time, the Hamas leadership repeatedly instructed its cadres to reiterate to the Palestinian public that the Oslo accord was illegitimate and inconsistent with resolution 242, which stipulated Israel's withdrawal to its 1967 borders, as opposed to the legitimacy and necessity of *jihad* under the continuing Israeli occupation. Subsequently, Hamas began to emphasize the PA's failures and mismanagement, particularly of the humiliating Israeli demand that Arafat and the PA act forcefully against the Islamic opposition. Hamas interpreted Israel's attempts to use the PA as a means to enhance its security as an absurdity that validated every attempt by Hamas to intensify the struggle against the Gaza-Jericho agreement by means of mass protest and violent struggle everywhere against the Israeli occupation.[26] Thus, whereas Hamas had been accelerating its attacks against Israel's forces withdrawing from the Gaza Strip, it adopted a "wait and see" position during the first few months of the PA, to test the limits of its freedom of action under the new authority.

Hamas's insistence on continuing the violent attacks against Israel was facilitated by the massacre at the Cave of the Patriarchs in Hebron in February 1994, committed by a Jewish settler, after which Hamas vowed vengeance in the name of the Palestinian people. The timing of the massacre, in the midst of the Israel-PLO negotiations on the implementation of the Gaza-Jericho phase of the DOP, gave Hamas an opportunity to enhance its popularity by escalating the violence against Israel in the form of suicidal car bombings in urban centers, toward the anticipated advent of a self-governing Palestinian authority. Furthermore, presenting Hamas's violent actions against Israel as a response in kind to the massacre in Hebron could mitigate criticism of Hamas following Israel's collective punitive measures against the Palestinian people.

The opportunity provided by the massacre in Hebron was doubly appealing to Hamas, due to indications that Arafat had been trying to prevent a head-on clash with the Islamists. This was indicated by the temporary arrests of Hamas and al-Jihad al-Islami members, and Arafat's permissive approach to attacks against Israeli targets in pre-1967 Israel.

Such an approach allowed the PA to deny responsibility, since the perpetrators had arguably launched their attacks from areas under Israel's administration.[27] Indeed, Hamas's concept of a continuous *jihad* was tacitly
acceptable to Fatah's leaders, who believed that it would also prevent a direct confrontation between Hamas and the PA.[28]

Israel's repeated retaliation for Hamas's suicide bombings by confining
the entire Palestinian population to the West Bank and Gaza Strip compelled the PA to reach an agreement with Hamas on the issue of armed
struggle. However, the PA-Hamas dialogue conducted in the summer and
fall of 1995 to settle their differences—including the dispute over the use
of violence against Israel—was marked by the PA's effort to buy time and
peace with Hamas at the expense of its commitment to Israel under the
terms of the 1994 Cairo agreement to prevent terrorist attacks from its areas. Hamas's and the PA's positions therefore may have been affected by
the relatively wide public support for violent actions against Israel.[29]

The difference between the PA and Hamas was demonstrated by the
PA's minister of planning, Nabil Sha'ath. Whereas Sha'ath called for freezing the armed operations and giving diplomacy a chance, Hamas leader
Mahmud al-Zahar insisted that the employment of arms was legitimate
and that the parallel use of war and peace was possible.[30] Hamas was willing to offer only to cease its military operations in and from the Gaza Strip
for a period to be agreed on by the two parties. In October 1995, before
the actual negotiations began, the PA's draft agreement had already taken
a vague position, contending that Hamas was committed "to put an end
to military operations in and from the PA's territory, or refrain from taking credit for them in any way."[31]

Despite lengthy negotiations, however, Hamas refused to give up the
armed struggle, and at the end of the Cairo talks in December 1995, the
two parties were unable to sign an agreement. Instead, the heads of the
two delegations issued only a joint communiqué, implying that Hamas
would try to avoid embarrassing the PA. Accordingly, Hamas would halt
military operations against Israel from PA-controlled areas and refrain
from publicly announcing or admitting responsibility for them.[32] The parties' reference to Hamas's continued violence under the Oslo process made
clear their mutual understanding that since the defense of Israel was not
the PA's responsibility, armed struggle against Israel could continue as
long as it was not waged from PA-controlled areas.[33]

That Hamas's armed struggle has been perceived as a means subordinate to political calculations was made clear by the movement's leading

figures in Gaza. Probably the most candid statement was by Mahmud al-Zahar:

> We must calculate the benefit and cost of continued armed operations. If we can fulfill our goals without violence, we will do so. Violence is a means, not a goal. Hamas's decision to adopt self-restraint does not contradict our aims, including the establishment of an Islamic state instead of Israel. . . . We will never recognize Israel, but it is possible that a truce [*muhadana*] could prevail between us for days, months, or years.[34]

From the outset, Hamas was aware of the possible consequences of continued armed struggle for its relations with the PA. Indeed, this became evident in view of the PA's rejection of any attempt to consolidate a legal opposition, Islamist or any other, and even used Hamas's armed operations against Israel as a pretext for suppressing the latter's activity. Nonetheless, senior Hamas members in the West Bank and Gaza Strip were divided between two major trends regarding the use of violence: a politically oriented position of being willing to adjust to the new political realities and, from the very establishment of the PA in June 1994, of striving to reach an agreement that would allow it a legal and open political presence and ways to share power through envisioned Islamic party; and a militant position, composed mainly of the military apparatuses, of insisting on continued armed struggle and objecting to any agreement with the PA that would end its activity and organization. The militant position was supported by the "outside" political leadership, whereas the "inside" political leaders in the West Bank and Gaza, weakened by the continued imprisonment of Sheikh Yasin and other leading figures, were paralyzed by pressures and threats from their local rivals. According to one report, these internal differences led to threats to political leaders like Mahmud al-Zahar from Gaza and Jamal Salim from Nablus by members of the Hamas military apparatus.[35]

It was against this backdrop and fear of confrontation with the PA as a result of Israeli pressures on Arafat to eliminate Hamas and its social and religious infrastructure that Hamas leaders had repeatedly proposed, since 1995, a conditional cease-fire with Israel, to stop the bloodshed of innocents on both sides. Although many of Hamas's political leaders spoke out in favor of such a cease-fire, they did not agree on its terms. The terms mentioned by Hamas's leaders in the West Bank and Gaza were the re-

lease of all prisoners, removal of the economic closure of the occupied territories, the eviction of all the settlers (sometimes the Jewish residents of
East Jerusalem were also included in this category), and an end to the persecution of Palestinians. In any case, such an agreement would have to be
signed by the PA—not Hamas—and Israel. Following a cease-fire, Hamas
was reportedly willing to negotiate indirectly with Israel on a time-
limited truce (*muhadana*) conditional on a full Israeli withdrawal to its 1967
borders, including Jerusalem, and the dismantling of all the Israeli settlements in the occupied territories.[36]

In September 1997, two days before the abortive assassination attempt
by Mossad agents in Amman against Khalid Mashʿal, the head of Hamas's
Political Bureau, Jordan's King Hussein delivered a message from the
Hamas leadership to Israel's Prime Minister Benjamin Netanyahu. In it,
Hamas suggested opening an indirect dialogue with the Israeli government, to be mediated by the king, toward achieving a cessation of violence, as well as a "discussion of all matters." But the message was ignored
or missed and, in any case, became irrelevant following the attempt on
Mashʿal's life. That such a message had indeed been delivered was revealed
by King Hussein himself in the aftermath of the Mashʿal affair, which led
to Yasin's release.[37]

The Dynamics of Controlled Violence

Hamas's policy of controlled violence should be examined in the context
of intra-Palestinian affairs and intra-Hamas considerations as much as in
the context of Israeli-Palestinian relations. However controlled and calculated, Hamas violence could be hardly anticipated, or prevented, raising
intriguing questions concerning the dynamics of Hamas's military operations: Given their critical impact on the movement's existence, the question is how much such operations were the result of political decisions
rather than local initiatives. What level in the movement's hierarchy, and
what considerations, determined the timing and type of the violent attacks
against Israel? Were the terrorist attacks a vindictive response to casualties among Palestinian civilians or perhaps to the elimination of senior
military figures of the Islamic movements by Israel's secret agencies?

Hamas perceived the Oslo accord and the 1994 Cairo agreement as a
strategic threat to its very existence. The more real this threat seemed—
as a result of the progress in the diplomacy between Israel and the PA—
the more willing Hamas was to resort to armed struggle despite the risk
to its dialogue with the PA. At the same time, Hamas sought to reduce

this risk by describing violent attacks against Israel as unavoidable acts of self-defense or as revenge for Israel's killing of Palestinians.

On April 6 and 13, 1994, shortly before the signing of the Cairo agreement on the establishment of a self-governing Palestinian authority in Gaza and Jericho, two suicide operations were carried out in 'Afula and Hadera, two Jewish towns in Israel, by the Battalions of 'Izz al-Din al-Qassam, Hamas's military wing. Publicly, these operations were portrayed as avenging the massacre in Hebron of thirty Palestinians by a Jewish settler on February 25 of that year. Although this argument was directed to the Palestinian people, these operations also were aimed at enhancing Hamas's bargaining position regarding the anticipated PLO-based PA, by pressuring Arafat to reckon with Hamas and seek political coexistence with it.[38]

Hamas's fears that any progress in the Israel-PA peace process would mean further restriction of its opportunities as a mass movement, as well as voices in Israel calling for its eradication, prompted Hamas and the Islamic Jihad to use even more violence and to urge their forces to carry out another wave of suicide attacks in Tel-Aviv (by Hamas) and Ha-Sharon Junction (by the Islamic Jihad) in October 1994, and January 1995, respectively. In the summer of 1995, Hamas carried out two more suicide bombings in Ramat Gan and Jerusalem, which coincided with the final phase of the Israeli-PA negotiations over Israel's withdrawal from all primary Palestinian towns in the West Bank, (concluded in the Taba accord, signed on September 28, 1995) and the general elections for the PA's Council to be held afterward. Taking into account Hamas's recognition that it must adjust to the new political reality, one may argue that beyond undermining the peace process, the suicidal attacks were meant to enhance Hamas's prestige among the Palestinians and to force Arafat to come to terms with Hamas as a legitimate opposition.

The signing of the Taba accord in late September 1995 apparently made Hamas's leaders inside the territories decide to suspend the terrorist attacks against Israel in order to avoid interrupting the Israeli withdrawal from the Palestinian cities and the preparation for elections to the PA Council, which could upset the Palestinian public. These calculations apparently underlay the limited understanding reached by Hamas and the PA in the talks conducted in Cairo in late 1995, according to which Hamas was to avoid embarrassing the PA by refraining from attacks against Israel from areas under the PA's control. Indeed, between August 1995 and February 1996, Hamas and the Islamic Jihad did not make any terrorist attacks against Israeli targets, a result of the pressure exerted by both Israel and the PA on Hamas's leaders and the fear of frustrating the Palestinian people's expectations of the new Israel-PA agreement. Accordingly, various groups of Hamas in the West Bank and Gaza Strip attempted to use this self-imposed truce as a trump card with the PA and, indirectly, with Israel.

One such attempt was Hamas's offer to stop military operations against Israel in return for the PA's ceasing to persecute members of 'Izz al-Din al-Qassam's battalions. The talks between Hamas and the PA were conducted with the participation of Muhammad Daif, Hamas's leading military figure in the Gaza Strip and first on Israel's list of wanted Palestinians, who expressed a willingness to accept the PA's demands, as follows:

1. A total cessation of military operations by Hamas against targets in Israel that do not serve Palestinian interests.
2. To help the PA prove that it has full control of the situation so as to prevent Israel from using this as a pretext to violate the agreement.[39]

Hamas leaders in the area controlled by the PA sought an agreement with Israel through the PA on a mutual cessation of hostilities. Hamas would sign a formal agreement with the PA, but not with Israel, and in return, Israel would stop pursuing the movement's activists and release Sheikh Yasin from prison. Prime Minister Shimon Peres and Chairman Yasir Arafat had been part of the effort to reach such an agreement, together with an Israeli rabbi residing in the West Bank.[40]

The PA's response to the Hamas leadership in the West Bank and Gaza Strip deepened the latter's split with Hamas's Political Bureau in Amman, whose attitude toward a cessation of violence and further accommodation with the PA remained negative. Thus, although "internal" Hamas activists supported an agreement with the PA for a total cessation of terrorist attacks against Israel, in the PA-Hamas talks held in Cairo in December 1995, the "outside" Hamas leaders refused to accept such a truce. All that they would agree to was a vaguely phrased commitment to temporarily halt military operations against Israel from the Palestinian self-governed areas and refrain from publicly announcing, or admitting to responsibility for, such attacks, in order to avoid embarrassing the PA. It is noteworthy that the PA had initially been willing to accept such a vague commitment by Hamas—apparently as the lesser evil—to ensure trouble-free general elections to the PA Council, scheduled for January 1996.[41]

Hamas's promise not to embarrass the PA by carrying out military operations against Israel from the territories under the PA's control left open the possibility of terrorist attacks from areas either still under Israeli control or, implicitly, even from the areas controlled by the PA. At the same time, Israel pursued its secret war against terrorism and continued to impose general closures on the Palestinian population in the West Bank and Gaza Strip in the wake of advance warnings of terrorist attacks. In short, Hamas's military apparatus could still justify, from its point of view, continuing its attacks against Israel. Specifically, when covert Israeli operations killed two leading Palestinian figures who were behind the suicide bombings—the Islamic Jihad leader Fathi Shiqaqi in Malta (October 26, 1995) and the so-called engineer of 'Izz al-Din al-Qassam, Yahya 'Ayyash, in Gaza (January 5, 1996)—their respective organizations vowed to retaliate, and the PA could hardly deny their right.

Shiqaqi's assassination clearly stiffened the PA's moral stand regarding the repression of Islamic terrorism in Palestinian society. Spokesmen for the PA claimed that the murder of Shiqaqi had undermined their efforts to reach an agreement with Hamas and Islamic Jihad to stop attacks against Israel.[42] Moreover, Hamas interpreted the murder as a "declaration of war" by Israel and declared that "the Palestinian people will avenge the murder," although it did not take any concrete measures. Then, however, the murder of Yahya 'Ayyash two weeks before the elections to the PA Council prompted Hamas spokesmen to announce unequivocally that his death would be avenged. Again they resorted to the argument that the *jihad* should be continued regardless of the Oslo process, as it complemented the diplomacy by expediting Israel's withdrawal from the West Bank and the establishment of Palestinian self-government. 'Ayyash's assassination in fact triggered a spate of suicide bombings in Israel. The actual instructions and means to implement the attacks were issued by Muhammad Daif, commander of 'Izz al-Din al-Qassam in the Gaza Strip, to a senior member of the West Bank military apparatus, Hasan Salama, who was responsible for recruiting and training candidates for these operations.

Thus, in February and March 1996, after a respite of six months, young Palestinians, supervised by Hasan Salama, carried out a series of suicide bombings in Jerusalem, Ashkelon, and Tel Aviv, calling themselves "Disciples of the Martyr Yahya 'Ayyash." The bombings brought the number of Israeli civilians and troops killed at the hands of the Islamic movements since the signing of the Oslo accord in September 1993 to more than one hundred. By using 'Ayyash's name, the perpetrators appeared to be fulfilling their duty of avenging his assassination and enhancing the movement's prestige. In addition, the wave of terrorism that jolted Israel served the purposes of intransigent elements in Hamas—the command in Amman and senior figures of the military apparatus in the Gaza Strip—who wanted to undermine the dialogue between the "inside" political leaders of the movement in the West Bank and Gaza Strip and the PA.[43] Indeed, the bombings revealed the weakness of the "inside" political leadership and its lack of control over the movement's armed apparatuses; at the same time, the "outside" leadership expressed uncertainty about the identity of the perpetrators, perhaps in order to blur their connection with Hamas and save the movement from possible punitive measures by the PA and Israel. Later it turned out that the idea of the bombings originated with a clandestine subgroup in the battalions of 'Izz al-Din al-Qassam, consisting of some ranking military figures of Hamas, such as Muhammad Daif and Ibrahim Maqadmah.[44]

In terms of lives lost, sheer horror, and the long-term impact on Israeli society, the February–March suicide bombings must be considered the worst terrorist assault ever unleashed against Israel. The repeated scenes of carnage in urban centers and the grief that followed generated worldwide solidarity with Israel and condemnations, culminating in an international summit conference at Sharm al-Sheikh in Sinai led by U.S. President Bill Clinton in mid-March. The PA, under heavy pressure to clamp down on Islamic terrorism, made extensive arrests and confiscated illegal arms, especially among the Hamas military apparatus, in coordination with the Israeli intelligence services. Under the heavy public criticism following the series of suicide bombings, Hamas took a passive line, reiterating that it would not veer from its policy of averting a full-blown internal Palestinian confrontation.

One reason for the PA's harsh reaction toward Hamas was the latter's violation of a tacit understanding reached in late December 1995, under which Hamas would not launch attacks on Israeli targets from the PA-controlled areas.[45] In addition, there was unprecedented condemnation by Palestinians of the carnage, and more broadly, the terrorist bloodbath sparked a public debate among Muslim scholars and theologians in the Arab world, revealing a range of attitudes toward legitimate means of struggle against Israel.[46] Criticism of suicide operations was supported by learned religious opinions (*fatawa*) by Muslim scholars, apparently issued at the behest of the PA. Such acts against civilians and unarmed people, they argued, could not be considered martyrdom (*istishhad*) in a holy war, thereby implying that they were, in fact, acts of individual suicide (*intihar*), forbidden in Islam as an act against God's will. This criticism was the reason for the publication in Damascus of an apologetic book on this theme, apparently at Hamas's initiative, if not by the movement itself, a few months after the February–March suicide bombings. The book's stated goal was to refute the criticism of the killing of innocent Israeli civilians and to establish the Islamic legitimacy of such acts, carried out by Hamas and the Islamic Jihad against Israel. Those who blew themselves up were made "martyrs" of *jihad*.[47]

Representing Hamas's militant viewpoint, the book ridiculed the scholarly Islamic opinions of those who opposed the suicide operations and questioned the writer's religious and moral authority. Hamas enlisted Islamic scholars in its cause as well, who maintained that self-sacrifice in the course of *jihad* had a sound historical and religious basis, representing the noblest expression of devotion and conferring the status of martyr (*shahid*) on those who fell. Giving up one's life in a holy war, these scholars held, was undertaken for the sake of Islam's domains and shrines, and the mission of every believer was to inflict as many casualties as possible on the enemies of Islam. Suicide for the sake of Islam was implicitly justified by the desperate reality of the Muslim world under the yoke of Western domination. Nonetheless, even this book set limits to suicide, emphasizing that it must be strictly subordinated to the public interest and not be based on emotion or unsound beliefs.[48]

The ascendancy of a right-wing government in Israel in May 1996, led by Benjamin Netanyahu, indicated a major shift in Israel's approach to the Oslo process, in which partnership with the PA was replaced by force and procrastination. The new Israeli approach was demonstrated by the delayed redeployment in Hebron; the opening of the Hashmonean tunnel in the Old City of Jerusalem in October 1996, which triggered armed clashes between the Israeli army and Palestinian police forces; and the decision to build a Jewish settlement in Har Homa (Jabal Ghneim) on the southern outskirts of Jerusalem. The tension and mistrust between the sides produced a convergence of interests, though not agreement, between Hamas and the PA in an effort to demonstrate "national unity" and a renewal of the intra-Palestinian dialogue. The stalled Oslo process alleviated Hamas's concerns, rendering the use of violence less necessary, while the nominal rapprochement with the PA meant an easing of the repressive measures taken against the Islamic opposition, enabling coexistence and uninterrupted development for Hamas. The result was that the first nine months of Netanyahu's government were marked by the absence of the kind of spectacular Islamic terrorist attacks that had taken place during the previous two years. But in March 1997, the bombing of a Tel Aviv coffee shop ended the respite. The operation, which had mistakenly ended with a suicide, indicated a new policy by Hamas to prevent its being identified with such attacks. Whether the March operation was an expression of despair at the economic deterioration and continued state of occupation,[49] the reflection of the availability of human and material resources, or the order of a Hamas decision maker in response to Israeli policy, it once again demonstrated the decisive weight of the local military squads in carrying out terrorist attacks inside Israel.

In two other suicide operations in August and September of that year, in Jerusalem, Hamas also tried to avoid being identified with the attacks, probably for tactical reasons involving Hamas-PA relations. Hamas was supported in this effort by the PA's senior spokesmen, including Arafat himself, who stated that the perpetrators had come from abroad. At the same time, unofficial announcements in the name of the military apparatus took responsibility for the suicide bombings, claiming they had been in reaction to the Israeli settlement in East Jerusalem.

The announcement by Hamas's headquarters in Amman regarding the suicide bombings was apologetic, trying to justify the return to armed struggle and suicide operations as the only way to block the Israeli settlement efforts and the "Judaization" of the Islamic holy places in Jerusalem. At the same time, the Hamas "inside" leaders demonstrated their solidarity with the PA as a gesture to Arafat, who had rebuffed Israeli pressure to take measures against Hamas's civilian institutions. However, in January 1998, the instigators of the suicide bombings were identified as members of 'Izz al-Din al-Qassam, and a well-organized Hamas "explosives laboratory" and operative cell were uncovered in PA-controlled territory near Nablus. The PA reacted by taking punitive measures against the Islamic movement. A number of Hamas's political leaders were arrested, and some of the movement's charitable organizations were closed down. Once again, the PA's harsh response was in answer to Hamas's violation of the 1995 understanding that barred it from launching operations against Israel from Palestinian-controlled areas.[50]

The interrogation of the Nablus group revealed an extensive, compartmentalized, military apparatus, which maintained close contact with the Hamas headquarters in the Gaza Strip, Jordan, and Lebanon using advanced communications methods, including the Internet. The activities of the 'Izz al-Din al-Qassam squads were divided among several senior regional commanders, whose names were on Israel's "wanted" list. They thus were constantly on the move from one district to another, assisted by the clergy and personnel of the mosques. These senior activists organized new military cadres and supervised their training for military operations. According to Israeli sources, students (including women) of Bir Zeit University in the West Bank also helped manufacture explosives in the "laboratory." Yet it still remained unclear whether the suicide bombings had been specifically ordered by the Political Bureau or were the result of local initiative and operational availability.[51]

On July 19, 1998, a van loaded with fuel, gas containers, and a large quantity of nails went up in flames in the heart of Jerusalem, seriously burning the Palestinian driver but not exploding. Subsequently it emerged that the man, a resident of a refugee camp north of Jerusalem and known to be a Hamas activist, had undertaken the presumed suicide bombing attempt on his own. Both Hamas and the PA charged that the incident had been provoked by the Israelis to justify the continuing stalemate in the peace process.[52]

Hamas's policy of controlled violence and its willingness to consider a cease-fire with Israel were also a function of internal Palestinian politics—both PA-Hamas relations and politics in Hamas itself. This connection was revealed after the assassination—apparently while he was preparing a car bomb—of one of Hamas's two senior military commanders in the West Bank, Muhyi al-Din al-Sharif, on March 29, 1998, in Ramallah, an area under full control of the PA. Spokesmen for the PA said that Sharif had been murdered by another senior member of 'Izz al-Din al-Qassam, 'Imad 'Awadallah, brother of 'Adel 'Awadallah, the central commander of Hamas's military apparatus in the West Bank, in the course of a power struggle in the organization. The incident exposed Hamas's political leaders' lack of control and information about the military apparatus. Thus, although Israel strongly denied any connection with the incident, Hamas declared it was responsible and vowed revenge. At the same time, Hamas rejected the PA's version of events, claiming that it was riddled with contradictions and hinting that the PA's security apparatus had tortured Sharif's assistant to obtain the alleged identity of the assassin. Furthermore, Hamas spokesmen implicitly accused the PA's security organizations of collaborating with Israel in Sharif's assassination. Hamas then organized protest demonstrations against the PA's continued persecution of its activists and its imprisonment of about two hundred Hamas members without trial. Hamas accused the PA of incompetence and corruption, claiming that its bureaucracy had stolen hundreds of millions of dollars. The PA took this as an attempt to question its legitimacy and authority and arrested some of Hamas's key figures, including 'Abd al-'Aziz Rantisi, as well as 'Imad 'Awadallah, who was suspected of murdering Sharif.[53]

The tension between the PA and Hamas flared up again after the murder of the 'Awadallah brothers ('Imad had escaped from a Palestinian prison in Jericho) by an Israeli force on September 10 in Hebron. This double murder, viewed by the Palestinians as an Israeli success—in eliminating the senior commanders of 'Izz al-Din al-Qassam and eroding Hamas's military capability—triggered new threats of revenge by Hamas leaders. They accused the PA of collaborating with Israel in trying to destroy Hamas's military apparatus, thereby forcing the PA itself to condemn Israel for killing the 'Awadallah brothers and accusing it of attempting to provoke another wave of violence that would end the American mediation efforts to bring about another Israeli redeployment in the West Bank, in accordance with the Oslo and Hebron accords.[54]

In October 1998, Israeli military sources reported that several attempts by Hamas to carry out mass terrorist attacks against Israel had been averted thanks to cooperation between Israeli and Palestinian security organizations. The PA's close collaboration with Israel reflected its anticipation of a positive conclusion of American diplomatic efforts to secure a redeployment of Israeli forces in the West Bank. The reports also suggested that despite the recent debacles, Hamas still possessed an impressive military infrastructure.[55] Thus, despite Hamas's policy of avoiding a head-on collision with the PA at this critical juncture, its military activists had still intended to carry out massive terrorist operations against Israel, with the declared blessing of Sheikh Ahmad Yasin. The explanation of this seeming contradiction may lie in Hamas's belief that it could take advantage of the murder of the 'Awadallah brothers by launching a massive strike against Israel, whose consequences—in the form of Israeli retaliation— could be justified to the Palestinian public.[56]

The terms of the Israel-PA Wye accord, signed in Washington on October 23, 1998, for a redeployment of Israeli forces in the West Bank, brought tension between the PA and Hamas, which had been mounting since March, to the verge of crisis. Not only did the agreement make Israel's transfer of land to the PA conditional on the latter's unequivocal commitment to fight terrorism and all forms of incitement and to collect illegal arms, but the PA also officially agreed to the United States' monitoring of their implementation, thus entailing the direct involvement and presence of American inspectors in Palestine. Six days after the accord was signed, a member of 'Izz al-Din al-Qassam attempted a suicide bombing of a school bus carrying Jewish children in the Gaza Strip; the attack was deflected at the last minute by the bus's military escort and ended with the death of the Palestinian driver and an Israeli soldier. The children were unharmed.

This incident, as well as the explosion of a car bomb in downtown Jerusalem a week later, in which two Palestinians from the Islamic Jihad were killed, indicated that both Islamic groups still possessed organizational and planning capability and had access to material and human resources. In fact, however, no clear information was available for Israel and the PA regarding the source of the initiative and authority for such actions, the underlying political considerations, or their timing. In any event, the Gaza bus incident constituted a clear violation of the 1995 understanding between Hamas and the PA. This situation was aggravated by another extensive roundup by the PA of senior Hamas leaders, with Sheikh Yasin himself placed under house arrest. This prompted a message by 'Izz al-Din al-Qassam threatening that further PA arrests and repressive actions against Hamas might lead to a clash with the PA's security arm, despite the instructions of the movement's leadership.[57]

It was apparently the deep involvement of the Clinton administration in the Wye agreement that accounted for the violent attack against the PA by Iran's supreme religious authority 'Ali Khamena'i, and a call by Hizballah's secretary-general, Hasan Nasrallah, to assassinate Arafat in order to foil the "treasonous agreement," which came a day after the PA began arresting Hamas activists in the wake of the attempted suicide bombing in the Gaza Strip.

Hamas, which was fully aware of the Palestinians' initial relief at Israel's withdrawal from the occupied territories, forged a strategy to secure its popularity among the Palestinians while arousing public resistance to the Oslo process, but without itself being accused of causing the process to fail. The idea was to demonstrate the inherent imbalance of the agreement with Israel, which would have the effect of perpetuating Israel's hegemony over and usurpation of Palestinian land. Hamas pursued a mixed policy of controlled violence against Israel and a willingness to maintain a dialogue and coexistence with the PA, despite the political difficulties this entailed. To offset the damage to Hamas's popularity—because its actions were perceived to cause adverse economic conditions and to delay the removal of the Israeli occupation—and to reduce the risk of a frontal clash with the PA, Hamas usually staged its violent attacks against Israel in reaction to Israeli operations against the Palestinians that called for vengeance.[58]

The two-track policy that Hamas adopted—controlled violence against Israel and dialogue with the PA—forced the movement to toe a fine line, which sometimes entailed contradictions that led to a temporary failure of the policy, by which Hamas avoided an irreversible collision with the PA. Hamas was able to sustain its policy not least because its spokesmen used different voices and represented different attitudes and environments that shielded the movement from repressive measures against its constant backbone: the civilian institutions. Hamas's communal infrastructure of mosques and social, educational, and welfare associations created a fertile soil from which the movement's military squads sprang and from which it drew moral as well as organizational sustenance. At the same time, the PA had limited options to uproot Islamic violence, not only because of the unclear chain of command in the Hamas hierarchy in PA areas, but also because it knew that the real power in Hamas resided with the Political Bureau, which was out of its reach. In this sense, as forged after 1989, Hamas's structure proved organizationally resilient for a policy marked by flexibility and political adjustment, which turned to be indispensable to survival in unfavorable conditions.

CHAPTER FOUR

Coexistence Within Conflict

The emergence of Hamas as a political alternative to the PLO intensified the tension between the two over how to shape the day-to-day activities of the Intifada and over the controversial peace process. Their rivalry grew rancorous following the Madrid peace conference in late October 1991. It has been argued that despite their divergence regarding ultimate objectives and means, the reality of occupation and the absence of a state structure accounted for the ideological and political proximity of Palestinian nationalists and Islamists, thus underscoring the distinctiveness of the Palestinian case.[1] But a close examination of the relationship between Hamas and the PLO during the Intifada and under the Palestinian Authority established in June 1994 shows that the patterns of negotiated coexistence and the continuation of their dialogue developed against the backdrop of intra-Palestinian politics, especially under the Palestinian Authority.

From the outset, Hamas was ambivalent toward the PLO, signaling, on the one hand, an interest in coexistence and, on the other, loyalty to its ideological distinction and political independence. Hamas's effort to maintain a dialogue and to ensure coexistence with the PLO, and later with the PA, reflected its political weakness in light of the growing international, regional, and local support for the Israeli-PLO peace process. It was this perception of the tenuousness of its position that induced Hamas to try to work out an understanding with the PLO that would enable it to gain time to expand its ranks and consolidate its power. At the same time, its quest for distinction and organizational independence led Hamas to search for a way to deflect the PLO's attempts at subordination and containment.

Flexibility Through Conformity

During the Intifada, Hamas took a conciliatory approach to the PLO, praising its historical record of armed struggle and political achievement in placing the Palestinian refugee problem on the international agenda as a national liberation issue.[2] That approach reflected Hamas's awareness of the PLO's prestige in the Palestinian society. Hamas, though, was eager to build its image as a movement seeking Palestinian national unity based on a militant Islamic agenda. Such an image would respond to the PLO's accusations that Hamas's insistence on preserving its independence and refusal to join the UNC had undermined the Palestinians' national unity and played into Israel's hands.[3] Thus, from the outset, Hamas criticized the PLO for its secular perception and its dearth of Islamic values. Although the Palestinian National Charter was consistent with its own national principles, Hamas argued that it could not join the PLO because the charter lacked the Islamic values that were essential to joint political action. Indeed, Hamas spared no effort to rebuke the PLO for its secular perceptions and disconnection from Islamic values.[4]

Following the resolutions adopted by the PLO at the nineteenth PNC session held in Algiers in November 1988,[5] Hamas's criticism of the PLO's secularism became a full-fledged condemnation of what it perceived as the PLO's abandonment of the armed struggle and deviation from its national platform. In a special leaflet, Hamas stated that the PLO was no longer a legitimate representative of the Palestinian people because it was willing to recognize the Jewish enemy and to abandon the greater part of Palestine. In contrast with the PLO's "deviation," Hamas portrayed itself as the authentic representative of the Palestinian people's national aspirations and collective needs. Taking credit for the eruption of the Intifada, Hamas expressed its determination to wage a *jihad* until all of Palestine was liberated.[6]

Although it stated that it was "not an alternative to anyone," Hamas's slogans, such as "the Qura'n is the sole legitimate representative of the Palestinian people,"[7] reflected its Islamic vision. Hamas's adherence to Islamic values prompted it to assert publicly that joint action with the PLO would be possible when the latter accepted three main principles: that the ultimate goal of their common struggle was to establish an Islamic state over the whole territory of Palestine "from the river to the sea," that a Jewish entity in any part of Palestine was inconceivable, and that *jihad* was the only way to attain this goal. Nevertheless, acknowledging the deep ideological differences with the mainstream Palestinian national movement, Hamas spokesmen often limited the possibility of agreement and cooperation with the PA to the prevention of mutual fighting (*taqtil*).[8]

Thus the profound differences between the two movements and Hamas's desire to avoid intra-Palestinian disputes did not prevent Hamas from demonstrating its willingness for controlled cooperation with the PLO on the loose basis of an agreed-on platform calling for the liberation of all of Palestine. Apart from explaining this willingness as stemming from the primacy of the Palestinian national interest and the necessity of internal unity against the common Israeli enemy, Hamas's attitude also derived from a realistic appraisal—both during the Intifada and following the establishment of the Palestinian Authority—of its military and popular inferiority to the PLO mainstream. Hence it adopted the principle of "prohibiting internal [Palestinian] fighting" (*hurmat al-iqtital al-dakhili*) and repeated proclamations regarding its willingness to cooperate with the PLO and, later, to accept the PA's power to prevent intra-Palestinian disputes.[9] Furthermore, Hamas's awareness of its limited ability to liberate Palestine or confront the PLO led it to take a rather realistic approach to a political settlement with Israel, which entailed a calculated deviation from its stated doctrine. In fact, the same pattern of controlled violence that Hamas had used against Israel also characterized its efforts to seek a flexible strategy by which it could coexist with the PLO without being identified with the peace process or seem to have abandoned its original goal of establishing an Islamic state in historic Palestine.

This approach was expressed during the Intifada in various statements made by its most prominent leader, Sheikh Ahmad Yasin, as the following three examples show: First, Hamas did not rule out the possibility of a Palestinian state in the West Bank and Gaza Strip, provided this was considered the first phase toward the establishment of a state in Palestine as a whole. Second, Hamas was ready to consider international supervision in the territories after the Israelis withdrew if it were limited in time and did not require direct concessions to Israel. Third, Hamas would reject any attempt to enter into political negotiations with Israel over a peace agreement as long as the Israeli occupation continued; however,

Hamas would not exclude such an initiative after a full Israeli with-drawal.[10]

Yasin's statements reflected a growing tendency within Hamas, even before the Oslo accord, to bridge the gulf between the movement's agreed-on prose of reality and the poetry of its ideology. By adopting a strategy of neither full acceptance nor total rejection of the PLO's program of po-litical settlement, Hamas was able to justify its position in normative terms, defining such "concessions" as tactical moves. It is here that we find a seemingly contradictory approach to the very idea of a political settlement with Israel. Thus, Hamas criticized the PLO's sanctioning of Palestinian participation in the Madrid conference of October 1991, calling it "a con-ference for the sellout of Palestine and Jerusalem," while leading Hamas figures kept open the admissibility, in principle, of a truce (*hudna* or *muhadana*) with the Jews. Although a final peace settlement with Israel was forbidden—and, if signed, would be null and void a priori—Hamas left open the option of a temporary agreement with Israel, provided it de-noted neither peace (*salam*) nor final conciliation (*sulh*). According to Hamas, such a relationship with Israel would coincide with the Muslims' interests (*maslaha*) and would not legitimize the enemy's presence on oc-cupied Islamic land. Similarly, Hamas rejected the PLO's legitimacy to represent the Palestinian people but at the same time stated that a polit-ical coalition was feasible if based "on an agreed program focused on *ji-had*."[11]

Hamas demonstrated its flexibility by differentiating between the short-term goal of a Palestinian state in the West Bank and Gaza and the long-term goal of establishing a Palestinian Islamic state on the whole territory of Palestine that would replace Israel. By accepting this order of goals, Hamas effectively subordinated the former to the latter by emphasizing the transitional nature and temporary status of any political settlement with Israel.

Hamas sought to enhance its social and political presence in the Pales-tinian population in the West Bank and Gaza Strip at the expense of the PLO, but without clashing with the secular forces, maintaining that it was for the Palestinian people to decide which course was preferable. In fact, the establishment of Hamas was a recognition of the Intifada's ability to widen the movement, at the expense of the PLO, and to achieve domi-nance among the Palestinians in the occupied territories by reasserting the rallying power of armed struggle, especially in its religious form of *jihad*. The realization of this goal necessitated a gradual approach of expansion and takeover of key positions by means of conviction and the use of existing democratic procedures while refraining from collision that could jeopardize the movement's future development.

The Struggle over Hegemony

The daily confrontation with Israel during the Intifada and the attendant agonies of the Palestinian population provided a favorable atmosphere for Hamas to challenge the PLO's claim of ideological hegemony and political domination. As mentioned earlier, even before the Intifada, members of al-Mujamma' al-islami had systematically tried to penetrate professional associations and other public institutions as part of their effort to attain political influence. This effort was redoubled during the Intifada when Hamas tried to gain official representation in all the leading local bodies in the West Bank and Gaza Strip. These included chambers of commerce, labor unions, professional organizations, and student associations. In addition, following Israel's massive arrests of the Hamas leadership, including Sheikh Ahmad Yasin himself, in May 1989, Hamas established its own international infrastructure, emulating the PLO's division of labor between "inside" and "outside" bases of power and its hierarchical structure. Reports of Hamas's attempts to establish contacts with the Iranian Revolutionary Guards in search of arms and training appeared as early as November 1989, and Hamas developed close ties with Syria, the Islamic movement in Jordan, and Hizballah in Lebanon.[12] Hamas's international alignment was based on ad hoc considerations of opposition to Israel and the PLO rather than on pure ideology. Thus Hamas allied itself with Iran and Syria and, after the Madrid peace conference in October 1991, joined in establishing the Syrian-based "Ten Front" together with other militant Palestinian factions, mostly nationalist and Marxist, that condemned the PLO's participation in the peace process.[13]

Hamas's reorganization sought to enhance the movement's political and military capabilities by obtaining funds from friendly governments and Islamic supporters, both regional and international. The regional infrastructure also provided military resources such as training facilities, mainly in Iran and Syria,[14] and operational networks necessary for enlisting manpower, trafficking arms and funds, and conducting secret communication. Yet unlike the PLO, Hamas initially derived most of its money from Palestinian sources, including Islamic institutions that received financial aid from external Arab and Islamic donors. According to unverified Israeli intelligence estimates, Hamas's overall annual budget in the years 1993/94 was $30 million to $50 million. According to these reports, about half this sum was collected directly from Palestinian Islamist associations in the diaspora, individuals, and business communities and indirectly from Arab and Islamic humanitarian foundations in the Middle East, western Europe, and the Americas. The rest was donated by the governments of Iran, Saudi Arabia, and Kuwait, and by private Middle Eastern donors. The flow of funds from the United States and western Europe was channeled through Islamic welfare organizations, including those of the Islamic movement in Israel, for ostensibly humanitarian purposes, such as support for families of the fallen and prisoners.[15]

The expansion of Hamas's activity to regional and international spheres weakened Hamas's coherence as a political movement. Its growing reliance on external financial and military resources effectively transferred the center of the movement's decision-making body from the occupied territories to Amman, where a new political body was established in 1992: The Political Bureau headed by Musa Abu Marzuq (who conducted much of the bureau's activity from his base in Springfield, Virginia) and its members were Hamas's representatives in the Arab states and Iran. The newly established institution, which as of 1993 was fully based in Amman, represented the "outside" leadership and derived its legitimacy and power from its control of financial resources, the military apparatus, and close relations with the Islamic movement in Jordan and with the Iranian and Syrian regimes. The "outside" center of power increasingly disagreed with the local "inside" Hamas leadership in the Gaza Strip and the West Bank over the benefit of continuing the armed struggle against Israel and its attitude toward the PA.[16]

Indeed, the Intifada contributed to the growing Islamization of the Palestinian public mood at the expense of the PLO's secular nationalism, which paralleled the deteriorating economic conditions of the Palestinians in the occupied territories. External developments also played a part: the fall of the Soviet Union tarnished the PLO's prestige by presenting its sole global ally as a broken reed and the frustrated hopes for substantial Arab funds to support the Intifada, which had to be channeled through the PLO. The prolonged violence and emerging conviction that the Intifada had reached an impasse forced the Palestinians to become more self-reliant and introverted, causing them to regard Islam as their main source of guidance.

The Kuwait crisis that led to the Gulf War of 1991, and Arafat's unrestricted support for Iraq, further aggravated the PLO's political and financial position both regionally and internationally. Concretely, this was manifested by the cessation of financial aid from the Gulf monarchies and the exodus of hundreds of thousands of Palestinians from these countries.

By 1991, the PLO's financial crisis forced Arafat to reduce the organization's international diplomatic presence and stop giving money to Palestinian institutions and welfare agencies in the occupied territories and even to victims of the national struggle and other needy groups. Immediately after the Gulf War, Palestinians, including Fatah activists, began to be more critical of Arafat's leadership and the PLO's political decision-making process and of Arafat's mismanagement of the organization's funds. Hamas lost no time in exploiting the opportunity to launch an indirect attack on the PLO's financial irregularities, contrasting this with the modesty and decency of Islamic schools and institutions.[17]

During the Intifada, Hamas grew stronger, building institutions and attracting young people to the mosques, as well as more pilgrims to Mecca. Since the beginning of the Intifada, most of the violent attacks against Israeli targets had been committed by Islamic combatants, whether Hamas, the Islamic Jihad, Islamic activists across the Jordan River, or Hizballah in southern Lebanon. Moreover, Hamas's grassroots leadership projected credibility, dedication, and integrity compared with the PLO's outdated and notoriously corrupt leadership, alleged unscrupulous bureaucracy, and abandonment of the armed struggle in favor of a luxurious lifestyle.

Hamas's burgeoning popularity was particularly pronounced after the Gulf War. The war had hurt the Palestinian economy in the West Bank and Gaza and greatly limited Fatah's financial ability to pay welfare subsidies or even salaries to its employees. At the same time, Hamas's charity committees (*lijan al-zakat*) and other Islamic associations continued their welfare activities. Indeed, besides foreign agencies, they were the only organizations that continued to dispense welfare, thus attracting many frustrated PLO supporters to the Islamic movement.[18] The Hamas welfare committees proceeded to tighten their local and international contacts, especially with Palestinian diaspora communities and Islamic associations in Israel and the Arab world, as well as with contacts in Europe and the United States. Hamas's agenda continued to focus on Islamic education, on the grounds that the "right education" was a prerequisite for building an Islamic society.

The impasse that followed the 1991 Madrid peace talks was another setback for Arafat's political position as a sponsor of the local Palestinian delegates (Faisal Hussaini, Haidar 'Abd al-Shafi, Hanan 'Ashrawi, and others) to the negotiations with Israel. Arafat's declining prestige in the West Bank and Gaza Strip reflected the Palestinians' disappointment in the peace process. The impasse in the peace negotiations left the PLO in an inferior position vis-à-vis Hamas and the leftist PFLP and DFLP, which, from the beginning, had rejected the Madrid conference's terms of reference and further heightened the tension in the PLO-Hamas relationship.[19]

The Hamas-Fatah rivalry reached a boiling point in 1992. The two organizations were locked in a struggle to acquire dominant positions in the Palestinian community in the West Bank and Gaza Strip. To obtain the advantage, Fatah enlisted the cooperation of the leftist PFLP, DFLP, and the communists. In Gaza, the nationalist bloc won the elections in the engineers', physicians', and lawyers' associations (65 percent in the last), although the Islamic movement won in the chamber of commerce. In the West Bank, the Islamic bloc was victorious in Hebron's chamber of commerce and the students' association of the city's Polytechnic Institute and its university. The exception, in the markedly religious-traditional city of Hebron, was the Red Crescent Association, in which the nationalist bloc gained a majority of seats. Hamas's most surprising victory came in the elections for Ramallah's chamber of commerce, a body that included a significant number of Christians and been considered a stronghold of secularism and nationalism.[20]

Hamas also won the elections for the teachers' seminary in Ramallah and for the committee of alumni of UNRWA institutes. The national bloc won the student elections at the local institute for refugees in Qalandia.[21] In Nablus, the nationalist list of candidates—from Fatah, the PFLP, DFLP, and the communists—was victorious in the chamber of commerce, though by only a narrow margin over Hamas (48 percent to 45 percent). The nationalists also won all the seats in the teachers' association at al-Najah University, although Hamas won 80 percent of the votes for the alumni association of the UNRWA institutes in Nablus.

In Jerusalem, the Islamists received 43 percent (versus 47 percent for the nationalists) of the votes of the electric company's workers. The nationalists won all the seats of the workers' union of al-Muttali' Hospital, and Hamas won a majority in the Maqasid Hospital. Hamas also won all the seats on the students' council of al-Umma College in Jerusalem (64.5 percent for the Islamic bloc versus 35.49 percent for the PLO's list).[22] So impressive were Hamas's growth and electoral achievements in the West Bank and Gaza Strip, especially after the 1991 Madrid peace conference, that in April 1992 the Palestinian delegation to the peace negotiations announced its objection, for the time being, to an Israeli initiative to hold municipal elections in the West Bank and Gaza.

The competition between Hamas and Fatah for leadership of Palestinian public institutions blurred the boundaries between the nationalist and the Islamist messages, which were invoked in the leaflets of both movements. Consequently, following its defeat in the 1992 elections in the Ramallah chamber of commerce, Fatah adopted an Islamic stance, creating the "Islamic national commercial and industrial coalition" which won a narrow victory in the 1992 elections for the chamber of commerce in Nablus. The rivalry between the organizations also led to a revolution in the use of slogans. Whereas Hamas had previously portrayed its rivals as "communists," its alignment with the leftist "fronts" after Madrid led Fatah supporters at al-Najah University to attack the communists and question the strange collaboration between Hamas and the left.[23]

The Struggle for Leadership

The competition between Hamas and Fatah to mobilize the masses by means of organized civil disobedience, boycotts, protests, and strikes deepened the animosity in their relations. Then in 1989, Fatah's pressuring of Hamas to accept the UNC's authority also exacerbated the tension between the two rival movements. The PLO was especially perturbed by Hamas's growing popularity, its independent decisions to execute collaborators, and its setting of separate dates for strikes and protests, which seemed to challenge the PLO's authority represented by the UNC. That Fatah and the leftists excluded Hamas from the prisoners' committees in Israeli incarceration facilities did not help the situation either.[24]

These circumstances became fertile soil for armed clashes between Fatah and Hamas activists in the occupied territories, and sporadic violence erupted in Tulkarm and Gaza. In September 1990, at the initiative of leading Muslim Brotherhood (MB) figures in Jordan, Hamas and Fatah signed a "charter of honor" recognizing Hamas's legitimate existence as an equal and independent faction and agreeing to refrain from hostilities. The charter was meant to address the immediate origins of the Hamas-Fatah clashes, especially Fatah's veto of Hamas's participation in the prisoners' committees. Although the charter paid lip service to the principle that "Islam is deeply rooted within us, it is our principle as Muslims, and way of our life," the main bone of political contention between Fatah and Hamas—the latter's independence and growing challenge to the PLO's authority—was not resolved and soon erupted again.[25]

Hamas's successes notwithstanding, it could not overlook the PLO's pressure to join the overall Palestinian national organization as a separate faction. In April 1990, Hamas—in what was probably a ploy to foil the idea rather than keen interest—applied to the PNC to join the PLO. But to avoid being co-opted and manipulated by Fatah, Hamas requested that general elections for the PNC be held among all Palestinians in the West Bank and Gaza and in the diaspora. If circumstances precluded holding such elections, Hamas insisted on being allotted at least 40 percent of the seats on the PNC, based on its proven power in elections to public institutions in the occupied territories. In addition, Hamas requested revisions in the Palestinian National Charter, rejection of political negotiations with Israel, and adoption of the *jihad* as the sole means to liberate Palestine. According to Hamas, since the PLO's policy was mistaken, it was the PLO that should adopt Hamas's strategy and not vice versa.[26]

Hamas also insisted on proportionate financial allocations and the inclusion of its representatives in the PLO's bureaucratic apparatus. Hamas's demands were effectively a claim for parity with Fatah that would end the latter's unchallenged domination in the PLO. At the least, it would give Hamas veto power over the PLO's decision making—hence Arafat's rejection of the demands and his counteroffer of no more than 20 percent. The dispute over Hamas's participation in the PLO remained unresolved until the Madrid peace conference in October 1991, when the issue was effectively dropped from the agenda. In the debate between the two movements, the PLO—actually Fatah—depicted its relations with Hamas in terms of a state vis-à-vis a splinter group that had rebelled against the state's legitimacy. According to Fatah, the PLO constituted the Palestinian homeland, entity, and state and so was above partisan debate. The PLO itself maintained that it was legitimate to criticize Fatah, but criticism of the PLO was tantamount to heresy (*ridda*) from Islam (for which the penalty was death).[27]

The PLO continued to press Hamas to accept its exclusive authority in the Palestinian arena and to try to delegitimize Hamas's independent existence. The PLO also criticized Hamas's conduct, implying that the MB was collaborating with Israel. At the same time, Hamas continued to present a judicious facade of adherence to the principle of willingness, in order to maintain a dialogue with the PLO for the sake of Palestinian national unity, avoidance of intra-Palestinian violence, and the quest for a joint struggle against Israel. In effect, however, Hamas insisted on the principle of sharing power equally with Fatah. Hamas's position was vividly expressed as well in its dialogue with Fatah on establishing a joint municipal council for the city of Gaza, an endeavor that foundered on Hamas's far-reaching claims for representation.

Responding to Fatah's campaign denouncing Hamas's refusal to join the PLO as a faction, Hamas's argumentation combined pragmatism and ideology. Hamas invoked democratic principles expressing a willingness to respect the majority decision of the Palestinian people. Yet Hamas also insisted that Islam was the only viable foundation for the Palestinian national effort. Like the Palestinian radical left, Hamas rejected the PLO's thrust for a negotiated Palestinian state in the occupied territories on grounds of Israeli hegemony and not necessarily because of any religious prohibition on negotiations and political settlement with Israel.

In conjunction with the 1991 Madrid peace conference, Hamas stated that the PLO's withdrawal from the peace talks was the principal prerequisite for "Palestinian unity." The issue of Hamas's representation on the PNC and other PLO institutions was ostensibly set aside once the controversy over Palestinian participation in the Madrid conference gave Arafat's opponents a potent argument against his criticism of Hamas for its reluctance to join the PLO. Hamas pointed to Fatah's support for the Madrid process at a time when Israel was still fighting the Intifada. Hamas contended, typically, that considerations of current Islamic, Arab, or Palestinian weakness vis-à-vis the enemy reflected a lack of faith in the will of Allah, warning that "history does not pardon the cowards and defeatists."[28]

Although Hamas had never officially recognized the PLO as the sole representative of the Palestinian people, after the PLO consented to participate in the Madrid peace conference, Hamas claimed that the majority of Palestinians rejected the "conference of wholesale of the land" and denied the PLO's legitimacy to represent the Palestinian people. Such legitimacy, Hamas reiterated, required the "Islamization" of the PLO's political program, meaning an unconditional return to the armed struggle for the liberation of all of Palestine.[29]

The relationship between the two organizations was strained further by their continuous competition at both the operational and political levels. Hamas's growth and electoral successes, and the erosion in Fatah's popularity with the Palestinian public due to its financial difficulties and support of a fruitless peace process, generated new tensions. Ostensibly the disputes revolved around the nature and course of the Intifada, but in fact they reflected a struggle for domination of the Palestinians' daily life through strikes, commemoration days, and commercial, educational, and social activities, as well as the tenets of individual moral conduct, especially women's modesty. Indeed, the Intifada was increasingly marked by internecine strife between Fatah and Hamas, which, although both accused Israel of provoking their differences, hurled mutual recriminations at each other over the discord within the Palestinian community.[30]

Fatah portrayed Hamas as a minority group, constituting no more than 15 percent of the population, which was attempting to foist its agenda on the Palestinian majority. Hamas, for its part, repeatedly pointed to the intolerable contradiction between the PLO's diplomatic negotiations with the "Zionist enemy" and the latter's continued repression of the Palestinian people by "iron and fire." Hamas gained momentum by its clear and unreserved adherence to the armed struggle as the essence of the Intifada and an antidote to the moribund Madrid process espoused by the PLO. Over and over, Hamas called on other Palestinian factions, especially Fatah, to refrain from intra-Palestinian violence, to respect signed agreements, and to coordinate Intifada activities according to the principle of armed struggle against Israel. However, Hamas itself came under attack by the PLO as well as by its closest partner, the Islamic Jihad, over its arbitrary execution of PLO activists for their alleged collaboration with Israel.[31]

The PLO became increasingly critical of Hamas's continued attempts to exploit the massive protests and strikes to enhance its political prestige at the expense of the national forces. The PLO was mainly concerned with solidifying its position as the sole legitimate national authority and the articulator of the norms and values that shaped Palestinian life under Israeli occupation. The marginal role that the armed struggle assumed in Fatah's agenda led to the inevitable conclusion that the PLO leadership had indeed viewed the Intifada as no more than a means to strengthen its position in the peace negotiations. Hamas, however, sought, according to its spokesman Ibrahim Ghawsha, to "nip it [the peace process] in the bud" by all possible means and to force Fatah to accept the "Islamic program."

Fatah tried to take full control of violent operations and mass protest actions in Palestine in order to prevent an interruption of the negotiations with Israel, as the collapse of the talks would provide Hamas further prestige. Capitalizing on this tendency, Hamas claimed that the "comical self-governing" (al-hukm al-dhati al-hazil) solution had tempted the supporters of the "capitulationist negotiations" (mufawadat al-istislam) to work toward "melting" the Intifada, that is, abandoning the idea of jihad. Both movements accused Israel of provoking their differences and clashes; however, since Madrid, the Intifada's agenda had become the crucial test for the PLO's control of the Palestinian arena.[32]

Fatah was apparently behind a leaflet of the "popular struggle committees" that asserted there was no alternative to the PLO and portrayed Hamas's insistent refusal to join the PLO as a provocation against the Palestinian people. The leaflet denounced Hamas for its inconsiderate policy of imposing strikes on workers and peasants who were struggling to eke out a living under harsh conditions. The leaflet warned that the "imaginary" rise of Hamas was dangerous, that this movement was to blame for the deportation of many PFLP fighters, and that it was sowing division and hatred in the "one nation."[33]

It was in this context that the two rival movements disagreed over the use of disciplinary violence against Palestinians in the name of the Intifada. Representing the PLO, Fatah clashed with Hamas over the latter's independent decisions to execute collaborators, an instrument that had apparently been used by both movements against each other's members. The troubled relations between activists of Fatah (and other secular factions) and Hamas deteriorated into the secularists' disruption of prayers, desecration of mosques, and attacks on clergy. There was a sporadic series of murders in the Tulkarm and Rafah areas, as well as street clashes between the 'Izz al-Din al-Qassam and the Fatah Hawks. Many activists on both sides were wounded, and threats were made against the life of leading figures of both movements in the Gaza Strip. The violent factional clashes spread to Hebron, where buses were torched as a result of a quarrel between Hamas and Fatah students over the latter's decision to permit male and female students to travel on buses together. Public figures, including delegates to the Madrid conference, appealed for an end to violence and a return to dialogue.[34]

On June 7, 1992, a "document of honor" was distributed in the name of Hamas and Fatah, reasserting their adherence to Palestinian national unity and proclaiming that Islam was the "nature . . . faith, and way of life" of the Palestinians. The document called on Fatah and Hamas to refrain from violence against each other. It also urged the establishment of joint committees to prevent conflicting Intifada activities by Hamas and Fatah, their entanglement in violent family and clan disputes, and the eviction of residents from their homes and villages in the wake of conflicts between the two movements. Fatah's renewed undertaking to incorporate Hamas into the prisoners' committees indicated that its previous commitments in this area had not been implemented. But Hamas immediately rejected the document, alleging that although it had been negotiating an agreement with Fatah, the latter had published the document without prior consultation with Hamas.[35]

In early July 1992, continued clashes between Hamas and Fatah activists intensified the efforts to end what seemed about to erupt into civil strife. The severity of the situation was indicated by the intervention of the "outside" leaders of both rival factions, who issued a joint call in Amman to cease all violent activities and warned that the internecine violence might diminish the Intifada's achievements. To contain the tension and clashes and preserve the agreement between the two movements, joint lo-cal conciliation and follow-up committees were set up, with representa-tives from the West Bank and Gaza as well as from Israel.[36]

But such measures could hardly erase the ideological cleavages or mit-igate the political competition. Toward the end of 1992, the PLO-Hamas relationship reached its lowest ebb as Arafat's attacks on Hamas became more vehement and humiliating. At one point, he called Hamas a "Zulu tribe," suggesting that Hamas's isolationism was like that of the Inkata movement, which had refused to accept the authority of the African Na-tional Congress under the leadership of Nelson Mandela during the talks with the white government of Frederik de Klerk. Arafat's hostility toward Hamas stemmed from his mounting concern over the latter's enhanced position in the Gaza Strip and the West Bank, which in turn was erod-ing public support for the peace process. Besides disparaging Hamas's gains in the elections to public institutions in the West Bank and Gaza, Arafat also endeavored to delegitimize the rival movement, suggesting that its close collaboration with Iran conflicted with the principle of independent Palestinian decision making. Arafat went as far as to accuse Hamas of serving Iranian foreign interests, which was infringing on Palestinian sov-ereignty and sabotaging the national struggle.[37]

An Antagonistic Collaboration

On December 17, 1992, Israel deported 415 Hamas and Islamic Jihad ac-tivists to south Lebanon, following the kidnapping and murder of an Is-raeli border policeman. It was Israel's largest deportation of Palestinians from the occupied territories since 1967. The deportees included Hamas's senior leaders, including 'Abd al-'Aziz al-Rantisi, the most prominent Hamas leader in the occupied territories, as well as the movement's local political, educational and religious activists, though none of them appar-ently had a military record.

The unprecedented deportation backfired almost immediately, demon-strating the limits to Israel's attempt to eliminate the movement's civic and political basis. Rather, the deportation was perceived as an acute violation of Palestinian human rights and a cynical exploitation of the occupation of Palestinian territories, and it triggered a harsh international reaction to Israel. In Palestine, rivals and supporters alike rallied to the cause of the deportees, reflecting their deep ideological opposition to such punishment and their familial and local solidarity with the deportees, who represented every segment of the Palestinian population. Thus, although the mass deportation temporarily paralyzed Hamas, it boosted Palestinian national solidarity with the deportees and their respective movements.

For the first time since the beginning of the Intifada, the PLO and Hamas issued a joint leaflet condemning the deportation. The Hamas-PLO initiative was followed by an ad hoc agreement among all the military organizations operating in the field—Fatah's Hawks, the PFLP's Red Eagles, and the Battalions of 'Izz al-Din al-Qassam—to cooperate in military operations against Israel. The public desire to resume the PLO-Hamas dialogue found Hamas in a favorable position vis-à-vis the PLO, with Hamas stating that a unified Palestinian position should be based on the PLO's correction of its mistake by withdrawing from the Madrid negotiations. Hamas's position on this issue was presented as "clear and non-negotiable." The pressure exerted by Hamas, the deportees' families, and the general public on the Palestinian delegates to the peace talks and on the PLO's leadership all but forced the latter to condition the renewal of the Washington talks—which had been adjourned for Christmas—on the deportees' return. For Hamas, it was a victory that neither Israel nor the PLO had desired.[38]

The mass deportation of Hamas activists came shortly after the movement reached a strategic agreement with Iran, according to which the Islamic republic would support Hamas politically and materially against Israel and the peace process. In November 1992, a year after Hamas had opened an official office in Teheran, a delegation of the movement, headed by spokesman Ibrahim Ghawsha, reportedly arrived in Iran and met with the revolution's spiritual guide 'Ali Khamena'i and with the commander of the Revolutionary Guards, Muhsin Rada'i. The two parties signed a draft agreement providing for a political and military alliance. Under its terms, Iran would give Hamas financial and military assistance, political facilities, and a radio station in southern Lebanon. The agreement was apparently confirmed during another visit of Hamas leaders to Teheran in early December 1992. It was this agreement that spurred Hamas to escalate its military operations against Israel—manifested in the murder of an Israeli policeman—in an attempt to derail the peace process.[39]

The Hamas-Iran alliance only deepened the Hamas-Fatah political cleavage. But Hamas's turn to Iran also caused discontent within Hamas. A minority faction, apparently associated with the "inside" leadership, advocated a "Palestinization" of the movement, cessation of the armed struggle, and a focus on open, peaceful efforts that would protect Hamas from Israeli repression and free it from the need to ally with the PLO as a shield. At the same time, the majority, representing primarily the "outside" leadership, accepted Hamas's Islamization of the conflict with Israel by making alliances with other Islamic movements, especially Iran. The proponents of Islamization regarded Hamas as the true representative of the Palestinian people and as a moral and political alternative to the PLO, whose collapse, they believed, was only a matter of time.[40]

Despite the manifestations of Palestinian solidarity with the deported Islamists, Israel's reaction presented Hamas with a dilemma in terms of its relations with the PLO. Hamas's appeal to the Arab and the international community, in the name of human rights and Palestinian legitimacy, represented its independence from the PLO but could be also interpreted as Hamas's readiness to cooperate with states and organizations maintaining close ties with Israel or strongly advocating the peace process. At the same time, the deportation offered the PLO an opportunity to lead the international diplomatic campaign against Israel and demand the immediate return of the deportees. The PLO tried to minimize Hamas's use of the deportation for political profit, playing on its status as the official representative of all the Palestinians, irrespective of political or ideological affiliation. It was against this backdrop that the PLO invited Hamas for a meeting in Tunis immediately after the deportation, ostensibly to persuade Hamas to join the PLO's efforts on behalf of the deportees but more likely as a step toward the co-option of Hamas through its incorporation into the PLO. Hamas's dilemma was evident in its reluctant acceptance of the PLO's invitation and its insistence on receiving a written invitation from Arafat himself before sending its delegates to Tunis.[41]

The Tunis talks in December 1992 were little more than a dialogue of the deaf. Each side repeated its own agenda, without resolving their differences. Besides the return of the deportees, Hamas repeated its demand that the PLO leave the peace talks and escalate the Intifada and the armed struggle in the occupied territories—proposals for which it gained the support of the PFLP and DFLP delegates. Although Arafat was willing to let Hamas decide on the form of its participation in the PLO's international efforts on behalf of the deportees, he firmly rejected Hamas's demand to withdraw from the peace negotiations. Arafat claimed that such a step could be decided only by the PNC, which was the forum that had sanctioned participation in the Madrid peace process. Avoiding the call to escalate the armed struggle, Arafat instead offered a constructive dialogue with Hamas in order to gain its cooperation in building institutions in the occupied territories. He repeated his offer to Hamas to join the PLO as the organization's second largest faction, with eighteen guaranteed seats in the PNC (compared with Fatah's thirty-three and the PFLP's fifteen).

Arafat also held out to Hamas the possibility of obtaining additional seats from among those allocated to popular associations and the Palestinian diaspora communities.

The Hamas delegation expressed no more than a willingness to study Arafat's proposals. From the PLO's viewpoint, however, the significance of the Tunis talks lay mainly in the fact that they had taken place. Hamas's acceptance of Arafat's invitation to visit the PLO's Tunis headquarters—despite internal reluctance and outspoken opposition by some of its allies in the Damascus-based "Ten Front"—seemed tantamount to tacit recognition of the PLO's status as the sole representative of the Palestinian people, and of Arafat's legitimate leadership. Hamas's decision to attend, despite Iranian and Syrian discontent, clearly resulted from consideration of its "inside" infrastructure's needs and expectations of accepting Arafat's outstretched hand as a manifestation of national solidarity. Yet the PLO's impression that it had gained the upper hand over Hamas and its expectation for positive results in the future talks between Hamas and Fatah scheduled to begin in Khartoum in early January proved to be overly optimistic.[42]

From January 1 to 4, 1993, representatives of Hamas and Fatah held a political dialogue in Khartoum under the supervision of Hasan al-Turabi, the spiritual leader of the Islamic regime in Sudan and an exemplary leader of political Islam. Contrary to Israeli and Palestinian commentaries at the time—which held that agreement was close—an unofficial version of the proceedings in Khartoum reveals the unbridgeable gap between Fatah and Hamas.[43] During the talks, Hamas expressed a willingness to join the PLO following the removal of obstacles such as the issue of representation and divergent political positions. The concluding statement revealed nothing of the tense atmosphere, which was reflected in Arafat's harsh language regarding the Hamas representatives. The PLO leader accused Hamas of undermining Palestine's national interests by accepting funds from Iran, Saudi Arabia, and Kuwait, which had the sole purpose of harming the PLO. Hamas's response was to reiterate its demands: withdrawal from the peace process, 40 percent representation on the PNC, and deep structural changes in the PLO, which Arafat vehemently rejected. Indeed, the main dispute in the Khartoum talks was over the PLO's participation in the peace negotiations with Israel, which Hamas castigated as heresy. Arafat, on the other hand, insisted that Hamas must accept unconditionally the PLO's status as the sole legitimate representative of the Palestinian people. However, it remained unclear whether he was willing to give a quid pro quo: recognizing Hamas as a legitimate, independent opposition within the PLO.

Although the dialogue was officially held between Hamas and Fatah, it was effectively a continuation of the Tunis talks. As in Tunis, Arafat himself took part in the meetings, representing the PLO's position, though from time to time he spoke also as Fatah's leader, and the main topics referred to the Tunis conference. Both sides were usually represented by their "outside" leaders. Fatah's delegation included military and political figures headed by Salim al-Za'nun, and Hamas was represented by the same figures who had been in Tunis, headed by Musa Abu Marzuq. The proceedings indicated that the Hamas delegates could not make a decision on their relations with Fatah without consulting Iran and Syria.

Faced with a political deadlock, Hamas and Fatah once again opted to paper over their differences. Hamas repeated its "adherence to the principle of affiliation to the PLO as a necessary framework for national unity," stressing the need to continue the dialogue on the issue of representation in order to achieve greater coordination. On a more practical level, Fatah and Hamas announced agreement on tactical issues such as establishing joint committees on the deportees, preventing violent clashes between the two movements, and even setting up a joint command for the Intifada. Yet despite its proclaimed agreement to coordinate action on the deportees, Hamas in fact rejected Fatah's suggestion that it should take part in a PLO-based committee on the subject, refusing to accept the PLO as the body's source of legitimacy.[44]

Hamas did not jettison its positions even when Hasan al-Turabi publicly recognized the 1967 United Nations Security Council (UNSC) resolution 242—shortly after the Fatah-Hamas dialogue—sending a clear message of support for Arafat. Furthermore, although Turabi reiterated that the ultimate Palestinian goal should be the recovery of all the occupied territories, he urged Hamas to soften its attitude and join the PLO. After becoming the first Islamic leader to publicly recognize resolution 242, Turabi also attempted to legitimize Arafat's leadership by referring to him as the symbol of the Palestinian cause and recalling his past affiliation with the Muslim Brotherhood movement.[45]

Turabi's overt support of resolution 242 and the peace negotiations apparently induced Hamas not to demand a total break in the peace talks. Furthermore, a public opinion poll conducted in the occupied territories in January 1993 revealed that only about 30 percent of the Palestinians there favored a withdrawal from the peace talks, although a majority were ready to boycott the imminent meeting scheduled for Washington. It was with this information that Hamas's spokesman and delegate to the Khartoum talks, Ibrahim Ghawsha, stated that his movement's willingness to join the PLO was "not a tactical maneuver" and explained that this would depend on whether Hamas could influence the PLO's organizational structure and decision making.[46]

Despite failing to reach a political agreement, both Fatah and Hamas preferred to maintain a dialogue and some collaboration rather than become enmeshed in an all-out confrontation. This position, which emerged during the Intifada, was maintained on the eve of the signing of the Oslo agreement. Rumors of a possible unilateral Israeli withdrawal from the Gaza Strip led Hamas to seek an agreement with the PLO, apparently in order to avert the use of force by the Fatah Hawks against its activists.[47] This objective became urgent following the Oslo agreement and the expected establishment of Palestinian self-government in the Gaza Strip.

The Inconclusive Post-Oslo Dialogue

The shock and sense of crisis in the Hamas leadership following the signing of the Oslo accords on September 13, 1993, did not change the basic pattern of the movement's response to the PLO's political moves. Hamas's response remained one of cautious rejection alongside a calculated acceptance of the new reality. Indeed, the opportunity to channel some of its opposition to Israel by means of violence allowed Hamas to show restraint in its dealings with the Palestinian self-government authorities. An internal political report prepared by Hamas shortly after the Declaration of Principles (DOP) was signed concluded that the movement faced two options, neither one of which was promising, namely, to take part in the establishment of a Palestinian self-government or to keep out of it.[48] The report noted the differences within Hamas over which option to choose and acknowledged the movement's inability either to prevent the agreement's implementation or to offer an alternative in line with national and Islamic principles. The document also conceded Hamas's limits in any confrontation with the PLO aimed at derailing the Oslo accord: "We opt for confrontation, but shall we confront our people? And can we tilt the balance in our favor? And if we succeed, will we be able to offer the people an alternative, or will our success only intensify the offensive of [the Israeli] occupation?" In a personal plea to the movement's activists and supporters a month after the DOP was signed, Abu Marzuq conveyed the sense of crisis within Hamas: the United States, now the world's sole superpower, strongly supported the Oslo agreement; the Arab world had been weakened by the Gulf War and had splintered into states, each of which had its own domestic problems to deal with while Arab and Islamic

parties became deeply involved in local politics; and the Palestinian people were still occupied, its leadership in the hands of a "defeated group"
that had forsaken both country and religion and put itself in the service
of the occupier.

In his plea, Abu Marzuq found consolation in history, in which Muslims had often overcome hardship and crisis by means of faith and perseverance. The key to survival, he maintained, was patience (*sabr*). More
specifically, Abu Marzuq called for the continuation of *jihad* and stressed
the need for sacrifice "under all circumstances and in every situation," as
well as for maintaining Palestinian unity and bringing together the forces
of resistance on the basis of Islamic and national principles while protecting the movement's existence (*al-hifaz 'ala al-dhat*) and its popular and
political gains. The strategy the Hamas leadership decided to adopt was
one of armed struggle against the occupation along with political confrontation with the signatory to the "shameful agreement," namely, the
Palestinian self-governing authority. In practice, this meant avoiding violence or political terrorism against Palestinian rivals while continuing the
Intifada by all possible means, penetrating the Palestinian self-government
institutions from the start, and exerting the utmost effort to secure public support for the Islamic movement.[49]

Hamas's tolerant attitude and disposition to collaborate with the PLO,
particularly Fatah, continued after the Oslo agreement was signed. True,
following the Israeli-Palestinian Declaration of Principles (DOP), Hamas
issued a statement expressing its "total rejection . . . of the 'Gaza-Jericho
First' [accord] for its conclusion of dangerous concessions, its total departure from national and legal norms, and its outright transgression of the
red lines agreed on by the Palestinian National Council." According to
Hamas, the accord "brings limited and fragmented self-administration in
Gaza and Jericho and represents an affront to our honor, a denial of our
sacrifices and years of struggle, and a violation of our established historic
rights to the land of Palestine."[50] Still, as in the pre-Oslo era, Hamas maintained a policy of controlled violence against Israel while demonstrating a
moderate attitude toward the Palestinian self-governing authority. Thus,
although Hamas's top leadership refused to meet with Arafat and Abu
Mazin because of their part in signing the DOP, it did issue instructions
prohibiting infighting and maintaining open channels with Fatah.[51]

Although the Oslo accord raised hopes for a better future among the
Palestinians in the occupied territories, especially the hope of an independent Palestinian state, uncertainties nevertheless marked the future of
the Oslo process and hence of the PLO's ability to fulfill the Palestinians'

expectations. Overall, though, the Oslo agreement was popular among the Palestinian public, and it was this, together with the uncertainties, that led Hamas to adopt a "wait-and-see" approach toward the PLO. Thus, as long as the peace process enjoyed broad public support, it would be best for Hamas to maintain a dialogue and limited collaboration with the PLO and thus ensure the continued smooth functioning of Hamas's communal activities, rather than to embark on a radical path with an uncertain outcome. As long as the PLO-PA had military strength and political control, Hamas's policy of coexistence within a negotiated order would minimize the threat of its marginalization.

The Oslo accord threatened Hamas's political maneuverability and independent existence because it stipulated replacing Israeli occupation with a PLO-led Palestinian Authority. Hamas was aware that now the Islamic movement would have to confront both Israel and the PLO if it were to remain loyal to its normative vision. After examining its limited options for political action and seeking to preserve its political position in Palestinian society, Hamas decided that it had to maintain its coexistence with the Palestinian Authority.[52]

The rationale for this was clear. An all-out confrontation would bolster the movement's principles and militant image but risk its freedom of action and possibly its very existence. More dangerous yet, it could erode Hamas's ability to underwrite social and economic services for the community, regarded as crucial to maintaining its popularity. A "successful" *jihad* against Israel—one that would end the peace process—would aggravate the Palestinians' socioeconomic plight—for which Hamas would be blamed—and turn people against the movement. But cooperation with the PLO might place Hamas in a "divide and rule" trap as a result of the co-option of segments of the movement's leadership into the system and thus undermine Hamas's bargaining position vis-à-vis Israel and the PLO.

The establishment of the PA in June 1994 made Hamas's dilemma even worse. Arafat's creation of a centralized authority with international moral and financial support was embodied concretely in the formation of a large security force, most of whose members had served in the PLO's military units and secret apparatuses in the Arab states and hence were loyal to Arafat. In addition, Arafat had exclusive control of the media and the financial flow into the West Bank and Gaza and was steadily tightening his collaboration with Israeli intelligence and security authorities. By moving quickly to consolidate its power and the means to uphold it, the PA became better able to mobilize public support and limit the Islamic movement's opportunities to act.[53] This institutionalization process by the PA deepened Hamas's awareness that it needed a new working formula to bridge the gap between its official ideology and the dramatically changing reality. As in Sheikh Yasin's early statements during the Intifada, Hamas displayed a sensitivity to and awareness of practical considerations of "here and now" that necessitated an indirect dialogue with Israel.

The main considerations favoring a pragmatic approach had been succinctly explained by Musa Abu Marzuq, head of the movement's Political Bureau, shortly before the Cairo agreement on the implementation of Palestinian autonomy in Gaza and Jericho. In an article published in the movement's internal organ, *al-Risala*,[54] Abu Marzuq expressed concern at the Israeli-PLO agreement and described three major threats that would require Hamas's continued rejection of the current process:

1. A threat to Hamas's presence in Jordan, the "second arena of action after Palestine," due to joint Israeli and American pressure.
2. A growing international negative perception of Hamas as a murderous terrorist movement that targeted civilians.
3. The exposure of Hamas to domestic Palestinian criticism because it had no positive alternative to the peace process.

According to Abu Marzuq, Hamas's difficulty in coping with these threats derived from

1. The similarity of interests of the United States, Israel, Jordan, and the PLO. In addition, most Arab states and the international community supported the peace process and agreed that Hamas posed the main threat to its success.
2. Hamas's military inferiority to the PA's police and security agencies.
3. The Hamas infrastructure's dependence on external financial resources, which could be easily curtailed by PA legislation and administrative restrictions.

Abu Marzuq's concern was expressed in an effort by Hamas, on the eve of the official establishment of the Palestinian Authority, to reach an agreement with Fatah on local matters in order to prevent a violent outbreak between the two movements. In early May 1994, shortly before the signing of the Cairo agreement on the establishment of the Palestinian Authority in Gaza and Jericho, a joint declaration was issued by the Battalions of 'Izz al-Din al-Qassam and the Fatah Hawks, announcing an agreement between them aimed at strengthening Palestinian national unity and preventing civil war. The six-issue document called for refraining from

rhetorical and violent polemics, using "constructive dialogue" and joint rec-
onciliation committees to settle disputes, calling a one-month moratorium
on executions of collaborators, cutting back the number of strike days, and
ending the interdiction on study in schools. This agreement became a blue-
print for a similar one between Islamic and Fatah activists in Hebron.[55]

Hamas also was aware that the strong international and regional support for the Oslo process meant that any attempt to derail it would be no
more than a "political illusion." The movement's leaders were familiar with
the international and regional trends that had forced Islamic movements
in almost all the Arab countries to go on the defensive. Hamas, for example, could not overlook the fact that the Sudanese Islamist leader Hasan
al-Turabi held back from denouncing the Oslo accords or that Egypt
seemed willing to support Arafat's tough policy against Hamas in the event
of a collision between the two movements. Hamas also lacked strategic
depth among the Palestinians: its supporters in the territories were in a
minority; the Islamic movement in Israel was closer to Arafat than to
Hamas; and the Islamic movement in Jordan was under the government's
strict control.[56] Conceding these weaknesses, Hamas had little choice but
to reach a limited understanding with the PA. A confrontational approach
would give the PA a pretext to deliver a serious blow to its main opposition, smoothing the way toward a permanent settlement of the Israeli-
Palestinian conflict.

Within a year of the PA's establishment, Hamas's influence had notice-
ably waned in the Gaza Strip in the wake of security operations by the PA
to suppress its activities. To prevent further damage, Hamas's religious and
political leaders strove not to give the PA cause to engage in a violent clash.
Hamas's local leadership also displayed an increasing interest in coexisting
with the PA on the basis of a temporary agreement, participation in the
elections, and independent political activity by Hamas. However, objections
to these conditions were raised by Hamas's "outside" political leaders and
its military wing, 'Izz al-Din al-Qassam. Threatened to be marginalized by
any agreement between the "inside" leaders and the PA, the "outside" leaders and the military apparatus defined the moderate line toward the PA as
a defeat. Indeed, the military wing may have stepped up the armed struggle in order to block an agreement between Hamas and the PA.[57]

Toward a Strategy of Mutual Restraint

Relations with Hamas had been at the top of the PA's agenda since the
signing of the DOP in September 1993. Notwithstanding Arafat's attempts

to enlist leading activists of the Muslim Brothers in Egypt to help persuade Hamas, and also the Islamic Jihad, to acknowledge the PA, Hamas remained adamant that it would accept no less than official recognition as a legitimate opposition that could continue its uninterrupted development under the PA. But Hamas's attempt to play it both ways—and, more particularly, its decision to continue the armed struggle against Israel—forced it into a head-on collision with the PA.

Even without the armed struggle against Israel, relations between Hamas and the PA might still have boiled over. Still, the presence of the Israeli occupation probably contributed to the Hamas leadership's loss of control over its military wing, which, in turn, increased the tension and conflict between the political leadership of the Hamas and the PA. Early in November 1994, a car bomb explosion killed Hani 'Abed, a military leader of the Islamic Jihad. Islamic activists attributed the killing to Israel, but crowds at the funeral directed their wrath at Arafat, calling him a traitor. The leader of the Islamic Jihad, 'Abdallah al-Shami, later apologized to Arafat and urged his own followers to avoid civil war. Earlier, however, he had issued a bellicose message, vowing that in the future "the guns of Jihad will not be able to distinguish between an Israeli soldier and the Palestinian police."[58]

The rising tension between Islamic Jihad and Hamas, on one hand, and the PA, on the other, reached a peak on November 18, 1994, a Friday, following prayers in Gaza's Filastin Mosque, when a violent clash erupted between the PA police and Islamic activists, who had planned a protest. The clash, which quickly developed into a full-fledged riot that targeted property and public buildings identified with the PA, resulted in fifteen deaths, some two hundred injuries, and the arrest of hundreds. The incident underscored the deep frustration within the Islamic movements over the Oslo agreement and conveyed dramatically their growing suspicion that the PA had helped Israel eliminate the leaders of Hamas's and the Islamic Jihad's military wings. Tension between the Islamic movements and the PA reached yet another crisis when Islamic Jihad activists assembled in Gaza and flaunted their weapons, threatening Arafat's security personnel and vowing to continue the violent struggle. In response, the PA outlawed unauthorized demonstrations and arrested about two hundred Islamic Jihad activists.[59]

The incident demonstrated the PA's newfound self-confidence and its determination to use arms to enforce its authority. Yet both sides demonstrated restraint, and Hamas said it was willing to open a dialogue with the PA. By pointing to Israel as the cause of the violent clash and by voicing common concerns such as "the homeland, Jerusalem, the [Palestinian] prisoners, [and Jewish] settlements," both parties were able to overcome the embarrassment that the incident had caused and demonstrate their unity.

The PA sought to stay above the fray, insisting that the dialogue be conducted between Fatah and Hamas, but Hamas insisted that talks with the PA be held on an equal footing, since the clash had occurred with the PA's police force. In addition, Hamas insisted that the dialogue be held outside the Palestinian autonomous areas and in the presence of Arab leaders, to ensure that the PA did not apply any pressure. The disagreement between the PA and Hamas was eventually resolved by Arafat's decision to accept Hamas's demand to conduct the dialogue with the PA outside the autonomous region, which was tantamount to recognizing Hamas's political status as a legitimate opposition.[60] In the PA-Hamas talks in Khartoum and Cairo in late 1995, Hamas raised concrete issues, such as the release of prisoners and an end to the persecution of its members, while requesting that the PA not support splinter groups of the movement. In return for its agreement on these points, the PA secured Hamas's commitment not to disrupt the general elections to the Palestinian Council. Hamas agreed not to boycott the elections and to take a neutral position.[61]

The PA's responsiveness toward the "inside" Hamas only aggravated the split within the movement, for then the "outside" tended to take a tougher attitude.[62] It was the fear of being ignored by the PA that induced elements of the "inside" Hamas to advocate participating in the emerging Palestinian bureaucracy and the elections to the PA Council (on the elections, see chapter 5). However, the more intransigent elements in the movement urged that the movement's authenticity be preserved and its original goals kept as a shield against internal erosion and containment by the central authority. Hamas's vacillation between these two approaches had been clearly reflected in its leadership's debate over means and strategies since the September 1993 Israeli-Palestinian DOP, and the uncertainty had a potent impact on the movement's practical politics. However persuasive the argument to become part of the PA and thus obtain access to resources and decision-making processes, this option also meant that Hamas might lose control over part of its military apparatus—a serious blow, as it was the military wing that had given the movement room for maneuver, legitimized its separate existence, and lent credibility to its claim to be an alternative to the PLO. Acquiescence in the peace process, therefore, could have severely threatened Hamas's ability to survive and develop into a moral and political alternative to the PA.

The cumulative effect of the internal debate within Hamas was to intensify its tendency to differentiate between an attitude toward the "objective," namely, Israel, and the perception of "actual situations."[63] Hamas repeated its rejection of Israel's legitimacy, maintaining that the solution to the conflict was a Palestinian Islamic state "from the river to the sea," that is, Mandatory Palestine. But a blind pursuit of this attitude could paralyze Hamas's political maneuverability and force it to fight the PA or abandon its quest to provide an alternative political frame of reference to the existing order. That this extreme scenario did not materialize was due to Hamas's attitude toward "actual situations," which revealed its political realism and a recognition of the constraints that consistently led Hamas to express its willingness to adopt the traditional Islamic concept of truce—*hudna*—with the infidels, in return for a Palestinian state in part of historic Palestine. Under these terms, the Hamas political leaders did not rule out an indirect dialogue with Israel. According to Sheikh Jamal Salim, head of the Palestine Muslim Scholar Association (Rabitat 'Ulama' Filastin) in Nablus, it would be possible to reach an agreement with Israel, similar to the truce of Hizballah with Israel in Lebanon, through any available mediation.[64] This attitude was supported by other leading figures, such as Sheikh Jamil Hamami, Sheikh Husain Abu Kuwaik, and Dr. Mahmud al-Zahar.[65]

As mentioned earlier in this chapter, even before the establishment of the PA in Gaza, Hamas's political leadership had announced a peace initiative of its own, which amounted to a "strategy of phases." Hamas's realpolitik extended to acceptance of a temporary agreement—*hudna*—with Israel if the latter withdrew fully and unconditionally to its pre-1967 borders and dismantled its settlements outside these borders. Hamas's leaders repeated this shift in their strategy in internal communications with the movement's activists, emphasizing the temporary nature of such an agreement and their continued adherence to the *jihad* and the ultimate goal of establishing an Islamic state of Palestine.[66]

The legitimacy of *hudna* as a phase in the course of a defensive *jihad* against the enemies of Islam has been widely discussed—and accepted—by both radical and more moderate Islamic scholars since Egypt's President Anwar Sadat signed a peace treaty with Israel in 1979. The concept has been justified by historical precedents ranging from the Prophet's treaties with his adversaries in Mecca (the Treaty of Hudaybiyya, 628 C.E.) and the Jews of al-Madina, to the treaties signed between Salah al-Din al-Ayyubi and other Muslim rulers and the Crusaders. The common denominator of these precedents is that they were caused by Muslim military weakness and concern for the well-being (*maslaha*) of the Islamic community and were later followed by the renewal of war and the defeat of Islam's enemies. In retrospect, these cases of *hudna* were legitimized in realpolitik terms and interpreted a priori as necessary and temporary pauses on the road of *jihad* against the infidels.[67]

Although the Oslo accord theoretically could be interpreted on the basis of the historical precedent of an Islamic state reaching an agreement with infidels, Hamas insisted on the religious illegality of the agreement with Israel, thus clearly distinguishing between Hamas and the PLO. Hamas spokesmen argued that any recognition of Israel's right to exist on Islamic land was irreconcilable with religious jurisprudence. Along with the religious argument, Hamas raised specific reservations regarding the content of the agreement and its failure to address basic claims of the Palestinians. According to Hamas, the PLO had made inordinate concessions to Israel, especially concerning the question of Jerusalem and Palestinian independence, and had displayed a willingness to settle for only two-thirds of the West Bank.

Hamas adopted the same line in its negative response to a religious opinion (*fatwa*) issued by the mufti of Saudi Arabia, Sheikh ʿAbd al-ʿAziz Ibn Baz, that permitted Arab leaders to make peace with Israel if and when it served Arab-Muslim interests. A peace of this kind, the mufti argued, would be contingent on the Jews' being inclined toward peace (*yajnahu lil-silm*) and would be temporary. This *fatwa* was sharply criticized by religious figures associated with Hamas. Prominent among these men was the Egyptian Sheikh Yusuf al-Qaradawi, who rejected the *fatwa* on the ground that Israel could not be considered to be leaning toward peace as long as it continued to occupy Islamic lands and to shed Muslim blood.[68]

Arafat's statements since signing the 1993 Israeli-Palestinian agreement seemed to support Hamas's phased strategy, enabling Hamas's leaders to maintain its coexistence with the PA. without necessarily legitimizing it. However apologetic, Arafat's statements nonetheless used militant Islamic terminology that, as Sadat had done after signing the Israel-Egypt peace treaty in 1979, tried to legitimize the Oslo process with Israel by relying on historic examples of temporary agreements between Muslim states and non-Muslims that ultimately ended in victory by the Muslims.[69]

By interpreting any political agreement involving the West Bank and Gaza Strip as merely a pause on the historic road of *jihad*, Hamas achieved political flexibility without losing its ideological credibility. In fact, Hamas emulated the PLO, which in the twelfth session of the PNC in June 1974 had set an interim national objective without abandoning the strategic goal of an independent Palestinian state covering all of Mandatory Palestine. In that session, the PNC decided that the PLO would, as an interim stage, establish a "national, independent and fighting authority on any part of Palestinian land to be liberated."[70] Hamas now adopted the same strategy, which would allow it to live with the post-Oslo reality without recognizing Israel; to support the establishment of a Palestinian state in the West Bank and Gaza Strip without ending the state of war or renouncing its ultimate goals; and to consider restraint, but not to give up the armed struggle, instead ascribing violent actions to uncontrollable groups and distinguishing between "political" and "military" wings within the movement while claiming the right to launch operations from areas under Israeli rule. In this way, Hamas hoped to retain both its credibility and organizational unity.

The differentiation between short-term needs and a long-term commitment to Palestinian national goals enabled Hamas to play the role of a "positive" opposition to the ruling power, focusing on social, economic, and political grievances that would underscore—and legitimize—its separate existence. Political activity here and now was thus justified in terms of hereafter. Acceptance of a political settlement in the short run was interpreted as being complementary, not contradictory, to long-term desires.

Indeed, Hamas did not miss an opportunity to criticize both the Oslo agreement and the disadvantages for the Palestinians, as well as the disappointing social and economic results. But Hamas was also attentive to the broad Palestinian public support for Oslo and the understanding of its irreversible nature. Hamas's critique, therefore, focused less on issues of principle and more on matters of economic, social, and security significance, referring especially to impoverished Palestinians. An example of the cautious line Hamas was walking was, as we saw in the previous chapter, its reaction to the assassination in March 1998 of Muhyi al-Din al-Sharif, a senior figure of 'Izz al-Din al-Qassam. Although Hamas leaders criticized the PA, accusing it of complicity in the killing, they were careful not to turn their public criticism into an all-out protest, which would have tested the PA's willingness to use force against Hamas.[71]

Hamas's inclination toward coexistence with the PA was due, first and foremost, to its recognition of its military inferiority to the PA. The Hamas leaders also realized that the PA's security and police forces were waiting for a pretext to abolish Hamas as a military movement, especially following the incorporation of Fatah into the PA's bureaucratic and security apparatus.[72] To these considerations were added strategic ones—namely, the collapse of the Soviet Union, the weakness of the movement's allies in the

Arab and Muslim world, and the need to adapt to the new reality, which meant narrowing the movement's activities to social and political domains.

Hamas's considerations in favor of coexistence with the PA despite the disagreements also derived from its assumption that the Oslo process was bound to founder against insurmountable future political obstacles, compounded by Palestine's myriad socioeconomic difficulties. The more apparent the PA's failure was, and the greater the people's grievances against it, the better Hamas's political cause would seem. Such considerations shaped the form, rather than the essence, of Hamas's critical response to the Oslo process and its hesitation to participate in the PA—a move that could cost Hamas popularity, since it would be perceived as a partner to power.[73] Moreover, the same considerations have guided Hamas's approach to the possible use of violence against the PA. Only if the PA were to take steps to undermine Hamas's civic infrastructure—its religious, educational, and social institutions and its public activities—would violence become inevitable.[74]

Hamas's willingness to acquiesce in a provisional political settlement with Israel, that is, without compromising its ultimate goals, have enabled it to consolidate a working formula of coexistence with the PA. This involved the creation of joint ad hoc conciliation forums with Fatah and committees on national concerns such as the Palestinian prisoners held by Israel. Hamas's willingness to maintain a negotiated coexistence with the PA has been reciprocated by the latter on grounds of cost-benefit calculations. True, Arafat has sought to weaken and divide Hamas and force it to join the PA, but his cautious policy also reflects a preference for dialogue over collision. Furthermore, gestures of temporary rapprochement with Hamas—such as meetings with Hamas leaders or the release of Hamas inmates from Palestinian prisons—have become a useful instrument by which the PA can curb internal criticism and win public support.[75]

This pattern of coexistence became critical following the release of Sheikh Ahmad Yasin from an Israeli prison and his return to Gaza at the beginning of October 1997. Yasin's release followed the Israeli Mossad's abortive attempt on the life of Khalid Mash'al, the head of Hamas's Political Bureau in Amman, and King Hussein's demand that Israel release the imprisoned symbol of Hamas (see also chapter 3). Whereas Yasin's return to social and political activity in Hamas allowed Arafat to maintain a close watch over the movement's spiritual leader, it also posed a challenge to the PA. In May and June 1997, Yasin visited Iran, Sudan, Syria, and the Gulf states for fund-raising purposes. After an absence of more

than eight years, Yasin was reestablishing his position within the movement and shifting Hamas's center of gravity back to the Palestinian territories. His visits to countries such as Syria, Saudi Arabia, and Kuwait (as
well as Iran) could be seen as part of a wider effort by Hamas to strengthen
its regional presence. In this sense, Yasin's return to activity posed a political threat to the PA—as well as to Hamas's Political Bureau in Jordan,
which was apprehensive that the weight of the movement would shift back
to the "inside" leadership.[76]

The preference of Hamas and the PA for cooperation over confrontation spawned a pattern of relations best described, as already noted, as coexistence within a prolonged conflict. Both sides were well aware of the
gulf dividing them and of the improbability that they could reach an agreement that would enable them to live side by side in political harmony. Yet
each side recognized the limits beyond which it could not press for a solution of "one in place of the other." Neither side would accept the other
fully, but both were equally loath to adopt a position of total rejection.
Given the social circumstances and political reality in which Hamas and
the PA operated, the price to be paid for in attempting to remove the
other from the political stage was intolerable. Both therefore preferred to
pursue a strategy that would mitigate the disadvantages of coexistence
rather than strive for a new political order that excluded the other side.
Underlying this pattern of relations was the sober perception that took
root in both camps, holding that the achievement of a clear decision in
their protracted dispute would never be more than wishful thinking and,
crucially, that a mode of action based on a zero-sum perception was likely
to end in tragedy. Hence, the most promising course was for each side to
concentrate on consolidating its position and to enhance its bargaining
ability vis-à-vis the other side, instead of pursuing an "all or nothing" policy to advance ultimate political goals.

CHAPTER FIVE

Calculated Participation

Islamic thinkers discern four main strategies that mark the political be-havior of Islamic movements: (1) reformist, operating through education, preaching, and guidance (*sabil al-wa'z wal-irshad*); (2) communal, focus-ing on the Muslim institution of welfare (*zakat*) and other social services; (3) political, operating through mass mobilization and public conviction aimed at pressuring rulers to implement the *shari'a*; and (4) combatant-political, using military force or violence against the ruling elites.[1] In fact, however, since the 1940s, Islamic movements, as demonstrated by Hasan al-Banna's Muslim Brotherhood Association (MB) in Egypt, which be-came a role model for similar movements across the Arab world, have shown flexibility, adopting mixed elements from these strategies under dif-ferent social and political conditions. Under al-Banna's guidance, the MB movement initially adopted a reformist approach but later also attempted to obtain political representation and prepared a military option by estab-lishing an armed militia.[2]

Islamic Movements and Strategies of Political Participation

Although Islamic movements have traditionally been divided by strategies of action even within the same state, the single most important variable determining their behavior has been the freedom of social action and access to power made available to them by the ruling elite. Contemporary Islamic movements have generally responded violently to violent repression, as shown at certain periods in the cases of Egypt, Syria, and Algeria, whereas in those states that tolerated Islamic political movements, they have been willing to accept the rules of the political game and refrain from violence, such as in the case of the MB in Egypt,[3] Jordan,[4] Sudan,[5] and Yemen.[6]

The reformist and communal approaches—often inseparable—have been the mainstay of the MB's activity since its founding in Egypt in the late 1920s and subsequent spread throughout the Arab world, whereas political and violent Islam remained on the margins in most Arab states until the late 1970s. The 1980s and 1990s, however, have witnessed a novel pattern of action of modern Islamic groups, a trend toward political parties and participation in the political process and even in power, even in non-Islamic regimes. Moreover, this trend has persisted despite the efforts of Arab regimes to slow down or backtrack on the process of controlled democratization, which usually was started under the pressure of the Islamic movements. This was the case in Egypt, Tunisia, and Jordan, whose regimes since the late 1980s have restricted freedom of speech and passed new election laws with the aim of reducing the Islamists' public power and presence in parliament. In Algeria, where the ruling FLN military elite overturned the victory of the Front islamique du salut (FIS) in the general parliamentary elections of December 1991—prompting militant Islamist groups to start a nationwide armed struggle against the regime— the Front hesitated to use violence and tried to find common ground.[7] In Lebanon, although Hizballah remained committed to armed struggle against Israel's presence in the south of the country, it took part in two consecutive parliamentary elections (1992 and 1996) and won representation.[8]

The scope of political participation and power sharing of Islamic movements in the Arab world since the 1980s—and the essential role they have been playing in the democratization of political life in Egypt, Jordan, Yemen, Morocco, Tunisia, Algeria, and Kuwait—became a focal point in the debate on Islam and democracy among students of the contemporary Middle East. Students of political Islam have been divided over the meaning of the growing participation of Islamic movements in the political process, which signals that they have accepted pluralism and the rules of the game determined by non-Islamic regimes. The focal point of the debate has been whether these movements represent a normative change in the attitude toward liberal democracy or a drive for power by exploiting opportunities afforded by the non-Islamic regime and under its terms. The underlying question is the extent to which such movements might be willing to accept democracy and apply its principles not only during the struggle for power but also after gaining power.[9]

The most conspicuous advocates of this increasingly dominant trend in the Arab world have been Hasan al-Turabi, leader of the Islamic National Front in Sudan, and Rashed Ghanouchi, the exiled leader of al-Nahda movement in Tunisia. These leaders adhere to active participation of the Islamic movements in the political process and accept the principle of a multiparty system (*ta'ddudiyya*). Drawing on pragmatic approaches used in the MB movement under Hasan al-Banna's lead, Turabi and Ghanouchi claimed legitimacy for the incorporation of Islamic movements in an ad hoc coalition (*tahaluf*) with non-Islamic parties, in order to exploit the opportunity of political participation to seize power and impose Islamization "from above" through official state machinery.[10] Although this approach recognized the crucial role of religious guidance and education as a necessary phase for creating a wide base of cadres for a mass Islamic movement, it also called for adopting modern strategies of mass mobilization rather than the elitist seclusion implied in Sayyid Qutb's writings.[11] According to this approach, although the use of violence is not illegitimate if the regime is repressive, it is not recommended because of the overwhelming power of the state and the danger of giving the ruling elite a pretext to wage an all-out war against the Islamic movement, as Nasser did in Egypt and Hafiz al-Assad did in Syria. This is why Turabi referred to the option of gradual penetration into the armed forces and bureaucratic apparatuses, parallel to participation in the political process (reflecting Turabi's experience and road to power in Sudan).[12]

The drive of Islamic movements for participation in non-Islamist power (*musharaka*)—preached and implemented by Turabi—has been further justified by Rashed al-Ghanouchi according to the normative principle of necessity (*fiqh al-darurat,* similar to the interest principle—*maslaha*). Drawing on Joseph's role in Pharaoh's administration and the Prophet's agreement with non-Muslim elements in Mecca, Ghanouchi maintains that such participation, or coalition (*tahaluf*) with non-Islamist movements, is a legitimate tactic to promote the Islamic movement's goals.[13] In this context, it is noteworthy that although Hamas boycotted the elections to the Palestinian Authority's Council held in January 1996, it did use Ghanouchi's pragmatic approach and collaborated with non-Islamic movements. In October 1991, on the eve of the international peace conference held in Madrid, Hamas joined a Syrian-based coalition composed of mostly radical-leftist Palestinian groups ("The Ten Front") opposed to the Israel-Palestinian peacemaking process.[14]

Under authoritarian regimes, opposition movements cannot gain much by joining the ruling system. Indeed, they might legitimize the regime while risking the loss of their constituency and becoming dependent on the ruler.[15] Similarly, Islamic movements have questioned their political participation and remained reluctant to turn into full-fledged political parties and share representation in non-Islamic institutions, thus legitimizing non-Islamic regimes. In addition to these reservations, Islamic movements—like other extraparliamentary opposition movements claiming to be an alternative to the ruling party—have found that a metamorphosis from a religious, social, voluntary movement into a political party includes, at best, not only prospects for representation and power sharing but also the possibility of being controlled, contained, and marginalized by the regime. As extraparliamentary movements, the Islamic groups have enjoyed considerable civic autonomy and direct contact with the masses through the mosques and charitable associations and through social services they provide, especially to the poor urban masses. Party politics (*hizbiyya*) has meant a loss of these relative advantages due to the acceptance of strict formal rules that require transparency and accountability to the regime. Moreover, whereas the earlier activities coincided with Islam's loftiest values—charity and social solidarity—reflecting honesty and service to the community of believers, official political activities have traditionally been identified with corruption and selfish interests.[16]

The prospect of gaining influence and power balanced against the limitations and risks of this option was the subject of much of the debate in Islamic movements in response to the new opportunity offered to them by the ruling elites in the form of "democratization from above." The crux of the matter, then, was cost-benefit considerations in the context of political freedom and restrictions determined by the regime.[17] As an official political party, the Islamists would be stifled by the regime, might suffer irreparable damage to their image, and were bound to lose supporters to more radical Islamic groups. However, failing to enter politics and take advantage of political pluralism could frustrate the expectations of the young generation of Islamists for participation in the political game and a shortcut to power.[18]

One way to resolve the dilemmas inherent in an Islamic party's political participation has been to create a "front" organization based on the communist model after World War II. This pattern of political action was used by communist parties in the Middle East, which until the 1950s refused to cooperate with the bourgeoisie, assigning the duty of social revolution exclusively to the proletariat. But in the wake of the European experience and awareness of the gap between Marxist theory and the sociopolitical structure in the countries of the Middle East, the communist parties there were permitted to align tactically with national and bourgeois groups. The result was the creation of temporary coalitions, known as "national fronts," combining communist and nationalist parties and movements such as the Ba'th, Nasserists, Arab Nationalists, and lower-middle-class socialist groups in Syria, Jordan, Iraq, and Lebanon. The alignment with the bourgeoisie was meant to topple the "reactionary" ruling elites closely connected with the West and in their place establish a "neutral national" regime. The communists believed that following the shift of power, they would be able to take over the state's centers of power and change the social and economic structure "from above."[19]

In the case of the Islamic party, such a front would include Islamists and potential opposition elements, though still Islamic, and would be considered as an extension, or instrument, of the main MB movement. This idea was successfully implemented by Turabi in Sudan in 1985 in the form of the Islamic National Front (al-Jabha al-islamiyya al-qawmiyya) and by the Algerian Front islamique du salut (FIS—Jabhat al-inqadh al-islami) in 1989. Similarly, the MB in Jordan formed the Islamic Action Front (Jabhat al-'amal al-islami) in 1992 to serve as the political arm of the Islamic movement there.[20]

By the early 1990s, however, Islamic movements were chafing under strictly controlled democratization in Egypt, Algeria, and Jordan. Participation in general elections and parliamentary life rarely brought the Islamic groups to real power sharing, that is, co-option to the government. The restrictions—in the guise of administrative regulations and discriminatory legislation—imposed by the ruling elite on these groups' freedom of political organization and speech limited their power in the representative institutions. The result was a retreat by the movements from participation in parliamentary elections. In 1990 the MB in Egypt boycotted the elections, as did the Islamic Action Front in Jordan in 1997. The decision by the Jordanian group followed a long and bitter debate triggered by the Islamic movement's declining representation in parliament after the general elections of 1993 when the government amended the election law, effectively marginalizing the Islamists.[21] The debate within the movement, which followed its participation in the general elections of 1993 and frustration at the disappointing results, revealed the split between Palestinians and Jordanians in the movement. Each side tried to justify its contradictory attitudes through Islamic argumentation and terminology while in practice representing different interests. Thus, the opponents of political participation, most of whom were Palestinian by origin, contended that to take part in elections and parliamentary life effectively legitimized the Jordan-Israel peace treaty, which contradicted Islamic principles. Conversely, the proponents of continued participation, a minority of mostly Jordanians by origin, displayed a willingness to cooperate with the nationalist and leftist forces, as well as with the regime itself—regardless of its commitment to the peace treaty with Israel—as long as their participation would lead to power sharing. As in the case of the Muslim Brotherhood in Egypt, the debate in Jordan culminated in a decision by the Islamic Action Front in July 1997 to boycott the elections that November. The decision, however, backfired on the militants, as more pragmatic elements were elected, forming a majority in the Front's institutions.[22]

The drive of Islamic movements to power sharing, justified on religious grounds and the Islamic community's well-being, is visible across the Arab world, from Algeria and Sudan through Yemen,[23] Lebanon, and Jordan. Even in Israel, officially defined as a Jewish state, a group from the Islamic movement decided—at the cost of splitting the movement—to run together with a non-Islamist party (the Arab Democratic Party) on a joint ticket and won two seats in the Knesset in the 1996 general elections.[24]

Besides reflecting the new opportunities for political participation afforded by most Arab regimes since the early 1980s, the Islamic movements also wanted to shorten the process of Islamizing the country by shifting from an evolutionary to a political strategy in order to gain access to power. Indeed, the very willingness of Islamic movements to take part in various levels of state-controlled and limited democratic systems demonstrated their belief that they could gain influence and promote their goals by operating within the existing political order.

A close study of Hamas's strategies of action reveals a similarity to those of other Islamic movements in the Arab world, as well as to those of the communist parties, concerning participation in the political process—in this case, entry into the PA's structural system—and its justification in normative terms. Hamas's posture of neither fully accepting nor totally rejecting the PA's legitimacy has been apparent in the movement's internal debate and its actual behavior over the issue of participating in the PA's executive and representative institutions. Hamas's wish to ensure its survival and continued growth necessitated its access to power and resources, based on coexistence with the PA. But Hamas also was eager to minimize the damage to its political stature as a result of collaborating with the PA and especially participating in its formal institutions, which might be interpreted as a deviation from its Islamic principles. It was this dilemma that underlay Hamas's strategy; it was a strategy that could be pursued only as long as it left intact, or at least ambiguous, the movement's commitment to its religious-national vision, on the one hand, and compromise with respect to the Oslo process, on the other.

Indeed, much of Hamas's approach to the issue of participation can be described as differentiating between participation through direct and official presence and participation through political involvement in the PA's representative and decision-making institutions. Taking into account Hamas's refusal to recognize the PA, involvement in its acting administrative apparatuses without an official presence and direct representation would provide a useful means to minimize the disadvantages of the existing post-Oslo processes without paying the political cost of its endorsement. Moreover, involvement would serve as a safety valve for Hamas, reducing the threats to its continued activities and public support.

Yet involvement without an official presence would be uncertain: it might provide political safety in the short run but would be exposed to threats of instability in the long run. An official presence, however, would increase the stability and continuity of resource allocation over the long run but might force Hamas to renounce or minimize its public rejection of Oslo and legitimization of the political and legal status of the PA. Given the growing conviction among both Palestinian and Israelis that the Oslo process was irreversible, the more that the PA tightened its grip on the society, the more intense the debate within Hamas became regarding its participation in the PA's executive institutions.

Alternatives and Preferred Options

The international peace conference held in Madrid in October 1991, with unprecedented PLO-backed Palestinian representation, was a clear indication to the Hamas leadership that the possibility of an Israeli-Palestinian-Jordanian settlement could not be ruled out, thus forcing it to clarify its position regarding that possibility. Hamas's dilemma was made worse by the anticipated establishment of a PLO-based self-governing authority in the West Bank and the Gaza Strip. The situation was further complicated by talks initiated by the U.S. State Department with Musa Abu Marzuq in the United States and Amman in the early fall of 1991, aimed at obtaining Hamas's support for the participation of a Palestinian delegation from the occupied territories in the Madrid conference. Hamas, however, had long objected to Palestinian participation in peace talks with Israel, calling instead for the escalation of the Intifada.[25]

This became Hamas's dominant public response to the Madrid talks (and afterward to the Oslo agreement) and to the establishment of the PA by the PLO, which it contemptuously dubbed "the Tunis command."[26] Internally, however, the period of the Madrid and Washington talks (1991–1993) was marked by a complex self-searching in the Hamas leadership and a review of alternative strategies, with a view to minimizing the repercussions of an Israel-PLO settlement on Hamas's communal infrastructure and political status. Specifically, Hamas examined its future strategy based on the premise that a confrontation with the Palestinian self-governing authority had to be avoided. Accordingly, Hamas's leaders looked at the experience of other Islamic movements that had entered the political process in their drive for Islamic legislation and power sharing. In the debate, in which Hamas's constituency was invited to take part, the movement's leaders considered establishing an Islamic party as a "front" organization to oppose the PA.

The debate underscored Hamas's essential difference from other Islamic movements in the Arab countries. In addition to its reformist religious character, Hamas was also a combatant movement, committed to liberating Palestine by means of a holy war. Indeed, although the movement's leaders refused to veer from its dogmatic doctrine of armed struggle toward social and political action, they occasionally demonstrated openness, flexibility, and willingness to adopt new options in accordance with the changing political circumstances. The prolonged debate over this issue shows unequivocally that Hamas's paramount concern was to ensure its future as a social and political movement within the framework of a Palestinian self-governing authority. The armed struggle against Israel was therefore not a strategic but a tactical goal, subordinated to the movement's needs in the Palestinian arena.

In April 1992 an internal Hamas bulletin stated that the movement's leadership had decided to object to a Jordanian-Palestinian confederation, "as it was being suggested." Hamas rejected the idea because it derived from the Madrid process, which the movement rejected on what it considered pragmatic political grounds, most notably that by attending the conference, both Jordan and the PLO had effectively deferred to Israeli prerequisites. In the bulletin, Hamas for the first time presented its position on elections to representative institutions in the West Bank and

Gaza Strip. It stated that it would not object to nonpolitical representative elections and that it would take part in such elections provided they were fair and just, were not conducted under Israeli occupation, were administered under appropriate international supervision, and were not conditioned on the candidates' commitment to support the peace process.[27] In July 1992, while Hamas and Fatah activists were still clashing and Hamas's leaflets fiercely and contemptuously attacked the negotiations with Israel, a secret document was circulated among Hamas senior members analyzing a spectrum of alternatives ranging from a total boycott of the PA to full and official participation in the election and the PA's institutions.[28]

The document assumed that the Israeli-Palestinian negotiations would lead to an agreement on establishing an interim Palestinian self-rule with general elections in the territories under its jurisdiction to be held shortly thereafter. Based on earlier consultations among leading Hamas figures in the West Bank, Gaza Strip, and the diaspora, the document presented a draft analysis of assumptions and a variety of considerations concerning Hamas's response to the new reality. In order to reach a decision regarding its position on participation, Hamas's policy paper examined its options in view of a possible PLO-Israel accord and the advantages and disadvantages of each, as well as the expected responses of the PA and the Palestinian public to each choice of action.

Besides its detailed discussion of Hamas's participation in the PA elections, this document offers a rare glimpse of decision making in the movement marked by careful consultation with the rank and file. The recipients of the document were asked to consider the suggested alternatives in accordance with the movement's goals and ideology and to prepare an answer within a week, to help the leadership decide on the most appropriate election strategy. The document set August 10, 1992, as the date for reaching a final decision.

The paper was classified, and its cover letter with directives to the recipient activists did not specifically mention Hamas (referring to it as "the movement"), even though the discussion clearly revolved around Hamas's prospective stand. The document's recipients were requested to consult with as many knowledgeable people as possible to ensure that the final decision would have wide support in Hamas, preserve the movement's achievements, and follow its principles. The document had a nonideological tone, bereft of the Islamic phrases and terminology of the delegitimization of Hamas's rivals and demonization of its enemies, particularly Israel and the Jews, usually referred to as descendants of Satan, monkeys, and pigs. Instead, Israel was referred to by its proper name, and terms such as "Zionists," "Jews," or the "enemies of Allah" were absent. Unlike the usual language of Hamas's leaflets and publications, saturated with Qur'anic verses and oral traditions (*hadith*), the document refrained from using even once terms such as "*shari'a*," "Qur'an," "Muhammad," or even "Islam."

The timing of the document suggests that it reflected the ascendancy of Israel's Labor-led government, which came to power in June 1992, and the high expectations for progress in the peace process that it had aroused. Thus, Hamas's positions toward Palestinian self-rule and the general elections were labeled "fateful" to the movement's future and defined as "the most dangerous and difficult" ever in its history. We have reproduced the full document here, owing to its significance as a reflection of the movement's modes of political thinking, its ability to adjust to changing circumstances, and its decision-making methods in evaluating and examining available alternatives.

In the name of Allah, the merciful, the compassionate

Re: The Position regarding the interim self-rule and the elections

Distinguished brothers,
   The l.s. [possibly referring to the political committee (*lajna siyasiyya*)] presented to you a paper on our position regarding the forthcoming development, assuming that the negotiations now being held succeed in bringing to the interim self-rule. We then started a debate over [our] position regarding the general elections that might be held in the [West] Bank and the [Gaza] Strip.

We have already received responses from Gaza and the [West] Bank and the brothers abroad. In this paper, we are trying to review the consolidation of opinion, suggesting . . . [sic] our decision making and examining the most influential factors in this regard. Following this [stage], a final proposal concerning the subject will be drawn up . . . [sic] the higher circles. We must arrive at a final draft resolution before 10.8.92 . . . [sic] on this paper and your evaluation of the most important elements affecting the decision and your opinion regarding the most appropriate position for the movement . . . [sic] within a week after receiving the paper.

Brothers!

We ask that you handle this paper with the utmost secrecy because the debate is continuing and no final decision has yet been reached. We also request that you study the paper carefully and consult with knowledgeable people in your area. [The reason is] that we wish to reach a decision acceptable to the widest possible basis of our ranks which, at the same time, would preserve the movement's achievements and remain faithful to its goals and principles. We also ask that you provide us with your elaborate rather than summarized opinion because we are about to make a fateful decision that will affect the future of our movement in the coming phase. We believe that this decision is absolutely the most crucial and difficult in the history of our movement. Hence, we hope that you give the issue your closest attention and respond within a week.

Peace be with you and Allah's mercy and blessings.

Our paper handles the following aspects:

First: Introduction to the Next Phase

Most of the analyses, including those of this movement, tend to [assume] that the peace process will culminate in an agreement between Israel and the Arab parties and that this agreement will result in the establishment of interim self-rule for the Palestinians. It has been suggested that elections will be conducted among the Palestinians with the possible goal of establishing a Palestinian authority to which the [Israeli] military government's powers and authorities will be transferred. This might be an administrative authority of a political nature and powers to oversee the daily affairs of Palestinians' lives. The [important working hypotheses are] that elections will be held; public institutions will be built; most of the powers and authorities of the military government will be transferred to the Palestinians; and it is possible that the first event will be the elections.

What is, then, the most appropriate position for the movement to take in view of what might happen?

Second: The Alternatives

There are four possible alternatives:

1. Hamas participates in the elections.
2. Hamas boycotts the elections and is contented with calling the people also to boycott the elections . . . [*sic*] against the elections.
3. Hamas boycotts the elections and also attempts to disrupt them by force in order to delegitimize them as well as the whole peace process.
4. Hamas participates under another name, the essence of which would be determined in accordance with the circumstances of the next phase and the results of the negotiations.

What are the advantages and disadvantages of the four alternatives? They are clarified in the following table:

TABLE 5.1 Third: Advantages and Disadvantages of the Alternative Positions Toward the Elections

The Alternative	Advantages	Disadvantages
First: Hamas participates in the elections	• Attaining the highest possible percentage of the votes. • Proving the movement's popularity. • Preventing political isolation. • Preserving the popular basis won by the movement during the Intifada and confronting the attempts to contain it. • Securing a greater chance to confront the concessions in the phase of final negotiations [acting] from a position of elected popular representation.	• It will be difficult for Hamas to play a role of political participation and [violent] resistance at the same time. • A significant legitimacy will be given to the elections, indicating Hamas's compromise of its objection to the self-government as a solution to the [Palestinian] problem. • If [Hamas] will not win a majority, which is most likely, the act [of elections] will appear as a [reflection of] popular consensus. • Its impact on the current of Jihadist Islam concerning Palestine.

TABLE 5.1 (Continued)

The Alternative	Advantages	Disadvantages
Second: Hamas Boycotts the elections and calls on the people also to boycott [the elections]	• An attempt to diminish the legitimacy of the elections and in effect also of the negotiating process and the concessions that it entails. • Political corroboration deriving from our objection to the self-rule and its consequences.	• Political isolation [of Hamas], facilitating the opportunity to Fatah to contain Hamas . . . (sic) • The movement loses the political warranty that supports the policy of resistance to the occupation.
Third: Boycott and attempt to disrupt the elections by force.	• If we win, it means foiling the process of negotiations. • Affirming the absence of legitimacy of negotiations and concessions. • Affirming Hamas's capability of political action. • Deepening Hamas's popularity and power.	• It might mean an entrance into a military confrontation with Fatah, that is, a civil war, for which we would be held responsible by the [Palestinian] people. • We might not succeed in foiling [the elections], which means, sustaining popular losses in addition to the human casualties, providing the future authority a pretext to adopt policies of striking the movement and forcing it into isolation.
Fourth: Political participation under another placard.	• Guaranteeing non-isolation. • Preservation of the popular basis attained by the Islamic movement during the Intifada. • Exercising a political role in support of the line of resistance, which Hamas continues to follow.	• It might not realize the same rate of votes, which we can attain through participation in the name of Hamas. • Confusing the public [due to the difference] between the position of resistance and the position of participation, even if there was a separation between the placard and the movement.

Fourth: The Elements of Decision Making

The responses to the initial document that have reached us presented many elements that should be taken into account in the decision-making process regarding our position on the self-rule and its institutions as well as the general elections that would take place. The following is a discussion of the key elements presented, in order of their significance:

1. What are our main interests and goals that we want to pursue in the next phase?
During the years of the Intifada, the Islamic movement has realized a great popular capital and attracted a large part of the people who have resisted the concessions and adhere to the Islamic rights in Palestine. The movement has built institutions and has trained many members and supporters to become leaders and exercise popular activities. Our basic interests might be summarized as follows:

a. Preserving the movement's popular base so that it can strongly support the continuation of the *jihad* in the next campaigns. This means that [if we were] politically isolated and absent [from the political arena], we would be deprived of the masses and lose much of the popular support that until now we have not been able to organize [*ta'tir*].

b. Adhering to *jihad* as the way to liberate Palestine from the [Israeli] occupation, which will remain during the implementation of the interim self-rule.

c. Resisting normalization and further negligence and surrender of the Palestinians' rights. This might be the most important factor in determining our choice . . . [*sic*]. It must be bound to our goals and interests in every historical phase . . . [*sic*].

In view of our alternative positions, we can say that . . . [sic]. [It would be difficult to disrupt] . . . [sic] the elections and be content with calling for a boycott because no matter how successful we may be in preventing people from participating, the voter turnout will be no less than 30 to 40 percent of the electorate. Although we might selfishly argue that this would support Hamas's position, it would not be enough to disrupt the elections. A low voter turnout, however, has not denied the legitimacy of elections in other states. The Islamic Salvation Front in Algeria won elections even when the voter turnout was less than a third of the electorate. The same situation [exists] even in the United States where the voter turnout is less than 50 percent of the electorate. Yet [choosing] this option certainly means abandoning the political arena to Fatah's leaders to do as they wish. We can expect that one of their priorities will be containing our movement, dismantling its institutions, and ending its activities, on the pretext of enforcing the self-rule's authority in order to be strong in confronting Israel in the final negotiations. Such an outcome would clearly be counterproductive to our interests and goals in the next stage.

2. The Movement's Ideological Position

The movement rejects self-rule as a solution to the [Palestinian] cause and insists on the liberation of the land and the purification of [its] sanctuaries. Some [people] maintain that participating in the elections means abandoning the movement's ultimate goals. Others maintain that participation will depend on whether the elections are held before or after the negotiations end. Also, participation will depend on whether it will be conditioned that the candidates recognize Israel or commit themselves to the negotiating process. Objectively, however, there is no doubt that it will be difficult for Hamas to bridge [the gap] between participation in the elections and what it requires in terms of altering our discourse and resisting the occupation and what it requires in terms of [adopting] a clear and unique discourse of *jihad*. This is a very important element because it might diminish the prospects of the first alternative, namely, Hamas's participation in the elections.

3. Our Capabilities and Power in Regard to the Internal and External Balances of Power

It is intended in this element to define the alternatives with which our power and capabilities enable us to cope. By our power and capabilities, we mean

a. The number of our members prepared physically and psychologically.
b. The proportion of popular support for any alternative that the movement might choose.
c. The quantity of arms and ammunition we possess.
d. Our ability to convey our position to the media so that we will not be the victim of false propaganda.

e. Our ability to persuade the Arab and Islamic sectors to support the alternative we choose.

We can say that our power enables us to undertake all the alternatives presented except for one, which we must avoid, namely, confrontation and disruption of the elections. The chances of success in realizing this goal seem poor and entail great risks, primarily entering into an armed struggle with Fatah which would be then supported by Israel and the international media. A large segment of the population might blame us because it will be easy for them to believe that Hamas first used force to impose its will on the others.

The predicament of this choice is that a decision on it seems to be most difficult while the other side . . . [sic] . . . the elections will be held without interruption. The result might be that we will defer to . . . [sic] . . . its boycott, which brings us back to the second choice, about which we concluded that it would not serve the goals of . . . [sic] . . . our capability in the context of the balance of power. In regard to the Palestinian arena, the movement confronts Fatah, which agrees with . . . [sic] and will not hesitate to use any method of elimination and bloodshed if Hamas tries to stop by force the implementation of the settlement, which would necessarily mean a civil war in which we would lose more [than Fatah would] because our real power is our popularity, whereas Fatah's power derives from a combination of both financial [resources] and control of the important institutions.

The other Palestinian parties will never enter the struggle but will try to pick up what the two [major] parties lose. These organizations' lack of power in the street and their affiliation with the PLO will make it incumbent on them to take part in the elections and in the institutions to be built. There is the risk that our movement will be on one side while the other forces and currents are on the other.

On the Arab and international level, if the negotiations are successful, the United States would exert a significant weight to help implement the accords, as occurred at Camp David, by way of [extending financial] aid to the Palestinian self-rule. In regard to the Arab and Islamic arena, it is expected that the Islamic movements will [be content with] issuing statements of rejection of the capitulationist accords, but we have no reason to believe that the Islamic movements in Jordan, Syria, or Lebanon will take a tougher position on the accords. In conclusion, this assumption disqualifies the third choice, namely, our most militant position, because we would be isolated even from the Islamic movements in other Arab states, which means that the most active Palestinian party (Fatah) could ignore us because the balance of power would be in its favor.

4. The Chances of Success and Failure in the Elections

Most of the estimates show that we might not be able to win a majority if we participate in the elections, which [means that] we would lose them and, at the same time, grant legitimacy to the negotiations. It is difficult to calculate the amount [of support] that we might have, as it will depend on the particular system of elections, the political alignments that we might initiate, and the level of organization and competence in conducting the election campaign. Yet the question here is whether we should decide on participation if we have a good chance of winning and decide on a boycott if we have a poor chance of winning a majority. Clearly, the elections will not be a one-time event, but the way in which we would tackle the next phase, primarily the elections, might be crucial to the movement. Our goal might not be to win a majority but, rather, to achieve a significant [political] presence, which would secure the movement's power and political weight. We believe that we can win a third of the votes, which would mean an excellent political presence, by which we could make sure we would not be overlooked. This [estimate of] one third is what we expect overall, whereas [the proportion of votes] might be higher in areas such as Hebron and Gaza and lower in others.

5. [People's Expectations]

We also must consider the people's expectations and wishes, the economic and security pressures [they suffer], and the assumption that they would support the [peaceful] solution once some gains in these areas had been achieved. Among these gains [might be] freezing [the Jewish] settlements—even gradually—and financial aid from America and Europe, some of the Gulf states, and Japan. Here we must remember that many of the people . . . [sic] . . . the negotiating delegation from Madrid for the first time. Local and international propaganda might ultimately focus on . . . [sic] [highlighting the future material gains] and amplifying them. Hence, we expect that a large segment of the people would accept participation in any elections . . . [sic] clear interests, regardless of their feelings toward the [Palestine] cause as a whole. This means that a boycott of the elections on our part . . . [*sic*] would be acceptable only to the close adherents familiar with the movement's position, who are the bulk of our supporters. The scope of the boycott would not be significant unless we used force, such as declaring a strike, preventing the people from reaching the voting places, or shutting down their means of transportation. This would mean leaning toward our third choice, which we have concluded would lead to a bloody confrontation with Fatah that we could not win. Then we would lose the people's support and thus would probably not be able to disrupt the elections or the self-rule and its institutions.

6. *The Connection Between the Elections and Self-Rule*

Some people believe that the connection between these two issues implies that participating in the elections means agreeing to self-rule as a solution to the Palestinian problem. Others maintain, however, that unless there is a condition to this effect, participation of the Palestinians in the elections does not necessarily mean voting for either confirmation or rejection of the negotiations conducted by the [Palestinian] delegation and the Fatah leadership. Although the coincidence [of the elections and self-rule] leaves a vague impression [that such a connection indeed exists], we should not count out any choice that the movement might consider appropriate in view of the more significant factors. As for the vague impression, we might be able to correct it through our political and propaganda input and our activity on the ground, which will continue the holy war (*jihad*) against the [Israeli] occupation. (End of document)

Hamas's policy paper outlines a range of alternatives from which decision makers were to decide the best approach to take with regard to elections. It is a document with a clear sense of political opportunities and constraints, and it offers an impartial, meticulous analysis of cost-benefit considerations, according to the movement's basic assumptions—such as Fatah's military superiority and the Palestinian public's likely massive support for elections—and the probable impact of each option. Unlike Hamas's public discourse, which is saturated with religious and historical symbols and norms defining the boundaries between right and wrong, this document (shown to senior figures only) is marked by political realism. The key question here is not the illegitimacy of the Declaration of Principles (DOP) but Hamas's future as a social and ideological movement and the policy it should adopt to preserve its political assets without losing its ideological distinctiveness.

A close examination of the document reveals that Hamas seems to have been caught in the middle of the spectrum of alternatives. Participating in the elections would legitimize the PLO, but if Hamas called for a boycott and the people voted anyway, it would lose its credibility. Hamas tried to cope with the dilemma of participation by adopting a strategy that combined elements of political involvement with mechanisms of indirect presence. Nowhere has this strategy of participation been better expressed than in regard to the general elections to the PA's Council, its incorporation into the PA's administration, and the establishment of a political party.

Elections to the PA's Council

Elections were held on January 20, 1996, in the Gaza Strip and the West Bank (including the Palestinians of East Jerusalem). The elections were based on the Declaration of Principles (DOP) of September 13, 1993, and on the Israeli-Palestinian agreement of September 28, 1995 (Taba accord, or Oslo 2).[29] According to article 3 of the DOP,

1. In order to enable the Palestinian people in the West Bank and the Gaza Strip to govern themselves in keeping with democratic principles, general, direct, and free political elections will be held for the Council, under agreed-on international supervision, and the Palestinian police will maintain public order.
2. The parties will agree on the definite form of the elections and the conditions in order to hold the elections within a period that shall not be more than nine months after the Agreement of Principles takes effect.
3. These elections will be an important preparatory step toward the attainment of the legitimate rights of the Palestinian people and their just demands.[30]

Hamas's position was tightly linked to two overriding questions: first, the PA's political program, that is, the grand policy with which Hamas would be identified by participating in elections that were bound to legitimize the PA and, implicitly, the DOP; second, Hamas's prospects of playing a significant political role in the PA. Hamas had been a fierce critic of the DOP and the elections, which it had urged the Palestinian public to boycott.

Hamas's first decision regarding the anticipated elections was apparently made on September 9. A year later, with Israeli-Palestinian negotiations progressing slowly, Hamas's leaders reaffirmed their previous decisions. Their explanation was an essentially pragmatic one: the movement ruled out participation because the elections were bound to be part of a "humiliating and shameful agreement" and because it was assumed that they would be held under Israeli domination.[31]

Hamas's spokesmen explained that the Palestinian signatories had made far-reaching territorial concessions: abandoned Arab Jerusalem; failed to secure a satisfactory solution to the predicament of the majority of Palestinians, particularly the refugees; and committed themselves to a process that would not lead to sovereignty and the establishment of a Palestinian state. Above all, the Hamas spokesmen declared that they would not be a party to an agreement that legitimized Israel's plundering of Islamic lands in Palestine.[32]

While constantly reviling the Oslo process, the debate within the movement remained unresolved, with Hamas trying to keep open all its options so as to be able to capitalize on future opportunities. Thus, despite the initial decision to boycott the elections, Sheikh Yasin announced shortly afterward that Hamas might participate in the elections after all, provided that the PA Council was given legislative power. Yasin explained that unless Hamas was represented, the Council might make laws detrimental to the Islamic movement. According to Yasin, the crucial elements were the interests of the Palestinian people and the uninterrupted development of the Islamic movement. From this point of view, participation in the PA's institutions would seem to serve Hamas's interests. At the same time, however, other spokesmen of the movement expressed an unequivocal, even ambivalent, position, ostensibly leaving open the question of Hamas's participation in the elections: "Everything is subject to consideration, including the possibility of participating in the elections."[33]

The statements by Yasin and other Hamas leaders reflected a position with broad support from Hamas's constituency. It held that participation was the lesser evil and could serve as a guarantee against an attempt to eliminate Hamas if there was strong domestic and international support for the PA. Nonetheless, the leaders set strict conditions for the movement's participation in the elections: that the elections be open to all Palestinian people and that the aim be the establishment of a sovereign and legislative council, not a powerless representative body under Israeli domination. In addition, they maintained that Hamas's participation in the elections was dependent on the extent of the agreement to their procedures and democratic nature. An opposing viewpoint maintained that such participation would cost Hamas its credibility and be tantamount to political suicide, by blurring the dividing lines between Hamas and the PA. Worse, it might imply Hamas's acceptance of the Oslo process. The Hamas approach, which combined political judiciousness and criticism of the PA, was succinctly expressed by the movement's spokesman in Amman, Ibrahim Ghawsha, who stated that Hamas "seeks no authority [*sulta*] and wants no part of the pie, or any position of power." According to Ghawsha, all Hamas wanted was to continue the *jihad* and the Intifada, which would oblige the Palestinian Authority to stop persecuting, arresting, and disarming members of 'Izz al-Din al-Qassam.[34]

Hamas as an ideological opposition movement distinguished by its adherence to the Palestinians' basic rights (*thawabit*), could not have it both ways and participate in elections that were broadly perceived as a vote of faith in the Oslo accords. Thus, in spite of the internal debate, the political leadership remained opposed to participation. There were, indeed, some practical considerations that Hamas could not escape. First, despite the intention to hold the elections under international supervision, it was doubtful that they would be fair. Hamas's and other opposition leaders realized that Arafat had stacked the deck against them by adopting a majoritarian method, rather than proportional representation, which would effectively strengthen Fatah as the ruling party at the expense of other popular political forces.[35] Second, even if the elections were relatively fair, Hamas had to calculate the potential scope of its success—in the case of both participation and boycott—and the results of each choice. According to a poll conducted in May 1995 by the Palestinian Research Center in Nablus, only 28 percent of the West Bank and Gaza Strip residents believed that the elections for the PA Council would be fair. At the same time, 20 percent were willing to boycott the elections if the opposition organizations called for that. Only 50 percent of the participants said that they felt free to criticize the PA. According to the poll, Hamas had only 12 percent of the population's support.[36]

Generally, the advantages and disadvantages were divided along regional lines. Due to the PA's tighter control in the Gaza Strip, Hamas leaders there were relatively more inclined to participate in the elections than were their colleagues in the West Bank. It was this same Gaza Strip leadership that had pressured the "outside" leadership to consider establishing an Islamic political movement like those in the neighboring Arab states, an issue that became an inseparable part of the debate over Hamas's participation in the elections and its relations with the PA (see later in this chapter). The Gaza leaders of Hamas also revealed a willingness to enter into negotiations with the PA over this issue, even without the consent of the "outside" leadership. In addition to the regional division, differences within Hamas apparently derived from socioeconomic disparities as well. In the Hamas-PA meeting in Khartoum in November 1995, the Hamas delegates, all from the autonomous Palestinian areas, were not conspicuous political leaders in the movement but members from a wealthy group of merchants in the movement. They supported participation in the elections, contrary to the view of many leading Hamas figures, especially outside the autonomous territory, as well as among the rank and file, who maintained a militant approach toward Israel and identified the elections with the Oslo accords.[37] It was from this reservoir that 'Izz al-Din al-Qassam, the military apparatus of Hamas, drew most of its recruits.

Hamas's dialogue with the PA did not induce the movement to change its essentially negative position on the elections, although it tempered it somewhat. At the PA's behest, Hamas agreed to do no more than passively boycott the elections and not to interfere with the Palestinian public's freedom to decide. By the end of October 1995, Hamas spokesmen no longer talked about boycotting the elections and urging the Palestinian public to do likewise, but only about "refraining" from participation.[38] In late October 1995, following the release of Hamas prisoners by the PA, 'Imad Faluji, editor in chief of the Hamas organ *al-Watan* and a leading supporter of Hamas's participation in the elections, explained that the movement's eventual decision would depend on certain assurances:

> We want to be convinced that any Palestinian parliament will be free. The elections must be independently planned and formulated by the Palestinians without any Israeli interference. And we insist that all unresolved questions must be up for discussion—though we flatly refuse any Israeli preconditions on the status of Jerusalem.[39]

Hamas's indecisive attitude represented the debate in which the movement's leadership had continued since the Oslo agreement, and the weakened position of the Islamic bloc following eighteen months of PA rule. In November 1995, for example, Hamas estimated that its support by the Palestinian people had dropped from 30 to 15 percent. This had been one result of Arafat's policy of "co-opt and divide," which included conditional tolerance of Hamas's public activity, cycles of short arrests and releases of leaders and activists, and recurrent closures of newspapers identified with Hamas.[40] But apart from Hamas's announced reasons for boycotting the elections, the movement's leaders were still in prison, including Yasin and Rantisi (by Israel), and Abu Marzuq (by the U.S. government), which apparently strengthened the outside leadership's militant voice and could further diminish the movement's prospects of success in the elections.

The vacillations that marked Hamas's attitude toward the elections since the signing of the Declaration of Principles (DOP) ultimately crystallized into a kind of "positive ambivalence." In practice, this meant avoiding official participation in the elections and hence the legitimization of the DOP but still displaying an informal presence in the election process to avoid risking political marginalization. In mid-November, Hamas announced its official decision to boycott the elections to the PA Council, though not actively, explaining that the movement was not against the principle of elections but against the dissatisfactory terms of the Oslo accords, especially Israel's insufficient withdrawal from the occupied territories and the inadequacy of the election law. Hamas made it clear that its boycott was not meant to prevent indirect participation, stating that "we have repeated the call to our members and to adherents of the Islamic bloc to register their names on the electoral roll."[41]

Hamas's decision not to participate officially in the elections remained unchanged in the talks held in Cairo on December 18–20, 1995, between its delegates and the PA's representatives. The main issues on the agenda were Hamas's participation in the elections and the PA's demand that Hamas should cease its military operations against Israel.[42] On the issue of elections, the PA urged Hamas to stop playing a negative role and to participate, at least in East Jerusalem, in order to bolster the Palestinians' position in their negotiations with Israel over the final status of the city, due to begin in May 1996. Hamas, however, refused to perceive Jerusalem as an exception and stuck to its boycott of the elections as a whole. On the issue of armed struggle against Israel, Hamas refused to halt its attacks against Israel completely, but it did agree to stop its violent attacks on Israel from the areas under the PA's control or those areas where the PA and Israel maintained joint patrols (areas A and B) (on the unwritten understanding between the PA and Hamas, see chapter 3).

Within the framework of a passive boycott of the elections, Hamas encouraged persons identified as Islamists, or even as its own members, to run as independents. Informally, Hamas also called on its followers to exercise their right to vote for Islamic candidates who had been associated or maintained good relations with the movement. This move represented a realistic approach that recognized the strong public excitement about exercising this unprecedented civil right. Indeed, if Hamas called for a boycott and people voted anyway, it would lose its credibility. Furthermore, the lists of registered voters for the general elections were to be used to determine the eligible electorate for the future municipal elections in which Hamas would be sure to take part officially, as they would have no connection to the Israeli-Palestinian peace process. Like the Islamic movements in Israel and in some of the neighboring Arab countries, Hamas was fully aware of the opportunity to be officially represented in the PA Council by committed Islamist independent delegates, thus preserving the ideological image of Hamas.

In accordance with the interim agreement, elections for the president of the PA were held simultaneously with those for the members of the Palestinian Council, using separate ballots. Participation was open to all Palestinians, eighteen years or older, who lived in their electoral district and whose names were on the voters' rolls. Candidacy for membership in the Assembly was open to every Palestinian who was thirty years or older on election day.

Election of the Council's members was regional, personal, and direct in each voting district. Although the elections were personal, the system permitted movements, parties, and individuals to organize and present joint lists from which the voter could choose the candidates he or she preferred. Every voter could vote for the same number of candidates as number of seats allotted to the district and could vote for candidates from different lists. The winning candidates were those who received the largest number of votes. Of the 725 candidates, 559 were independents who ran on the basis of their established reputations as national or social activists, personal wealth, or relationship to one of the larger clans in a specific district. There were 166 candidates up for election, 36 on new lists that had been drawn up as the elections approached, and 130 representing preexisting movements and parties.[43]

By adopting a strategy of unofficially participating in the elections, Hamas could urge its supporters to take part and to help them get to their voting place. Hamas advised its followers to vote for the seven candidates whom the movement supported as close adherents and of whom five (according to another version, six) were elected. Also, Hamas supported several independents and even a number of Fatah candidates who were known for their good relations with the Islamic opposition. An exit poll of 3,200 voters by the Palestinian Research Center in Nablus found that 60 to 70 percent of Hamas supporters participated in the elections, whereas the general level of participation ranged between 88 percent in the Gaza Strip and 70 percent in the West Bank (Hamas's participation was still lower than that of the PFLP and the DFLP whose participation was closer to the general level).[44]

A regime can manipulate elections in three main ways to favor itself: (1) by deciding on a propitious time for the elections; (2) by instituting an electoral system highly favorable to itself, harassing and intimidating the opposition, and employing government resources in the campaign; and (3) by outright fraud and theft.[45] In the January 1996 elections in Palestine, Arafat engaged in at least the first two, if not all three of these techniques.[46] First, Arafat appointed his long-time confidant and Fatah member Sa'ib 'Ariqat to head the Central Election Commission that was to pass the electoral laws and oversee the elections. The commission set the election date for January 20, one day before the start of the Muslim holy month of Ramadan. Had the elections been held after Ramadan, Hamas would have had a chance to reach the masses through the daily prayers and Friday sermons, though principally through its charity and welfare committees, which tended to be especially active during this month among the poor. The Palestinian vote, then, demonstrates one method by which elections can be strategically set to benefit one specific party.[47]

In addition, the (PA) Council of eighty-eight members was chosen by majority winner-take-all elections in sixteen districts. But not all the seats allotted to a region represented the same number of people in each district. For example, in the region of the Gaza Strip, the number of seats allotted was based on 8,730 voters per seat, whereas in the region of Salfit, in the West Bank, 18,996 voters vied for the one seat allotted.[48] Three districts had a single member, and thirteen had several members. Six seats were reserved for Christian candidates and one for a Samaritan candidate. Candidates could run as individuals or as members of a party, and voters could split their tickets across parties. Voters were allotted the same number of votes as slots for their district. For example, a voter in Gaza City had twelve votes, one for one candidate, and he could vote for candidates of different parties. With the polls a month before the election showing Fatah running at 40 to 45 percent and Hamas at 15 percent,[49] Arafat must have known that a majority system would greatly favor his party. If the polls were correct, a proportional system would have required Arafat to share power with thirteen or more Islamic Council members. Moreover, multimember districts further favored Arafat's party, since, as Lijphart writes, "all majoritarian systems tend to systematically favor the larger parties, to produce disproportional election outcomes, and to discourage multipartyism. District magnitudes larger than 1 tend to reinforce these tendencies."[50]

Not only did the electoral system itself benefit Arafat, but so did the conduct of the campaign. The Central Election Commission was appointed only a few weeks before the vote, and up until the last few days, it continued to announce new arrangements. Even the district boundaries were uncertain until the last moment. Furthermore, the official campaign period was reduced to just over two weeks from the planned twenty-two days, a very short length of time for an election in which 725 candidates were running for office. One of the few well-known campaign rules was that political speeches were forbidden in mosques, a clear attempt to diminish Hamas's chances of success if it decided to participate.[51] There were also reports that Palestinian police patrolling the streets at night were tearing down posters for any non-Fatah candidates. Some observers noted that if all these advantages were not enough, then the presence of at least three PA policemen at every polling station would probably help persuade Palestinians to vote for Arafat and Fatah.[52]

Incorporation Without Identification: Hamas and the PA's Institutions

The strategy of unofficial participation also determined Hamas's stand on placing its members in the PA's executive apparatuses. Similarly to its attitude toward participating in the elections, Hamas encouraged its adherents to join the PA's administrative organizations on their own. Hamas justified this by distinguishing between two perceptions of the PA, as a sovereign political power and as an administrative organization to provide services to the people. Whereas the former represented political principles and national symbols, the latter was seen as instrumental, linked to daily life. As Mahmud al-Zahar explained,

> There is a difference between [being] a clerk in the educational department and applying a policy to the educational department. Members of Hamas work in the departments of education, health, agriculture, and everywhere . . . but everyone knows that we do not take part in those departments whose task is to implement the political Oslo agreements.[53]

Citing the Oslo accord the PA had signed with Israel, Hamas remained adamant in its refusal to grant the PA legitimacy as a national center which, besides its authority to enforce the law, would also articulate the people's ideas, symbols, and beliefs. But Hamas was willing to recognize the PA as an administrative entity with the duty of maintaining law and order and providing employment and services to the community. Hamas, for its part, regarded its active presence in the PA's administrative organization not only as a means to exercise its social influence but also as a guarantee against any attempt by the PA to impede the Islamic movement.[54]

Hamas justified this position by pointing to the necessity of avoiding civil strife, a position the movement had taken from the start. Hamas leaders admitted, however, explicitly as well as implicitly, that their acquiescence to the PA and their willingness to accept "the Palestinian people's democratic decision" reflected the movement's strategic weakness in view of the intra-Palestinian, regional, and international reality created by the Oslo agreement. Accordingly, Islamic spokesmen suggested a "wait and see" tactic, maintaining that the amount of criticism on both the Israeli and Palestinian sides meant that the agreement's collapse was only a matter of time. Meanwhile, patience and flexibility on Hamas's part were needed to guarantee the movement's uninterrupted communal activity. Indeed, after the signing of the Oslo agreement, both Hamas and the Islamic Jihad repeatedly called for patience as a manifestation of true Islam and adherence to its long-term goals. Preaching patience (*sabr*) as a religious norm thus helped justify a policy of coexistence with the PA despite the latter's commitment to a political settlement with Israel.[55]

The distinction between long-term ideological commitment and here-and-now needs had already been affirmed years before when Israel imposed a series of closures on the Palestinians in the occupied territories, citing security. At the same time, Israel incrementally limited the number of permits for Palestinians working in Israel. Although this policy had been initially adopted in response to terrorist attacks by Palestinians, mainly Islamists, in Israel in late 1990, with the availability of an alternative labor force of newcomers from the Soviet Union and the continuation of violence, those restrictions turned into a de facto Israeli policy that has remained in place despite the Oslo accord and the economic agreement between Israel and the PA signed in April 1994 (the Paris Protocol). In late 1994, the demand for day jobs by Palestinians in Gaza Strip alone was 60,000 while the demand by Israelis had dropped below the number of permits issued by the Israeli authorities. In January 1995, before the ha-Sharon Junction (Beit Lid) suicide attack and consequent closure, the Israeli demand was for only 22,000 workers, 10,000 fewer than the permitted quota of workers. Consequently, despite its scarce resources, the PA became the largest employer in the Gaza Strip.[56]

This is why and how Hamas's position toward the PA's institutions was marked by an attempt to differentiate between the political and the executive. Whereas Hamas's propaganda elaborated on ways to discredit and delegitimize the PA's leadership, it was careful not to alienate the Palestinian public and especially the rank and file in the PA administration. Already in October 1993, Hamas had instructed its followers not to antagonize the Palestinian police officers. Indeed, these police officers were to be encouraged to collaborate with Hamas's armed activities against Israel and even to "initiate suicide actions . . . exploiting their possibilities of [available] weapons, and freedom of maneuver to support the resistance."[57]

Despite the poor prospects of achieving a tangible influence on the PA, Hamas leaders could not ignore the advantages of having a political presence in PA institutions. In particular, they sought a voice in the construction and functioning of legislative, judicial, and educational institutions, whose impact on the social and religious aims of the Islamic movement was undeniable. Such participation was also intended to prevent legislation that might be incompatible with Islam. In the same vein, Hamas asserted its intention to take an active part in municipal elections and repeatedly urged Arafat to hold them. Unlike the elections to the PA's representative institutions, which were perceived as part of the Oslo process, municipal elections were considered directly related to the service of society. Arafat, however, preferred to appoint municipal councils in Gaza, Nablus, Hebron, and other cities rather than to hold elections, which Hamas believed would enable it to demonstrate its popularity and record of achievements at the local and communal levels.[58]

Because of this approach and the PA's policy of preferring coexistence to confrontation with Hamas, the latter encouraged its followers to take official positions in the religious establishment in the West Bank, explaining that these positions were administrative, providing services to the community, but had no representative significance. Thus, by reducing the significance of participating in the PA's administration to the individual-level and executive positions, Hamas could portray its participation as unofficial, with no political or symbolic meaning. "If the Islamists [directly] participate in the government, it would mean that they have become part of it and would not be able to return to the slogan 'Islam is the solution' [*islam huwa al-ḥall*]."[59]

Presence by Proxy: Establishing a Political Party

As the Hamas paper of alternative strategies cited earlier showed, already in the summer of 1992, the movement had considered establishing a political party as a way to participate indirectly in the elections to the PA Council. Hamas renewed its interest in this option in early 1993 following the deportation by Israel of 415 leading members of the Islamic movements. It was, however, the signing of the Oslo accord later in the year that triggered an intensive public debate over this issue in Hamas circles. According to one of the figures who advocated the idea, Fakhri ʿAbd al-Latif, the Oslo agreement obligated Hamas to consider a new political strategy in which a legal party could better serve the Islamic movement's interests and preserve its achievements.[60]

The proponents of an Islamic party argued for maintaining an official political presence by means of a legal instrument that would serve as a security net for the Islamic movement in case of an attempt by the PA to suppress Hamas. The envisaged party was to offer Islamic followers a legitimate framework for participating in elections and political life in general, including serving on the Legislative Council. The party was not supposed to replace Hamas but, rather, to "serve as its instrument, just like the Islamic University in education and charity associations in the welfare sphere."[61] The opponents of the idea claimed that establishing an Islamic party might cause Hamas to lose its combatant (*jihadi*) character and also identify it with mere politics, thereby perhaps pushing militant followers out of the movement. Thus, under self-government and as long as the struggle for Palestinian national liberation and statehood continued, Hamas was obligated to remain a clandestine movement with no organizational link to a political party.[62]

Support for establishing an Islamic political party came mainly from senior figures of the Islamic movement in the Gaza Strip, who in the summer and fall of 1994 wrote a series of preliminary draft papers on various aspects of the question. The papers explained the necessity of a political party and the best time to form it, defined its relations with Hamas and other elements of the Islamic movement, and determined its basic guidelines. One of the documents urged quick action, before the PA had consolidated its position.[63] According to the Hamas spokesman, in the summer of 1995 the consultative bodies of Hamas—possibly the Consultative Council (Majlis shura)—resolved in principle to establish an Islamic political party, though when was not decided.[64] The decision was clearly made with a view to the elections to the PA Council, which were then thought to be imminent. The party was envisaged as a political arm of the Islamic movement, hence the issue of armed struggle against Israel would not be affected.

According to these documents, the party would have four main tasks:[65]

1. Provision of a countrywide political umbrella for all those Palestinians who agreed with the Islamic vision, not only for Hamas

members. The party would operate legally and democratically in support of Hamas's political opposition to the PA. The party would seek to play a role in decision making, protect the social and political rights of the Palestinian people, and Hamas's right to continue the armed struggle against Israel, especially in view of the PA's anticipated persecution and repression of Hamas. The party would separate political, social, and military activities.

2. Promotion of general Islamist values and goals, particularly the establishment of an Islamic society and state in Palestine. The Islamic party would play a pivotal role in the relations between the public and the PA and coexist with the latter in order to diminish the "negative effects" of the accords with Israel; build a civic society based on the Islamic law (*shari'a*), and provide social and economic services to the public. The party would organize public activities among youth, trade unions, and students' associations in preparation for their joining the movement. It would engage in indoctrination, including the publication of Islamic ideological studies.

3. Political mobilization for support of Hamas, thus ridding the latter of the problem of the elections. Hamas, as explained earlier, could neither participate in the elections nor boycott them without paying a political price. Although participation would mean indirectly legitimizing the Oslo process and harming the movement's ideological reputation, a boycott of the elections would mean political isolation and a loss of influence on future relations between the PA and Israel. The party could legitimize the Oslo process without "staining" Hamas or directly committing it to the party's platform and policies.

4. A major political framework for participating in elections to public organizations, such as municipal government, trade unions, and professional associations. Given its reputable record in providing communal services, Hamas leaders could expect to gain wide public support, especially in local government elections. Taking over local governments was particularly attractive, as it seemed to have no ideological significance, such as shaping the basic beliefs and values of the future Palestinian state and its relations with Israel. Thus, according to one of Hamas's leaders in Gaza, Mahmud al-Zahar, the establishment of a political party and its participation in the elections for the Palestinian Council would not legitimize the PA, just as Hamas's previous participation in elections for professional and social associations had not legitimized the Israeli occupation.[66]

In its platform, the proposed Islamic party would struggle for the liberation of the Palestinian people from the yoke of the "Zionist occupation" and implement the "right of return" of the 1948 and 1967 Palestinian refugees. Although trying not to contradict the Hamas charter, the documents' framers did not define its territorial aims in line with the charter, which strove for the liberation of all of Palestine by means of armed struggle. Rather, the party borrowed the pragmatic goal set by Hamas, bringing about a full Israeli withdrawal from the Palestinian territories occupied in 1967, including the removal of all the Jewish settlements in those territories. That aim coincided with Hamas's statements about its willingness to accept a "temporary truce" (*hudna*) with Israel, though not peace. The proposed Islamic party would work to block all normalization with the "Zionist entity" and halt the PA's policy of political concessions in negotiations with it. The party would also respect human rights, freedom of political organization and association, political pluralism, and the majority decision in selecting the Palestinian people's leaders and its representatives in "inside" and "outside" institutions. Another plank in the platform called for an effort to remedy the PA's hostility toward Islam and the Islamic movement and to minimize the chances of an armed clash between the two. The platform committed the Islamic party to refrain from employing violence and force to reach its goals. At the same time, the platform made clear that the party supported all the national and Islamic bodies striving to realize the Palestinian people's full rights in a strategy of armed resistance to the Israeli occupation.[67]

Structurally, the party was to be made up of a founding committee, a general assembly, a consultative council (*majlis shura*), and a political bureau. Representation would be based on geography, "sectoral affiliation," past activity in Hamas and its communal institutions, public status, and administrative and organizational skills. Consequently, an Islamic party would require a restructuring of the Islamic movement, which under the new dispensation would consist of three-tiered functional institutions. Hamas would be responsible for clandestine and military activities, maintaining an institutional separation from the Muslim Brothers, who would continue to maintain the *da'wa* (Islamic preaching) infrastructure, and the Islamic party. The Islamic party would secure political backing for the other two arms of the Islamic movement and thus forestall any attempts by the PA to suppress Hamas and *da'wa* activities by cooperating with the PA and maintaining an official presence in its institutions. Under the new structure, the Islamic movement would be managed directly by a supreme political leadership, which for security considerations would be located outside the Palestinian territories and would be the source of legitimacy for all parts of the movement. To ensure the party's Islamic character, it would always have a majority of MB (51 percent or more) among its cadres, and the MB would have the final say regarding the admission of members to the party.[68]

In mid-November 1995, shortly after Hamas's spokesman announced the decision in principle to establish a party, Arafat announced the foundation of the National Islamic Salvation Party (Hizb al-khalas al-watani al-islami). Arafat had an obvious interest in publicizing the new party, to demonstrate his success in persuading the Islamic opposition to take part in the elections, thus legitimizing the Oslo process. In a meeting with Arafat, the party's founders, all well-known Islamist figures in Gaza Strip, stated that they were not connected with any existing political body. The new party's spokesman, Fakhri 'Abd al-Latif, conceded that his party and Hamas were based on the same principles, although they were structurally independent. He also revealed that the new party's Political Bureau was composed of members of Hamas, but not all the founders were originally from Hamas.[69]

Despite the practical reasons for its foundation, a month before the elections the new party still had not officially announced its participation, apparently because of the delay in the political talks between Hamas and the PA. Meanwhile, reservations grew within Hamas about taking part in the elections. Other reasons for its reluctance to participate in the elections, apart from rejection of the Oslo accord, were the party's incomplete preparations for the elections and insufficient time for preparations, and the limited power allotted to the Council. At a massive rally in Gaza on its eighth anniversary in mid-December 1995, Hamas's leaders officially announced that the movement would not take part in the elections on the grounds that the "Oslo elections" would not guarantee the Palestinian rights for sovereignty and a state for the Palestinian people. But they repeated their commitment to avoid infighting and to contribute to building a civic and secure society through dialogue with the PA. Hamas's decision not to participate in the elections was announced again at the Cairo talks, yet it implied that candidates identified with Hamas—understood as the newly established National Islamic Salvation Party—would take part.[70] But with the registration of candidates for the elections closed, it was clear that the National Islamic Salvation Party would not take part officially in the elections, leaving them to Fatah and its two marginal political partners: the People's Party (Hizb al-sha'b—previously the Communist Party) and the Palestinian Democratic Union (al-Ittihad al-dimuqrati al-filastini—FDA).

In the final analysis, the abstention of the Islamic party from participation in the elections derived from a combination of internal and external causes. Certainly, the timing and system of the elections were designed
to give Arafat an advantage. These circumstances apparently provided
Hamas's "outside" leadership with strong reason to reject the participation
of an Islamic party in the elections, beyond its initial concern lest such
participation strengthen the "inside" leadership at its own expense. Furthermore, given the symbolic significance of the elections, the expected
decisive victory of Arafat and Fatah, participation of the Islamic party in
the elections would only have called attention to Hamas's public weakness
and present it as a marginal movement. Such results could weaken Hamas's
bargaining position with the PA and encourage the latter to take further
steps to reduce the movement's public influence.

In March 1996, two months after the elections, the National Islamic
Salvation Party officially announced its founding after receiving the PA's
approval. The announcement was accompanied by a list of the names of
the nineteen members of the Political Bureau, emphasizing the party's
openness, as opposed to Hamas's secret character. The members of the
Political Bureau were well-known figures with a record of activity in
Hamas; indeed, some of them were in prison when the party's founding
was announced. The party would accept political pluralism, conduct its activities by legal political means, and respect human rights.[71]

In the first two years following its foundation, the National Islamic Salvation Party gained little public attention or political significance and, in
fact, remained a footnote in Palestinian politics. The party's poor organizational and political performance might be traced to the changing
Israeli-Palestinian and intra-Palestinian relations. First, in 1996, Hamas's
concern that the PA might take strict measures to isolate it socially and politically and suppress its activities faded, owing to the stalemated Israel-PA
negotiations following the election of Netanyahu's right-wing government
in Israel. Moreover, weakened by this stalemate and the growing economic
and social hardships of the Palestinians under its jurisdiction, the PA sought
to reach a tactical rapprochement with Hamas. Second, the long-delayed
municipal elections were postponed indefinitely, stripping the party of a
major task it had counted on. Nonetheless, the party did undertake certain
activities, especially propaganda, occasionally issuing statements of protest
and criticism of the PA, and recruitment of youth by, among other means,
opening summer camps for children.[72] At the same time, Hamas continued to play openly its political role, with its leaders referring to military issues as well, while its communal activities continued to prosper.

The absence of a Hamas-based Islamic party in the elections might indicate the main considerations determining Hamas's political behavior regarding participation in the PA institutions. The fear that refusing to cooperate with the PA would cause the movement irreversible damage and that participating might be interpreted as legitimizing the Oslo process obligated Hamas to opt for unofficial participation. Such a mode of participation was subject to three considerations:

1. Practically, whether it might help Hamas, at least help secure its achievements and bargaining position.
2. Symbolically, whether it would be seen as an instrumental act with minimal symbolic significance attached to recognizing the PA.
3. Organizationally, whether it would be likely to win the support of the movement's leadership, both "inside" and "outside" the homeland.

These are the reasons for Hamas's decision to encourage its members to vote in the elections and support the candidates identified with Hamas—but as individuals, not as members of a party. In the same vein, Hamas encouraged its members to join the PA's executive offices, but not to accept any position with political significance. In both cases, Hamas's chance of scoring gains without paying a symbolic price seemed possible, and the likelihood of consent by Hamas leaders both "inside" and "outside" was thought to be high.

CHAPTER SIX

Patterns of Adjustment:
Opportunities and Constraints

Adjustment had become the main feature of Hamas's political conduct. Its strategies of controlled violence, negotiated coexistence, and calculated participation all reflected Hamas's effort to avoid making a decision about its conflicting commitments to an all-Islamic vision and a Palestinian nation, on the one hand, and to communal interests, on the other. Whereas an all-Islamic vision would mean a strategy of confrontation with Israel, the PLO, and the PA, local communal considerations would encourage Hamas to adjust to the changing circumstances and acquiesce in the political reality.

Hamas's strategies reflected a perception based on neither a full acceptance nor a total rejection of the political order emanating from the Oslo accords and the establishment of the PA. Although Hamas made its struggle with Israel a religious duty, it did not lose sight of its sociopolitical interests. A sense of political realism and "here and now" considerations were signs of pragmatism. Hamas's thrust toward extremism was balanced by its awareness of political constraints and structural limitations. Hamas refused to accept the basic assumptions or to officially recognize the consequences of the peace process. But it did not seek an all-out confrontation with the emerging new political order prompted by the PA-Israeli dialogue. Thus the Hamas discourse represented its inclination to stick to its ideological premises and pursue its long-term goal of establishing an alternative social and moral order, but it also demonstrated its implicit acceptance of the current political circumstances. And as Hamas strove to preserve its image as a highly doctrinaire, activist movement, it displayed considerable ability to adjust to the new reality. Hamas, then, continued to name armed struggle as its sole strategy of national liberation from the Israeli occupation, but it did not rule out the possibility of indirectly joining the new Palestinian political order. Hamas refused to accord legitimacy to the PA and yet recognized it as a fait accompli; it rejected Israel's right of existence and yet showed its pragmatism by being willing under certain conditions to tolerate a temporary coexistence. For the same reasons, Hamas publicly rejected official participation in the PA's institutions because of the symbolic ramifications of such a move. In practice, however, Hamas encouraged its members to take part as individuals in building the Palestinian society by joining the civil service and the PA's operational apparatus.

In a cost-benefit analysis, Hamas's politics of adjustment carried tangible advantages at a minimal organizational price and at a tolerable normative sacrifice. A policy of adjustment protected Hamas from being marginalized because of its dogmatic adherence to maximalist goals or because of its ignoring the far-reaching changes in Israeli-Palestinian relations. At the same time, it prevented a head-on collision with Israel and the PA, which could have caused the movement's demise. From Hamas's viewpoint, there were certainly enough incentives for following a strategy of political adjustment. The question is how the movement managed to find a middle way between the two radical options, each of which could have exacted an intolerable price. How could Hamas maintain its militant, uncompromising image and continue to take pride in its public achievements in the face of deep disagreement and bitter conflicts between internal rivals that sometimes erupted into violence? To answer these questions, we must examine Hamas's structural and organizational characteristics, their effect on the decision-making processes, and the leadership's ability to justify pragmatic moves in religious terms.

Compared with the PLO, Hamas was at a marked disadvantage. Hamas was a newly established political movement whose leaders were local and inexperienced. Its material resources were limited, and its international contacts were few. In contrast, by the 1980s the PLO was widely recognized and diplomatically established in both the Middle East and the rest of the world, having been granted official diplomatic recognition or some form of representation by more than eighty nations.[1] In many political circles, the idea that a political settlement of the Palestinian problem could be achieved without the PLO's participation had become inconceivable. The PLO was the only nongovernmental body to gain observer status in the United Nations, and it had managed to get a series of anti-Israeli resolutions passed by the General Assembly.[2] It also had emerged as a significant force in Middle East politics; thus the notion that a peaceful settlement to the Arab-Israeli conflict would require a solution to the Palestinian problem had firmly taken root. After losing its territorial stronghold in Lebanon in the 1982 war, the PLO nevertheless was able to maintain its position as a key player in Middle East politics, and its status as the "sole legitimate representative" of the Palestinian people remained unchallenged.

The PLO's political achievements reflected primarily the efforts of its largest and dominant faction, Fatah. Under Arafat's leadership, Fatah managed to unify the main Palestinian groups under a national umbrella organization and achieve a consensus around a common national platform. The PLO sanctioned each faction's autonomy and, under Fatah's leadership, insisted on the principle of independence of Palestinian decision making, despite the tireless efforts of Arab states to dominate the PLO and impose their preferences on it. The PLO's achievements were echoed by its intensive political activities in the West Bank and Gaza Strip, especially after the 1973 war. These activities took the form of political, social, and political penetration; institution building; and the control of students, workers, and welfare and charity associations. The PLO thus became a symbol of Palestinian national identity and of aspirations for independence and statehood.

During the 1970s, the PLO also created interorganizational mechanisms of collaboration to mitigate conflicts, manage tensions, and deal effectively with noncompliance. Although ideological cleavages, political mistrust, and suspicion had not disappeared, no serious Palestinian political or military group existed outside the PLO's sphere of influence. All the major groups were either affiliated with or identified with the PLO. It had become the dominant force in Palestinian political life, and its symbolic status, charismatic leadership, and political influence among the Palestinian people were beyond question.

In the late 1980s, when Hamas emerged as a significant political element in the occupied territories, the PLO was already internationally recognized and represented as a state-in-the-making in control of military and civil institutions and financial resources. Moreover, despite the loss of its Lebanese territorial base in 1982, the PLO continued to maintain an institutional presence in refugee camps, among students, and in other

Palestinian communities in the diaspora. Despite not having sovereignty, the PLO became the supreme national authority and the nucleus of the Palestinian state-to-be. Indeed, even though the Intifada accorded Hamas clear advantages—simply for having its leadership and institutions in the territories—Hamas could not match Fatah in terms of human, military, and political resources. Under these circumstances, an all-out confrontation with Fatah would have been disastrous for Hamas's social and communal institutions. Hence, Hamas repeatedly warned its activists against internal violence, turning this prohibition into a normative limitation in its rivalry with Fatah.

The potential for such a confrontation, and the damage that it would cause, soared after the Oslo agreement was signed, when the Fatah leadership, with its military and civilian apparatuses, moved into the Gaza Strip and Jericho and assumed the status of a self-governing authority backed by Israel. Moreover, as Hamas was aware, the PLO's political experience with the West Bank after 1973 suggested that whenever the PLO adopted a pragmatic approach and preferred "here and now" considerations over "hereafter" calculations, it won broad public support. Supported by the PLO's institutional penetration, the notion of a Palestinian state in the West Bank and Gaza was deemed by the Palestinian inhabitants to be a realistic solution. This shift in the PLO's policy during the 1970s enhanced its stature in the occupied territories in the face of the prevalent pro-Hashemite political sentiments. The Oslo accords produced the same impact, as they represented a historical rapprochement between the PLO and Israel. Taking into account the balance of power between Hamas and the PLO, one may argue (1) that Hamas had a sufficient incentive to pursue the politics of adjustment that represented pragmatism and compromise and (2) that a prolonged adoption of strategies of political adjustment could lead to greater institutionalization and routinization at the expense of revolutionary fervor and political and military activism. More specifically, a policy of adjustment might lead gradually to Hamas's acceptance of the PA as a legitimate authority and to its direct participation in PA institutions. In the long run, such a development might diminish Hamas's claim to be a normative and political alternative to the PA. Yet, however persuasive the arguments for being pragmatic, we cannot exclude the possibility that under certain circumstances, Hamas turn to a policy of confrontation with either or both Israel and the PA. So, to answer the question of whether Hamas would follow pragmatic strategies or turn to violence, we must examine the movement's structural features and organizational tenets that affected its political thinking, shaped its conduct, and influenced its strategic choices.

Strategies and Structures

Hamas's adoption of a strategy of political adjustment can be explained in terms of its ability to bridge the gap between opposing considerations of practical needs and normative requirements, representing its dual commitment to both sociocommunal values and religious-nationalist beliefs. As a religious and national movement self-perceived as the sole moral and political alternative to the existing order, Hamas had to maintain its radical image, which is identified with a strategy of all-out confrontation. Yet as a social movement, Hamas had to take into account issues closer to home. Accordingly, Hamas was effectively compelled to develop a way to maneuver politically despite its radical Islamic and national vision and its claim to be able to realize its vision through violent means.

Hamas was able to bridge the gap between its official dogma and "here and now" considerations as long as it justified pragmatic moves in normative terms and engaged in pragmatic initiatives that carried tolerable organizational risks. Islamic argumentation played an important role in legitimizing its pragmatic conduct. Such argumentation probably helped the rank and file accept these moves and reduced the risk of division within the movement. The concept of *sabr* is a typical example of Hamas's inclination to use a normative justification for its political inaction toward, or acquiescence in, an accepted reality that might have been regarded as a deviation from religious dogma.

Sabr enabled the Hamas leadership to justify its ongoing efforts to build an Islamic society from below, according legitimacy to the movement's preference for long-term religious and communal activities over a short-term, avant-garde vision of revolution from above. It was in this context that Hamas distinguished between a permanent settlement of the Israeli-Palestinian dispute, which it unequivocally rejected, and a temporary settlement, which it deemed tolerable; between a short-term policy necessitating the temporary delay of its ultimate goals in accordance with circumstances and constraints and a long-term strategy based on firm adherence to Islamic radical vision; and between willingness to accept ad hoc arrangements of coexistence as the lesser evil and denial of the PLO's and PA's legitimacy. *Sabr* thus served as a normative device of legal interpretation, providing Hamas with a measure of maneuverability to minimize the negative effects of deviating from the official dogma, which called for pragmatic moves and responses. At the same time, this device reduced the chance of effective, prolonged opposition from within.

Nevertheless, Hamas's institutional landscape and its structure indicate that the movement suffered from intrinsic limitations in ensuring a viable base of support for its strategy of political adjustment. If Hamas did succeed in turning to pragmatic action without being seriously hurt by accusations of deviating from Islamic dogma and Palestinian nationalist norms, this would be the result of the surrounding political environment rather than Hamas's own institutional capabilities. Arguably, then, far-reaching developments in the region's political environment and significant local changes might weaken Hamas's ability to maintain a strategy of political adjustment and pragmatic thinking.

Like other social movements and political organizations, much of Hamas's inter- and intraorganizational activity is grounded in its hierarchical structure and interpersonal relations. Without sovereignty and political independence, traditional affiliations and loyalties have become critical factors in Hamas's public activities, as they are often based on personal acquaintance, family blood, or physical proximity to or close affiliation with a site of prayer or a religious figure. But compared with other organizations, what stands out in the case of Hamas is the tension between the movement's formal and informal elements, between its religious-national vision and communal needs, as well as the tension emanating from the power struggle between "outside" and "inside" over Hamas's leadership and institutions. This tension increased significantly after 1989 when the movement's headquarters and staff gradually moved abroad as a defensive measure to secure freedom of action and reduce its susceptibility to Israeli repressive measures. The technocratic, "outside" leadership preferred a formal and hierarchical structure, choosing clandestine activities and organizations like the secular revolutionary movements to which some of Hamas's senior members had belonged before shifting to Islamic radicalism. Hamas's organizational structure made the "outside" leaders paramount, and the local leaders were organized informally based on ties of solidarity and traditional attachments.

Therefore, much of Hamas's structure during this formative period continued to play a significant role afterward as well. Its characteristics derived from the activity of al-Mujamma' al-Islami, which was established in Gaza in 1973. As a popular religious organization, the Mujamma' strove to create an Islamic space in which to build a community of believers to be ruled by the *shari'a*. The Mujamma''s activities were aimed toward preparing the way for the establishment—at an indefinite time—of an Islamic state.

The Mujamma' focused on education, preaching, and communal activity, leading to an increased effort to form autonomous social enclaves based on the principle of self-sufficient systems parallel to those of the state. The Mujamma' formed institutions to provide educational, medical, sports, and material services for the needy, most of which revolved around the mosques in the main refugee camps of the Gaza Strip—Jabaliya, Nusairat, Shati', Dair al-Balah, Khan Yunis, and Rafah.[3]

As a local movement, the Mujamma''s interpersonal networks and interactions, based on friendship, reputation, and trust rather than on hierarchy, played an important role in building organizational infrastructure and mobilizing resources and public support. Indeed, the Mujamma' was affected less by authoritative, bureaucratic, and vertical relations and a hierarchical chain of command than by group interaction and lateral relations based primarily on solidarity among the participants, self-identification as a collective unit, a common background, and a sharing of basic knowledge and values.[4]

The informal relations within the Mujamma' also determined its organization. Thus, the leaders' success in attracting new members, expanding its popular support, and securing obedience and compliance from its followers depended on personal, charismatic virtues rather than coercive means. The archetypal leader was Sheikh Ahmad Yasin, the founder of the Mujamma' together with others such as Ibrahim al-Yazuri, Mahmud al-Zahar, and 'Abd al-'Aziz Rantisi. The ability of these charismatic leaders to command both obedience and compliance depended more on persuasive ability and less on coercion, more on the controlled use of symbolic and beneficial rewards than on the threat of sanctions and punishment. This pattern of informal activity derived also from the Muslim Brothers' tradition which, under the influence of Sufism, remained aloof from politics and formal state institutions, emphasizing instead education and elitist Islamic scholarship.[5]

Hamas was founded as an Islamic and Palestinian nationalist movement at the beginning of the Intifada, reflecting a turn to territorialization. Its quest for the establishment of an Islamic Palestinian state covering all of Mandatory Palestine by means of armed struggle—as an alternative to the PLO's two-state solution—encouraged the movement to develop formal civilian and military institutional capabilities.

Hamas's emphasis on a popular uprising and controlled violence to mobilize the people required a structure based on vertical relations and a hierarchical chain of command. Moreover, Hamas's goal of political domination and normative hegemony led to its expansion from the Gaza Strip to the West Bank. To the intensified mass action that characterized the Intifada, Hamas responded with more bureaucracy and a more formal structure than the pre-Intifada al-Mujamma' al-Islami featured.

Hamas's need for a more formal structure was also dictated by external constraints. Israel's repressive policy during the Intifada, especially after the outlawing of Hamas and the massive arrests of its cadres in May and June 1989, led the movement to seek more effective measures to secure its survival and continue its activities, hence its emphasis on discipline, secrecy, compartmentalization, and hierarchy. Interpersonal interactions based on trust and persuasion were no longer sufficient, although they continued to affect relationships in regard to both civil and military actions.

Hamas's competition with the PLO also drove it toward a hierarchical structure and infrastructure building. It was after the Yom Kippur War of October 1973 that the PLO began its intensive political activity in the occupied territories. In later years, the organization gained popular support and secured powerful positions in municipal bodies, student groups, trade unions, and charity and welfare organizations. Its institutional inroads were matched by its ideological success, and the PLO emerged as a source of political inspiration for the population, as both the embodiment of Palestinian national aspirations and an ideological guide to the labyrinthine politics of the Palestinian and inter-Arab systems. More often than not, the PLO and the Palestinian issue were seen as inseparable.

The PLO's institutional domination of the occupied territories became clear during the Intifada. And it was this institutional penetration that enabled the PLO to mobilize public support for both violent and nonviolent measures initiated by local activists. Therefore, in order for Hamas to secure a prominent position in the Palestinian population, it had to establish a countrywide bureaucratic apparatus and an institutional network. These could improve Hamas's capability to compete with the PLO for public support, using both practical and coercive means to ensure the population's compliance.

In addition to the military and organizational constraints imposed on Hamas by Israel and the PLO, a key factor was the geographic separation and sociopolitical differences between the West Bank and Gaza Strip. As a result of the Israeli-Arab war of 1948, the West Bank became part of Jordan, and the Gaza Strip was governed by Egypt. The unique political conditions and particular social and economic circumstances that developed in each region resulted in two different communities. True, following the Arab-Israeli war of 1967 the enforced unification of the West Bank and Gaza Strip under Israeli occupation helped narrow the differences and strengthen common political and social values. But the new political circumstances could not obliterate the differences between and contradictory interests of the two regions. Since 1967, the Gaza Strip had been a more violent society than the West Bank. Gaza was more economically distressed, demographically saturated, dense with refugees, and more religious than the West Bank.

Politically, the differences between the West Bank and Gaza Strip after 1967 were reflected in the continuing Jordanian influence over the Islamic establishment in East Jerusalem and the West Bank. With Israel's tacit agreement, the Muslim *waqf*—the body in charge of religious endowments—and Muslim judicial apparatuses continued to operate as part of the Jordanian Ministry of the Awqaf, leaving the Haram al-Sharif (the Temple Mount) under Jordan's supervision.[6] Since the West Bank was made part of the Hashemite Kingdom in April 1950, Amman's official policy had been marked by a tacit alliance with the Muslim Brothers (MB) against both pan-Arab movements and communism. In East Jerusalem and the West Bank, the *waqf* apparatus supported the MB through charitable committees (*lijan al-zakat*) which operated in most of the towns and villages, as well as through appointments of preachers and other clergy.[7] Following the war of 1967, Jordan's efforts to preserve its standing in the religious establishment and the PLO's struggle for the civic domain led the MB to increase its organizational efforts and to restructure its institutions in order to compete with the PLO.

The record of Hamas's activities, both violent and nonviolent, during the Intifada indicated its awareness of the need to design those activities according to its formal organizational structure. Hamas's growing involvement with the people in the Gaza Strip and the West Bank amid competition with the United National Command (UNC) and confrontation with Israel, encouraged it to become less complex, avoid conflicting commands, and ensure control by the leadership. Similarly, Hamas created an organizational infrastructure based on horizontally and vertically differentiated positions. Vertically, positions are linked to a hierarchical chain of command—instructions go down and compliance reports go up—and are controlled by supervisors with a fixed number of subordinates, each of whom has one clearly identified supervisor to whom he is responsible. Horizontally, various tasks are grouped according to the functions performed for the organization.[8]

Hamas's organizational infrastructure is meant to function in accordance with the principles of bureaucratic hierarchy. It includes internal security, military activities, political activities (protests, demonstrations, etc.), and Islamic preaching (*da'wa*). All four units have separate regional headquarters in the Gaza Strip and the West Bank. The security apparatus (*al-majd*) was first established in 1986 as part of the Mujamma', its main function to gain control of the local population, to "gather information on suspected collaborators with the [Israeli] authorities and [those] who deviated from the Islamic path—thieves, drug dealers, pimps, and traffickers in alcohol drinks and pornographic videocassettes—and their punishment by physical damage to their bodies or property."[9] During the Intifada, the security apparatus's functions expanded to include the printing and distribution of Hamas leaflets as well as the execution of Palestinians suspected of collaborating with Israel.[10] The military apparatus had already been established before the Intifada, as secret military cells of al-Mujamma' al-islami, known as "the Islamic Holy Warriors." During the first three years of the Intifada, the military squads were operated by separate regional headquarters in both the West Bank and the Gaza Strip. The military apparatus, however, came to be associated with 'Izz al-Din al-Qassam units, which were established in 1992 and were immediately identified with the spectacular terrorist attacks on Israeli civilians. Hamas set up its political activity unit in the early days of the Intifada. Its assignment was to be "responsible for the daily activity of the Intifada: stoning, building barricades, burning tires, starting demonstrations, writing slogans, enforcing strikes, extending first aid to the wounded during curfews, and making peace among the residents."[11]

Unlike other Hamas activities, the main role of the *da'wa* is the Islamization of the community by means of social mobilization and religious preaching. The *da'wa* was mentioned in the Qur'an (14: 46) as God's "call" to humans to find in Islam their true religion. The *da'wa* activities are concentrated around the mosques and include religious, educational, sports, and social activities, as well as the recruitment of candidates for training as members of Hamas.

From the outset, Hamas invested its chief organizational efforts and financial resources in education, religious preaching, and welfare (including support for families of martyrs and of prisoners in Israeli jails). Hamas's educational activities are offered to children and youth from kindergarten through primary and secondary school all the way to postsecondary education. "A Guide for the Muslim Student," distributed to students involved in *da'wa* in 1992, states:

The student should say: I did not come to school only to study . . .
even if I have to do that as a Muslim, for I must find the narrow
path between my studies and the *da'wa* for Allah, for which we were
created by Allah. Always remember! The *da'wa* for Allah is the
highest and most honorable act—it is the duty of the Prophet and
his followers; those preaching for *da'wa* are like the stars in heaven
leading the errant back to the straight and narrow path.[12]

In an internal document dating from the middle of 1992 and entitled
"A General Plan for da'wa Activity," Hamas outlined its annual program
to teach Islam to schoolchildren. The program includes producing a
monthly publication, organizing competitions on religious topics, enlisting Muslim Brothers to teach in the schools, and arranging activities for
students in their free time. It also calls for establishing "houses of the
Qur'an," a network operating from mosques and serving as a forum for
public seminars and setting up extracurricular workshops in Qur'anic studies for children and youth after school.

Aside from disseminating *da'wa* through written publications—books,
pamphlets, personal letters, and articles in widely circulating newspapers—
Hamas attributes great importance to oral communication, using public
occasions for religious preaching. These occasions include family events
such as weddings or funerals, reconciliations between rival families, participation in public lectures and symposia, lectures on religious issues, sermons (especially on Fridays and holidays), and plays bearing a religious
message. Hamas also organizes discounted book sales and distributed stick-
ers and cassettes and movies of religious interest.

The movement has formed administrative bodies to provide medical
and educational services, which constitute the core of its communal infrastructure. The Scientific Medical Association, which was established as a
counter to the Palestinian Red Crescent—a stronghold of the left in Gaza
Strip—coordinates the activities of medical infirmaries, dental facilities, and
the blood bank. The association charges a nominal fee for its services or
offers them free of charge to the needy. In addition, Hamas operates the
Association for Sciences and Culture, which coordinates education from
kindergarten up to secondary school, taking care to include Islamic religious values at all levels of schooling. As a popular movement, Hamas operates a vast propaganda machine, coordinated by the Supreme Council for
Islamic Information, which is in charge of media coverage of Hamas and
its activities, relations with the international press, and a press agency (al-
Quds Press), with bureaus abroad and in major Palestinian cities.[13]

In addition, Hamas is broadly involved with the workers, especially in urban neighborhoods. The Islamic Workers Union, which Hamas established in July 1992, organizes lectures on Islamic labor laws, which are accompanied by religious preaching. Hamas also works closely with graduates of Islamic universities and colleges, in both the West Bank and the Gaza Strip. The Association of the [Islamic] Scholars of Palestine (Rabitat 'ulama' filastin), which was formed in the summer of 1991, later was established as an official institution with eighty members. It was to serve as the supreme religious authority in charge of persuading the educated classes of Islam's superiority as a way of life. But it disbanded shortly after it was established, perhaps because of the "outside" leadership's opposition. The latter apparently preferred to rely on an external religious advisory council (*majlis shura*, see later)—whether really existing or just imagined—that would be more amenable to its influence.

To consolidate its civilian activities, Hamas offers a training program for members who are then assigned various public responsibilities. The trainees fast for three days a month, and within two months each trainee must complete the following tasks: read a book, organize a meeting on a religious topic, watch a video movie, participate in an outing with other trainees, take part in religious lessons for the public, and contribute to a cultural publication by writing for it or distributing it.

In addition to labor's functional division, there was also a vertical geographical division. The Gaza Strip was divided into seven districts and the West Bank into five. Each district was divided into subdistricts, which were further divided into local units of villages or refugee camps. Each unit was headed by a supervisor who was responsible for two or three cells. At the district level, there also were committees on education, publications, finance, and prisoners. The prisoners' committee was established to support prisoners' families financially, paying for detainees' legal defense, and transferring "canteen money" to jails.[14]

Hamas's units are carefully compartmentalized.

Every drafted person, every district and unit, was identified by a number and a code. Members of each cell knew only their cellmates and their supervisor. Members of each unit could communicate with one another but not with members in other districts. Communication between different units operating in separate districts was to be conducted through the security apparatus's members, who acted as couriers.[15]

In practice, Hamas's political leadership in the West Bank, the Gaza Strip, and abroad is occasionally surprised by military actions against Israel about which it had no prior knowledge. Some of the "inside" leaders often claim that the military units were operating independently rather than on external or high-level political orders.[16] Such claims are meant, first, to give the impression that the political leadership has nothing to do with terrorist actions and thus should be exempt from accusations that could make Hamas's community infrastructure vulnerable to retaliation by Israel or the PA. In fact, such claims are not entirely groundless. At least some terrorist acts against Israelis were carried out by individuals acting on their own for religious or personal reasons.

Indeed, during the Intifada, Hamas's ability to operate as a hierarchical organization suffered serious damage. Despite the difficulties of penetrating such a highly motivated movement as Hams, Israel's intelligence agencies repeatedly exposed Hamas's planning or operational military groups while its repressive measures of detainment and deportation weakened the senior and middle leadership. Consequently, the grassroots activists—young, educated, militant, charismatic figures, often from the lower middle class— had a disproportionate amount of influence and freedom of action in their constituencies. That these men were willing to risk their lives in military activities against Israel and then to go underground for months or years to escape detainment by the Israelis have made them national heroes.

The members of the military apparatus are thus distinctly different from both the "inside" and "outside" political leaders because of their age as well as their social and professional background. This discrepancy might help explain the frequent irregularities in Hamas's hierarchical order and even the violations of its official leadership's policies. Hamas's pattern of decentralized organization is expressed in local initiatives that often contradict the official policy and instructions of the top leadership. This is most strikingly manifested in the execution of Palestinians suspected of collaborating with Israel or of immoral conduct and violation of Islamic norms. These individual initiatives occasionally embroil the movement as a whole in conflict with other organizations, primarily Fatah.

The diminished ability of Hamas's senior leaders to maintain control over the rank and file, and the growing stature of the young local activists, underscores the organic nature of Hamas's structure:

1. Tasks are defined more "through the interaction of [local] members than . . . by the organization's top leaders."

2. Local activists are encouraged to "accept broader responsibilities and commitments than those prescribed by their role descriptions."
3. Decisions are driven more by "interaction among peers than strictly by hierarchical authority and control."
4. Activities are based more on information from local members than on formal leaders.
5. Lateral communications and consultation among members in different local positions have become more common than reliance on vertical communications between superiors and subordinates.
6. Local activists are committed "to performing tasks and fulfilling responsibilities effectively . . . rather than to blind loyalty and obedience to superiors."[17]
7. Local leaders and activists participate more in daily decisions about changes in the movement's missions, goals, and functions.

The organic nature of local activities sometimes has led to dramatic results, highlighting the discrepancy between the activists' low hierarchical status and the outcome of their nonauthorized initiatives. Furthermore, given the absence of clear hierarchical norms, so prevalent in Islamic movements, it is likely that the thrust toward an organic structure will widen the gulf between the central leadership and the rank and file, resulting in the local power centers challenging the leaders' moral and political status.

What prevented this organizational disharmony between the central and local leaders from deteriorating even further is the fact that it is operational rather than ideological. As long as the Intifada continued and the expulsion of Israel from the occupied territories topped Hamas's agenda, differences and disagreements among the movement's various groups were treated more as tactics than as principle. Indeed, during the Intifada it was because of external political developments that Hamas, despite the gap between radical militancy and more controlled activity, was spared the need to adopt policies that might have been interpreted as a major deviation from its religious dogma. Consequently, the possibility that the differences would lead to an organizational split and cause structural chaos was drastically diminished.

The Logic of Structural Reorganization

The arrest in 1989 of Hamas's leader, Ahmad Yasin, brought to an end the era during which the movement's leaders came exclusively from within. The vacuum that opened in the senior- and middle-level leadership was filled mostly by deportees from the territories, technocrats in liberal professions, mostly in their late thirties and early forties. Many were former disciples of Yasin, and some had been granted scholarships by the Mujamma' to study abroad. These men, of whom Abu Marzuq was typical, were able to gain legitimacy and assume authority based on the organizational and leadership skills they demonstrated when the movement experienced crises, as well as their ability to raise funds from supportive governments and communities worldwide for "inside" civilian and military activities. Here, too, the links between the delegates outside the leadership and the local activists are based on personal acquaintances and are supported by Hamas's senior activists in Israeli prisons. Indeed, activists from abroad often come to the West Bank and Gaza with lists of names of the movement's members or of those tapped for key positions, along with instructions and ready cash.[18]

Compared with the "inside" members, the "outside" leadership consists of relatively young, educated technocrats who belong to the radical groups within Hamas. The "outside" activists subscribe to a vision of political Islamism—that is, a revolution from above—rather than with religious revelation through ordinary processes of communal activity. However, they do not have to cope with the reality of Israeli occupation, the PA's domination, and the daily hardships of the Palestinian community, which might explain why they can afford to adopt a harder line concerning the armed struggle and the Oslo process. This radical perception, coinciding with the militancy of the rank and file in the occupied territories, helped the "outside" Hamas to reorganize the movement's activity into a hierarchical order following the mass arrests of 1989. This initiative was designed to give the "outside" leadership control over the "inside" and secure the subordination of the latter's operational ranks.

Standing at the top of the pyramid in Hamas's new organizational order are two bodies, both based outside the occupied territories: the Advisory Council (Majlis shura), and the Political Bureau (al-Maktab al-siyasi). The Advisory Council is thought to have twelve members, the majority non-Palestinians.[19] It serves as the supreme religious authority, its principal role being to provide normative backing and moral justification for Hamas's political conduct and major decisions. Officially, the council's decisions are based on a majority vote.[20] In practice, however, the council does not operate as a collective body; rather, issues under discussion are referred to a council member able to offer expert advice.

Unlike the amorphous structure of the Advisory Council, the Political Bureau functions as an executive body that has obtained more control over and greater obedience and compliance from Hamas's rank and file. The bureau's ten members are responsible for directing Hamas policies and adjusting them to conform with the shifting realities. Until his deportation from Jordan and subsequent arrest in the United States in 1995, Dr. Musa Abu Marzuq served as the head of the Political Bureau. It was under his energetic leadership that Hamas became capable once more of acting and conducting a dialogue with the PLO, other Islamic movements, and Arab governments.[21] The acting head of the bureau was Khalid Mash'al, who replaced Abu Marzuq following the latter's arrest, and a failed attempt on his life was made by the Israeli Mossad in October 1997. Other leading figures were the Hamas spokesman Ibrahim Ghawsha and Hamas's representatives in Jordan (Muhammad Nazzal), Iran ('Imad al-'Alami, until early 1998), Syria (Mustafa Qanu', until early 1998), Lebanon, and Sudan.

Like the members of the Advisory Council, all the bureau's members reside outside the occupied territories, mainly in neighboring Arab countries. Usually they are well educated and in white-collar professions and maintain close contact with other Islamic movements as well as with Palestinian communities abroad. Jordan, Syria, Iran, Saudi Arabia, Yemen, Algeria, and Tunisia are among the states helping, or encouraging, Hamas to maintain a visible presence. In addition, members of the Political Bureau have been able to obtain financial support from Palestinian and Muslim communities in the United States and Britain. It is this fund-raising ability that may explain the bureau's primacy in the movement following the Israeli sweep in 1989.[122] The bureau supervised the local activity of Hamas through three committees: *da'wa*, finance, and internal affairs.[23]

To ensure control over Hamas's local units and their daily activities, the Political Bureau established two coordinating bodies: the Administrative Unit, and the West Bank and Gaza Office. The former body is responsible for coordinating the *da'wa* activities and the Security and Events Units. In addition, the units make the appointments to command roles, formulate plans in coordination with the representatives of other units, and recruit new members. The West Bank and Gaza Office acts as a liaison between the headquarters of the two regions.[24] The reorganization of Hamas also included the establishment of an overall military apparatus in charge of both the West Bank and the Gaza Strip.

Since 1989, Hamas's "outside" leaders have worked hard to institutionalize the movement's presence in Arab and Palestinian communities in the United States and Europe, especially Britain and Germany. Focusing on Muslim community centers, these efforts have included organizing conventions, issuing pamphlets and publications, and raising money for supposedly humanitarian purposes. The largest center was in Dallas, Texas, and was responsible for publishing periodicals of the Palestinian Islamic movement in North America, such as *al-Zaituna, Ila Filastin*, and *The Palestine Monitor*. At the end of 1991, a Hamas center opened in Springfield, Virginia, Musa Abu Marzuq's hometown, but both centers were shut down in 1993 when the U.S. government declared Hamas a terrorist organization.

Like the PLO, Hamas has two sets of leaders, those "outside" and "inside" the territories, with the former in control of the latter. The outside group is more closely identified with Hamas's ultimate goals and grand vision, and the inside group focuses on local grievances and close-to-home issues. Also similar to the PLO, Hamas's operational networks, both inside and outside the occupied territories, have strengthened its quest for an all-Palestinian movement.

Oslo and the Future of Hamas-PA Relations

The establishment in May 1994 of the PA in Gaza and Jericho threatened Hamas's popular position, especially the "outside" leadership's domination of the movement in the PA-controlled areas. Indeed, the PA's growing penetration of the Palestinian population in Gaza heightened the tension between Hamas's "outside" and local leaders regarding the strategy to be used in response to the newly established political order. Both groups knew that Oslo might enhance the prestige of the PA, to the detriment of Hamas, and both recognized the importance of a dialogue with the PA. Nevertheless, each group came to a different conclusion. Hamas's "outside" leaders preferred a strategy of avoidance, or an absence of response, to initiatives geared to assimilate Hamas into the new political reality and thus implicitly legitimize the PA. By contrast, the "inside" leaders were willing to consider such initiatives while downplaying their significance. Nowhere were these differences over Hamas's preferred strategy and conduct toward the PA more vividly expressed than in the issue of a political party to be formed by Hamas in order to participate in the general elections to the Palestinian Authority's Council held in January 1996.

Whereas the "outside" was more reluctant, the "inside" leadership took a more positive approach to the idea of establishing a political party and running in the elections. Ibrahaim Ghawsha, the Amman-based official Hamas spokesman, clarified the "outside" leaders' position in several statements made to the Palestinian, Arab, and international media. In an interview with a Kuwaiti newspaper, Ghawshah stated:

> Hamas will not be transformed into a political party. . . . We know how much the Zionist and American quarters and those who rotate in their orbits would like that. Containing Hamas politically, folding its resistance and *jihad* banner, and involving it in the Oslo agreements are their ultimate hope.

> Hamas indeed discussed the establishment of a political party more than three years ago. It is no secret that the idea was discussed with the deportees in 1992. Several months ago, the movement's consultative institutions approved the establishment of a political party not to replace Hamas and not to contradict its political program and strategic objectives. It was left for the movement to choose the appropriate time to announce the establishment of this party. The movement's consultative institutions also decided not to participate in the Oslo agreement, which the movement rejects. It regards the elections as one of the mechanisms of the Oslo agreement. They are not comprehensive legislative elections open to the Palestinian people at home and abroad, as the movement wants, but are connected with the settlement plans.[25]

A month later, in a radio interview, Ghawshah added the following to his arguments against Hamas's participation in the elections:

> In light of the recent developments in the Gaza Strip, [where a] grave crisis and tension [prevail], to overcome this crisis matters should take the correct course. In other words, a million Palestinian people in the Gaza Strip should be allowed to elect their true leadership from among the people, under the auspices of a neutral party. . . . We want the world to know who represents the Palestinian people by holding free and fair direct elections for the people, outside the framework of the Oslo and Cairo agreement. Afterward, elections can spread to all Palestinians inside and outside [the occupied territories].[26]

Mahmud al-Zahar, a pediatrician from Gaza and a prominent Hamas leader, took the opposite position. As for the establishment of a political party, al-Zahar stated,

Islam has come to tackle realities on the ground. As a body which seeks to apply Islam to reality, Hamas has stated from the beginning, and from the moment the PA was established, that it is ready to participate in the process of construction. However, it has some controls which govern its religiously based political ideology. Participation in the process of construction does not mean that one accepts the Oslo agreements; nor does it necessarily mean one rejects them. It means we have to find a suitable formula that reconciles the two realities so that the requirements for construction may be placed above ideological or political differences. This calls for the establishment of a body that works to further enhance the concept of institutions. Let us view things on the ground to clarify the picture. As Palestinian people, comprising all affiliations, including Fatah and Hamas, we now need to pass a law on political parties that would meet all the requirements and that all parties will approve. Parties will then be formed. These parties have programs, ideologies, and projects and can participate in the construction operation either from within the PA or from outside it through voluntary work or parallel services work. Thus, the construction process does not mean restricting the issue to those who accepted Oslo and that everything else is rejected.

First of all, Hamas was, and is still, a militant [jihadiyyah] organization acting against the occupation. Now, if a new reality is imposed that requires the establishment of parties, then parties will participate. We do not now have a law that specifies or regulates the way to establish parties. We need a law, which must be approved by all Palestinian factions and the Palestinian public, that can entrench the concept of pluralism. After that, these bodies which will be established, be they parties or political or ideological organizations, can preset their ideas and decide to participate or not participate in the elections.[27]

In response, Hamas's spokesman, Ghawashah, flatly rejected al-Zahar's position:

No change has taken place in the position of Hamas. The movement refuses to participate in the self-rule elections for many reasons. These elections are an implementation of the Oslo agreements, which are incomplete agreements. Only two million Palestinian people will participate, excluding the four million who are abroad. Besides, the

Zionist occupation will be the final authority of the council to be elected. For these reasons, the Islamic Resistance Movement still stands by its position of not participating in the self-rule elections and calling on the Palestinian people to boycott these elections, which we believe do not express in a free and fair manner what these people want.

With respect to the local elections, we called on the Palestinian Authority, from the very first day, to conduct fair and free municipal elections. Unfortunately, the Authority appointed the municipalities in Gaza, Nablus, Hebron, and others, and refused to hold democratic elections.[28]

Underlying the differences between the "inside" and the "outside" leaders were two issues. First, the "outside" leaders were inspired by an avant-garde vision and advocated a revolution from above; the local leaders, however, preferred to focus more on immediate communal interests and re-formist processes from within. Second, as a result of uncertain external political developments in which other parties were involved, the "outside" leaders feared they would be marginalized by the "inside."

We could argue that the PA's growing political control and the differences between Hamas's "inside" and "outside" leaders would intensify the latter's effort to secure its influence within the movement by escalating the military effort and thereby driving a wedge between the military command and the "inside" political leadership. However, Israel's and the PA's pressure on Hamas, particularly on its military apparatus, would weaken the "outside" control over the local leadership. Accordingly, the tension between the "outside" and "inside" leaders could adversely affect Hamas's organizational unity, putting at risk the fragile coexistence between the two parties. In turn, such developments could undermine Hamas's ability to turn to a policy of adjusting to the new political reality.

There are three reasons that Hamas managed to avoid an organizational split and structural chaos. First is the PA's policy, which, as a matter of tactics, prefers dialogue and coexistence to a military confrontation with Hamas. Second is the fact that Israel, under the Labor government that took office in 1992, withdrew the demand that the PA dismantle Hamas and now is willing to accept the PA's preventive steps against radical Islamic terrorism. Third is the provisional character of the Oslo accords, which have left unresolved until the final status talks key issues such as the Palestinian refugees of 1948 and 1967, the future of Jewish settlements beyond Israel's 1967 borders, Jerusalem, the PA's permanent political status, and the demarcation of Palestinian territory. In addition, Arafat's repeated commitment to establish an independent Palestinian state with East Jerusalem as its capital has helped bridge part of the gap between Hamas and the PA pertaining to the political goals of the peace process.

It is Hamas's internal weakness and the PA's and Israel's perception of the Oslo accords—and the role of Hamas in this context—that made its policy of adjustment a preferable option to both Hamas's "inside" and "outside" leaders. A strategy of all-out confrontation by the "outside" leaders in an attempt to undermine the Israeli-Palestinian Oslo process, would exact a high cost. In the short run, uncontrolled violence against Israel and the PA could disrupt implementation of the accords. In the long run, however, the deterioration of the Oslo accords would trigger violent retaliations by Israel—including a tighter closure of the Palestinian-inhabited areas—and the PA, thereby adding to the public's resentment of Hamas, which could alienate its local, nonmilitary leadership. Thus, the effect of a policy of all-out confrontation by Hamas's "outside" faction could help consolidate the position of the PA and the "inside" Hamas leaders.

If the "inside" Hamas leaders collaborated with the PA, or participated in its institutions to the point of de facto recognition of the PA, thereby defying the "outside" leadership, they might obtain personal political benefits. But this would generate extensive opposition among Hamas's rank and file, undermining the legitimacy of the "inside" leadership. Arguably, then, despite the "outside" leadership's control of material resources and the civil and military apparatus, as long as the outlook of the permanent Israeli-Palestinian settlement remains vague and the PA maintains its tolerant policy toward Hamas, the movement will probably continue to adhere to its policy of adjustment as a guiding political strategy.

Apart from the "push" factors, "pull" forces also have encouraged Hamas to seek a policy of adjustment as the preferred alternative. Strategies of controlled violence, negotiated coexistence, and calculated participation have helped the movement stick to its official dogma, which calls for the establishment of Palestine as an Islamic state. At the same time, strategies of political adjustment have enabled Hamas to maintain its involvement in a broad variety of civil activities in the Palestinian community in the West Bank and Gaza Strip, through its welfare and social services, parallel to those of the PA.

Hamas's adoption of a policy of adjustment also has enabled it to perceive its relationship with the PA as an intermediate situation of prolonged tensions and contradictions, to be dealt with by institutional arrangements and normative devices that mitigate the antagonism rather than resolve it. In this respect, Hamas has usually avoided adopting rigid political doctrines regarding its relations with the PLO, and later with the PA, opting instead for temporary accommodation.

The perception of Hamas's relations with the PA as temporary has two aspects. First, it reflects Hamas's sense that it is engaged in an unresolved conflict, and so it should not view the existing political order represented by the PA as a permanent peace solution. Second, groups within Hamas have been able to accept the existing situation in the short term until they acquire the means to realize their ultimate goals.

The perception that the political order established by the Oslo accord is temporary, then, offers both the potential for change and the possibility of somehow maintaining the existing political order in the Palestinian autonomous areas. By regarding their political existence under the PA as temporary, groups within Hamas can delay confronting the PA over issues of symbolic significance that in the past led to a violent showdown. These patterns of relations contradict less nuanced generalizations such as T. E. Lawrence's statement that "semites had no half-tones in their register of vision. . . . They never compromised: they pursued the logic of several incompatible opinions to absurd ends."[29]

True, compared with other Islamic movements in the Arab states, Hamas has operated in a political arena characterized by a limited self-governing authority and overall Israeli domination. This has resulted in, simultaneously, an armed struggle against Israel and a political struggle against the PA. One can argue that major changes in this situation might question the feasibility and benefit of Hamas's continued policy of adjustment and the preference for it to other tactics. Rapid progress in the Israeli-Palestinian negotiations toward a permanent settlement with clear territorial, institutional, and economic gains for the Palestinians would increase the PA's chances of obtaining wider support from the Palestinian communities in the West Bank and the Gaza Strip.

In such a scenario, Hamas's justification for continued coexistence with the PA, as well as its civic activities, could be expected to be diminished, intensifying the differences both internally and with the PA. Such a development might lead to one or all the possibilities of direct confrontation between Hamas and the PA, a split within Hamas, within the autonomous areas, as well as between the "inside" and "outside" leaderships. But stagnation or a regression in the Israeli-Palestinian diplomatic process would make the Palestinians even more frustrated, forcing the PA to close ranks with Hamas and other radical opposition movements.

Still, given the complexity of Palestinian politics, we could argue that accelerated progress toward a permanent settlement would not automatically lead Hamas to confrontation with the PA. Hamas is more reformist than revolutionary, more populist than avant-garde, more political than military, more communal than universalist. Hamas is aware of cost-benefit considerations and has made its decisions accordingly. Similarly, the PA has chosen pragmatism over extremism and has subscribed to the prose of reality rather than the poetry of ideology. Hamas has been cognizant of its limitations, though without admitting it; anxious to preserve Palestinian national unity—hence its extreme sensitivity to public opinion—particularly in view of the PA's volatile diplomatic negotiations with Israel. Thus, we might assume that even if PA-Hamas relations were in crisis, both sides would remain faithful to their basic inclination to avert a total showdown. Admittedly, this inclination tends to weaken when Hamas's hostility toward Israel grows or it feels threatened.

Various structural and cultural conditions might strengthen Hamas's and the PA's desire to maintain their coexistence. Unlike Arab revolutionary regimes such as those in Syria, Iraq, and Algeria, the PA has traditionally tolerated Islamist elements. In contrast to Syria or Iraq, where the reins of power are held by an ethnic minority group, nearly all Palestinians are Sunni Arabs. Above all, unlike Syria's and Iraq's policy of excluding an Islamic opposition, the PA's policy toward opposition movements has been characterized by an inclusive approach generally aimed at co-opting the opposition to minimize its effects on the decision-making process.

The PA's policy toward the Islamic opposition resembles the negotiated coexistence adopted by Jordan and Saudi Arabia toward the Islamic opposition in those countries. Under these circumstances, a deterioration in PA-Hamas relations would be probably approached by the two parties more in terms of redefining their power relations rather than leading them to confront each other. The history of Hamas's relations with the PLO, and later with the PA, shows that seeming rivals and enemies can find ways to co-exist even if they cannot resolve basic conflicts.

Hamas and Israel: Indirect Dialogue

The coexistence of Hamas and the PA as well as significant progress in the Israeli-Palestinian peace negotiations may strengthen trends in Hamas favoring political dialogue with Israel with the possibility of coexistence. As our study has shown, Hamas is far from being fixated on unrealistic "all or nothing" objectives. Despite the perception that Hamas caters only to fantasies, it has demonstrated an awareness of the shifting political circumstances and a willingness to base its policies on cost-benefit calculations. Hamas, then, does not live up to its world image of a one-track organization with a monolithic, fanatic vision; unshakable fundamentalist interests; rigidly binary perceptions; and intransigent preferences. In fact, if Hamas were to adopt such an unbending approach, it would be counterproductive, increasing its isolation in the local Palestinian, inter-Arab, and international arenas.

A comparison of Hamas's declared principles with its concrete actions shows that it has been in Hamas's interest to become politically active and not to exclude the possibility of a settlement—albeit temporary—through nonviolent means. Consequently, Hamas's political imagination and its organizational energies have generally been directed toward striking a balance among constantly growing conflicting considerations, competing demands, and contradictory needs.

Taking into account Hamas's fears that a strategy of clear-cut decisions would lead to a point of no return, as well as its structural need to search for a policy that balances national and local interests and maintains an equilibrium among multiple normative commitments, we cannot exclude the possibility that a continuation of the Israeli-Palestinian peace negotiations and of the coexistence of Hamas and the PA may encourage the organization to search for a political understanding with Israel. Probably Hamas's ability to justify such a move in the eyes of the radicals and gain the rank and file's support as well, would depend largely on its leaders' ability to adopt a strategy of political ambiguity. In such a strategy Hamas would rely on a third party—the PA and/or Jordan—to negotiate the political understanding and a workable coexistence with Israel.

The use of politically ambiguous strategies to address otherwise irreconcilable issues includes the following problems:

> Participants do not know exactly where they stand. It is not clear
> what they or their antagonists may do. There are no fixed boundaries
> or guidelines to behaviour that can be described as legitimate,
> reasonable, or acceptable. At the very least, ambiguity produces the
> stress of not knowing one's own limits or those of one's adversaries.

Moreover, the Israeli-Palestinian history of violence renders a situation of ambiguous guidelines doubly problematic. "If good fences make good neighbours, a situation of undefined boundaries between hostile communities raises the possibility of bloodshed."[30]

Hamas has no guarantee that relying on politically ambiguous strategies and on the services of a third party would preclude such problems. Hamas might have to pay a heavy price for the assistance of the Palestinian Authority (PA) or Jordan. In return for their services, they might try to restrict Hamas's freedom of action or, if Hamas were to act against their will, refuse to help. Hamas also cannot rule out the possibility that the PA or Amman would hold talks with Israel behind its back to reach agreement on disposing of Hamas if its social status and political influence were deemed to have become too powerful.

Nevertheless, a political understanding with Israel, achieved through a third party, remains Hamas's lesser-evil alternative, so to speak. Certainly, such a course would minimize the intensity of the shock to its supporters if it entered into a public dialogue with Israel. A slower pace would mean better management of events and allow for modifications as needed. Hamas would also have an opportunity to take safety measures and plan its responses in advance.

In the dusty reality of the Middle East, politically ambiguous strategies and reliance on a third party to enhance the possibility of an understanding and a workable coexistence between the Palestinian Hamas and the Jewish-Israeli state seem unattainable. Yet looking at the dramatic shift in Israeli-Egyptian relations in the late 1970s and at the developments in the Israeli-PLO conflict during the early 1990s, we cannot escape the conclusion that what once seemed improbable might become inevitable. Often, people, movements, and nations terrorize the entire world just to become part of it.

Hamas's Internal Structure[1]

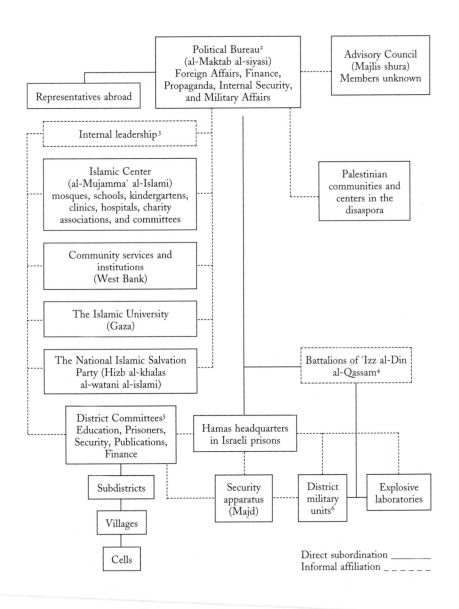

Political Bureau[2]
(al-Maktab al-siyasi)
Foreign Affairs, Finance,
Propaganda, Internal Security,
and Military Affairs

Advisory Council
(Majlis shura)
Members unknown

Representatives abroad

Internal leadership[3]

Islamic Center
(al-Mujamma' al-Islami)
mosques, schools, kindergartens,
clinics, hospitals, charity
associations, and committees

Palestinian
communities and
centers in the
disaspora

Community services and
institutions
(West Bank)

The Islamic University
(Gaza)

The National Islamic Salvation
Party (Hizb al-khalas
al-watani al-islami)

Battalions of 'Izz al-Din
al-Qassam[4]

District Committees[5]
Education, Prisoners,
Security, Publications,
Finance

Hamas headquarters
in Israeli prisons

Subdistricts

Security
apparatus
(Majd)

District
military
units[6]

Explosive
laboratories

Villages

Cells

Direct subordination _____
Informal affiliation _ _ _ _ _ _

The Charter of the Islamic Resistance Movement (Hamas)

In the Name of Allah, the Merciful, the Compassionate.[1]

Ye are the best nation that hath been raised up unto mankind: ye command that which is just, and ye forbid that which is unjust, and ye believe in Allah. And if they who have received the scriptures had believed, it had surely been the better for them: there are believers among them, but the greater part of them are transgressors. They shall not hurt you, unless with a slight hurt; and if they fight against you, they shall turn their backs to you, and they shall not be helped. They are smitten with vileness wheresoever they are found; unless they obtain security by entering into a treaty with Allah, and a treaty with men; and they draw on themselves indignation from Allah, and they are afflicted with poverty. This they suffer, because they disbelieved the signs of Allah, and slew the prophets unjustly; this, because they were rebellious, and transgressed. (SURA 3, AL 'IMRAN, vv. 109–111)

Israel will be established and will stay established until Islam nullifies it as it nullified what was before it. (The martyred Imam Hasan al-Banna, may Allah have mercy on him)

Indeed, the Islamic world is burning, therefore it is obligatory on every one to put a little of it out so he can extinguish what he is able to do without waiting for anyone else. (Sheikh Amjad al-Zahawee, may Allah have mercy on him)

Introduction

In the name of Allah, the Merciful, the Compassionate, all praise is to Allah. We seek his aid, forgiveness, and guidance, and on him do we rely. We send peace and blessings to Allah's messenger—his family, companions, those who follow him, called with his message, and adhered to his way—may the blessing and peace be continued for as long as the heavens and earth last. And after.

O People:

From the midst of troubles, from the sea of suffering, from the beats of believing hearts and emasculated arms, out of the sense of duty, and in response to the decree of Allah, the call has gone out rallying people together and making them follow the ways of Allah so that they will fulfill their role in life, overcome all obstacles, and surmount the difficulties on the way. Our preparation has been constant and so has our readiness to sacrifice life and all that is precious, for the sake of Allah.

Thus it was that the seed [of the movement] was formed and began to travel through this tempestuous sea of hopes and expectations, wishes and yearnings, troubles and obstacles, pain and challenges, both inside and outside.

When the idea matured, the seed grew, and the plant rooted in the soil of reality, away from passing emotions and hateful haste, and the Islamic Resistance Movement emerged to carry out its role, struggling (mujahida) for the sake of its Lord. The movement joined hands with all the warriors (mujahidin) who are striving to liberate Palestine. The souls of its fighters joined all the souls of the fighters who have sacrificed their lives on the soil of Palestine ever since it was conquered by the companions of the Messenger of Allah—may Allah's prayers and peace be with him—until this very day.

This covenant of the Islamic Resistance Movement (HAMAS)[2] has taken shape, unveiling its identity, stating its position, clarifying its expectations, discussing its hopes, and calling for aid, support, and additions to its ranks. Our battle with the Jews is very long and dangerous, requiring the dedication of all of us. It is a phase that must be followed by succeeding phases, a battalion that must be supported by battalion after battalion of the divided Arab and Islamic world until the enemy is vanquished and the victory of Allah is sure.

Thus we shall see them approaching over the horizon.

And you shall learn about it hereafter. (Sura 38, al-Sadd, v. 88)

Allah hath written, Verily I will prevail, and my apostles: for Allah is strong and mighty. (Sura 58, al-Mujadila, v. 107)

Say to them, This is my way: I invite you unto Allah, by an evident demonstration: both I and he who followeth me; and, praise be unto Allah! I am not an idolator. (Sura 12, Yusuf, v. 107)

CHAPTER ONE

Introduction to the Movement

Ideological Origins

Article 1

The basis of the Islamic Resistance Movement is Islam. From Islam it derives its ideas and its fundamental precepts and view of life, the universe, and humanity; and it judges all its actions according to Islam and is inspired by Islam to correct its errors.

The Islamic Resistance Movement's Connection to the Society of the Muslim Brotherhood

Article 2

The Islamic Resistance Movement is one of the wings [chapters] of the Muslim Brotherhood in Palestine. The Muslim Brotherhood Movement is a world organization, one of the largest Islamic movements in the modern era. It is characterized by profound understanding, precise notions, and a total comprehension of all Islamic concepts in all domains of life: views and beliefs, politics and economics, education and society, jurisdiction and law, exhortation and teaching, communication and art, the seen and the unseen, and in all the other spheres of life.

Structure and Formation

Article 3

The Islamic Resistance Movement consists of Muslims who have devoted themselves to Allah and truly worshiped him—"I have created the jinn and humans only for the purpose of worshiping" [of Allah]—and who have known their obligation toward themselves, their people, and country. In all that, they have feared Allah and raised the banner of Jihad in the face of the oppressors, in order to extricate the country and the people from the [oppressor's] filth, impurity, and evil.

> But we will oppose truth to vanity, and it shall confound the same; and behold, it shall vanish away. (Sura 21, al-Anbiya', v. 18)

Article 4
The Islamic Resistance Movement welcomes all Muslims who adopt its belief and ideology, enact its program, keep its secrets, and desire to join its ranks in order to perform its obligations. Allah will reward them.

The Islamic Resistance Movement's Conceptions of Time and Space

Article 5
Because the Islamic Resistance Movement adopts Islam as it way of life, its historical conception extends back as far as the birth of the Islamic message, of the Righteous Ancestors (al-Salaf al-Salih). [Therefore], Allah is its goal, the Prophet is its model, and the Qur'an is its constitution. Its spatial conception extends wherever Muslims—who adopt Islam as their way of life—are found, in any place on the face of the earth. Thus, it reaches both the depths of the earth and the highest spheres of heavens.

> Dost thou not see how Allah putteth forth a parable; representing a good word, as a good tree, whose root is firmly fixed in the earth, and whose branches reach unto heaven; which bringeth forth its fruit in all seasons, by the will of its Lord? Allah propoundeth parables unto men, that they may be instructed. (Sura 14, Ibrahim, vv. 24–25)

Uniqueness and Independence

Article 6
The Islamic Resistance Movement is a unique Palestinian movement. It owes its loyalty to Allah, derives from Islam its way of life, and strives to raise the banner of Allah over every inch of Palestine. Under the shadow of Islam, it is possible for followers of all religions to coexist in safety and with security for their lives, property, and rights. In the absence of Islam, strife arises, oppression and destruction are rampant, and wars and battles take place.

How eloquent was the Muslim poet, Muhammad Iqkbal,[3] when he said

When faith is lost, there is no security
There is no life for those who have no faith
And whoever is satisfied with life without religion
Then he would have let annihilation be his companion for life.

The Universality of the Islamic Resistance Movement

Article 7
Because of the [wide] distribution of Muslims who have adopted the doctrine of the Islamic Resistance Movement throughout the world, working to support it, taking its positions, and reinforcing its Jihad, the movement is a universal one. It has wide appeal because of the clarity of its thought, the nobility of its goal, and the loftiness of its objectives.

It is on this basis that the movement should be viewed, given a fair evaluation and acknowledgment of its role. Whoever denies its rights or avoids supporting it or is so blind as to hide its role is challenging fate (qadr) itself. And whoever closes his eyes to reality, whether intentionally or not, will wake up to find himself overtaken by the events and will have no excuse to justify his position. The reward is for those who are early comers.

Oppression by one's next of kin is more painful to the soul than the assault of an Indian sword.

We have also sent down unto thee the book of the Koran with truth,
confirming that scripture which was revealed before it; and
preserving the same safe from corruption. Judge therefore between
them according to that which Allah hath revealed; and follow not
their desires, by swerving from the truth which hath come unto thee.
Unto every of you have we given a law, and an open path; and if
Allah had pleased, he had surely made you one people; but he hath
thought fit to give you different laws, that he might try you in that
which he hath given you respectively. Therefore strive to excel each
other in good works; unto Allah shall ye all return, and then will he
declare unto you that concerning which ye have disagreed. (Sura 5,
al-Ma'ida, v. 48)

The Islamic Resistance Movement is one of the links in the chain of Jihad in the confrontation with the Zionist invasion. It is connected to and tied with the setting out of the martyr 'Izz al-Din al-Qassam and his brethren the Mujahidin, of the Muslim Brothers, in 1936.[4] And [the chain] continues to connect to and tie with another link of Jihad of the Palestinians, the Jihad and efforts of the Muslim Brotherhood in the war of 1948,[5] and the Jihad operations of the Muslim Brotherhood in 1968 and after.

Even though the links have been far away from one another, and even though the obstacles, placed by those who revolve in the orbit of Zionism in the face of the Mujahidin, have rendered impossible the pursuit of Jihad; nevertheless, the Islamic Resistance Movement has been looking forward to fulfilling the promise of Allah, no matter how long that might take. The Prophet—Allah's prayers and peace be with him—stated:

> The Last Hour would not come until the Muslims fight against the Jews and the Muslims would kill them, and until the Jews would hide themselves behind a stone or a tree and a stone or a tree would say: Muslim or Servant of Allah[!] there is a Jew behind me; come and kill him; but the tree of Gharqad would not say it, for it is the tree of the Jews. (cited by al-Bukhari and Muslim)[6]

The Motto of the Islamic Resistance Movement

Article 8
Allah is its goal, the Prophet is its model, the Qur'an is its constitution, Jihad is its path, and death for the sake of Allah is its most coveted desire.

CHAPTER TWO

Objectives

Motives and Objectives

Article 9
The Islamic Resistance Movement has evolved at a time when Islam has moved away from everyday life. Thus judgment has been upset, concepts have become confused, and values have been transformed; evil prevails, oppression and obscurity have become rampant, and cowards have turned into tigers. Homelands have been usurped, and people have been expelled and fallen on their face [in humiliation] everywhere on earth. The state of truth has disappeared and been replaced by the state of evil. Nothing has remained in its right place, for when Islam is absent from the scene, everything changes. These are the motives.

As for the objectives: fighting evil, crushing it, and vanquishing it so that truth may prevail; homelands will revert [to their rightful owners]; and calls for prayer will be heard from their mosques, proclaiming the institution of the Islamic state. Thus, people and things will return, each to their right place. And aid is sought from Allah.

And if Allah had not prevented men, the one by the other, verily the earth had not been corrupted: but Allah is beneficent towards his creatures. (Sura 2, al-Baqara, v. 251)

Article 10
While the Islamic Resistance Movement is creating its own path, it provides a support for the deprived and a defense for all the oppressed, with all its might. It will spare no effort to establish the truth and defeat falsehood, by words and deeds, here and everywhere it can reach and have influence.

CHAPTER THREE
Strategies and Means

Strategies of the Islamic Resistance Movement: Palestine Is an Islamic Endowment (waqf)

Article 11
The Islamic Resistance Movement believes that the land of Palestine is an Islamic Waqf [endowed] to all Muslim generations until the day of resurrection. It is not right to give up it or any part of it. Neither a single Arab state nor all the Arab states, neither a king nor a president, not all the kings or presidents, not any organization or all of them—be they Palestinian or Arab—have such authority, because the land of Palestine is an Islamic Waqf [endowed] to all Muslim generations until the day of resurrection. [So] who has the legitimate right to represent all Islamic generations until the day of resurrection?

This is the rule [of the land] in the Islamic Shari'a, and the same [rule] applies to any land that the Muslims have conquered by force, because at the time of conquest the Muslims consecrated it for all Muslim generations until the day of resurrection.

And so it was that when the leaders of the Muslim armies conquered Syria and Iraq, they sent for the caliph of the Muslims, 'Umar Ibn al-

Khattab, asking for his advice concerning the conquered lands: should they divide it among the troops or leave it for its owners or what? After consultations and discussions between the caliph of the Muslims, 'Umar Ibn al-Khattab, and the companions of the Messenger of Allah—may Allah's prayers and peace be with him—they decided that the land should remain in the hands of its owners to benefit from it and from its wealth. As for the guardianship of the land and the land itself, it should be considered as a Waqf [endowed] to Muslim generations until the day of resurrection. The ownership of the land by its owners [applies] only to its benefit, and this Waqf will endure as long as heaven and earth last. Any action taken in regard to Palestine in violation of this law of Islam, is null and void and will be taken back by its claimants.

> Verily this is a certain truth. Wherefore praise the name of thy Lord, the great Allah. (Sura 56, al-Waqi'a, v. 95)

The Islamic Resistance Movement's View of Homeland (watan) and Nationalism (wataniyya)

Article 12

According to the Islamic Resistance Movement, nationalism is part and parcel of its religious creed. Nothing is loftier or deeper in nationalism than [waging] a holy war (jihad) against the enemy and confronting him when he sets foot on the land of the Muslims. This becomes an individual obligation (fard 'ayn) of every Muslim man and woman: the woman is allowed to fight the enemy [even] without her husband's permission, and the slave without his master's permission.

Nothing of the sort is to be found in any other system; this is an undoubted fact. Whereas other nationalisms consist of material, human, or territorial considerations, the Islamic Resistance Movement's nationalism carries all of that plus all the more important divine factors, providing it with spirit and life, since it is connected with the origin of the spirit and life-giver, raising in the sky of the homeland the divine banner to connect earth to heaven with a strong bond. When Moses comes and throws his staff, indeed the magic and magician are nullified.

> Now is the right direction manifestly distinguished from deceit: whoever therefore shall deny Tagut, and believe in Allah, he shall surely take hold on a strong handle, which shall not be broken; Allah is he who heareth and seeth. (Sura 2, al-Baqara, v. 256)

Peaceful Solutions, [Peace] Initiatives, and International Conferences

Article 13

[Peace] initiatives, the so-called peaceful solutions, and international conferences to resolve the Palestinian problem all contradict the beliefs of the Islamic Resistance Movement. Indeed, giving up any part of Palestine is tantamount to giving up part of its religion. The nationalism of the Islamic Resistance Movement is part of its religion, and it instructs its members to [adhere] to that and to raise the banner of Allah over their homeland as they wage their Jihad.

> . . . for Allah is well able to effect his purpose; but the greater part of men do not understand. (Sura 12, Yusuf, v. 21)

From time to time, a call goes out to hold an international conference to search for a solution to the [Palestinian] problem. Some accept the idea, and others reject it for one reason or another, demanding the fulfillment of a condition or conditions [as a prerequisite] for agreeing to convene the conference and to participate in it. [But] the Islamic Resistance Movement—knowing the parties comprising the conference and their past and present attitudes toward the problems of the Muslims—does not believe that the conferences are capable of fulfilling the demands or restoring the rights of or doing justice to the oppressed. Those conferences are nothing but a means of enforcing the rule of the unbelievers in the land of the Muslims. And when did the unbelievers do justice to the believers?

> But the Jews will not be pleased with thee, neither the Christians, until thou follow their religion; say, The direction of Allah is the true direction. And verily if thou follow their desires, after the knowledge which hath been given thee, thou shalt find no patron or protector against Allah. (Sura 2, al-Baqara, v. 120)

There is no solution to the Palestinian problem except by Jihad. The initiative, proposals, and international conferences are but a waste of time and sheer futility. The Palestinian people are too noble to have their future, rights, and destiny [subjected to] vanity. As the noble hadith states:

> The people of Syria (Sham) are Allah's whip on his earth. With them He takes revenge on whom He pleases of his worshipers. It is

forbidden on their hypocrites to be ruling over their believers and they will die in anxiety and sorrow. (Told by al-Tabarani as traceable in the ascending order of tellers to the Prophet[7] and by Ahmad whose chain of transmission is incomplete.[8] But it is bound to be [a] true [hadith] for their stories are reliable, and Allah knows best.

The Three Circles

Article 14

The liberation of Palestine is bound to three circles: the Palestinian circle, the Arab circle, and the Islamic circle. Each one has a role to play in the struggle against Zionism and has duties to fulfill. It is a grave mistake and a horrendous [act of] ignorance to ignore any of these circles, for Palestine is an Islamic land where the first of the two Qiblas[9] and the third holiest sanctuaries[10] are located, as well as the [place] where the Prophet—may Allah's prayers and peace be with him—ascended to heavens.

> Praise be unto him who transported his servant by night, from the sacred temple [of Mecca] to the farther temple [of Jerusalem], the circuit of which we have blessed, that we might show him some of our signs; for Allah is he who heareth, and seeth [all things]. (Sura 17, al-Isra', v. 1)

In view of this state of affairs, the liberation [of Palestine] is an individual duty, binding on every Muslim wherever he may be. It is on this basis that the problem [of Palestine] should be viewed and every Muslim must know it.

When the problem is dealt with on this basis, when the full potential of the three circles is mobilized, then the current circumstances will change, and the day of liberation will be nearer.

> Verily ye are stronger than they, by reason of the terror cast into their breasts from Allah. This, because they are not people of prudence. (Sura 59, Hashr, v. 13)

The Jihad for the Liberation of Palestine Is an Individual Obligation

Article 15

Once the enemies usurp some of the Muslim lands, Jihad becomes an individual obligation for every Muslim. In the confrontation with the usurpation of Palestine by the Jews, we must raise the banner of Jihad. This requires the propagation of Islamic consciousness among the people, on the local, Arab, and Islamic levels. It is necessary to spread the spirit of Jihad among the Umma,[11] clash with the enemies, and join the ranks of the [Jihad] fighters.

The process of education must involve the 'Ulama' as well as educators and teachers, and publicity and media men as well as the educated people and especially the youth of the Islamic movements and their scholars. Introducing fundamental changes into the educational curricula is necessary to cleanse them of the traces of the ideological invasion by orientalists and missionaries. Their invasion began overtaking the [Arab] region after the defeat of the Crusader armies by Salah al-Din al-Ayyubi [Saladin]. The Crusaders realized that it was impossible to defeat the Muslims unless they prepared for an ideological invasion that would confuse their [the Muslims'] thinking, stain their heritage, and discredit their ideals, after which a military invasion would take place. This was to pave the way for the imperialistic invasion, as in fact [General] Allenby[12] declared upon entering Jerusalem: "Now the Crusades are over." And [General] Gouraud[13] stood at Salah al-Din's grave, saying: "Here we have returned, O Salah al-Din." Imperialism helped advance the ideological invasion and deepened its roots, and it continues to do so. All this led to the loss of Palestine.

We must instill in the minds of the generations of Muslims that the Palestinian cause is a religious one and should be dealt with on this basis. It [Palestine] includes Islamic shrines such as the al-Aqsa Mosque, which is linked to the Holy Mosque in Mecca in an inseparable bond as long as heaven and earth last, by the journey (isra') of the Messenger of Allah— may Allah's prayers and peace be with him—to it, and his ascension (mi'raj) from it.[14]

> To guard Muslims from infidels in Allah's cause for one day is better
> than the world and whatever is on its surface, and a place in paradise
> as small as that occupied by the whip of one of you is better than
> the world and what ever is on its surface; and a morning's or an
> evening's journey which the worshiper [person] in Allah's cause is
> better than the world and what is on its surface (told by al-Bukhari,
> Muslim, al-Tirmidhi, and Ibn Maja).[15]

> By him in whose hand is Muhammad's life, I love to be killed in the
> way of Allah then to be revived to life again, then to be killed and
> then to be revived to life and then to be killed (told by al-Bukhari
> and Muslim).[16]

Education of the [Young] Generations

Article 16

We must give the [young] Islamic generations in our area an Islamic education based on the implementation of [our] religious precepts, a conscientious study of the Book of Allah, the study of the Prophetic narration (sunna),[17] and the study of Islamic history and heritage from its reliable sources, under the guidance of experts and [Muslim] scholars and using a curriculum that will give Muslims the correct concept of thinking and faith. It is also necessary to study conscientiously the enemy and its material and human potential, to identify its weaknesses and strengths, and to recognize the powers that support it and stand by it. It is necessary too to be aware of current events, to follow the news and study analyses of and commentaries on it, as well as plan for the present and the future and examine every [new] phenomenon, so that the fighting (mujahid) Muslim will live his life aware of his purpose, objective, way, and what happens around him.

> O my son, verily every matter, whether good or bad, though it be of the weight of a grain of mustard-seed, and be hidden in a rock, or in the heavens, or in the earth, Allah will bring the same to light; for Allah is clear-sighted and knowing. O my son, be constant at prayer, and command that which is just, and forbid that which is evil: and be patient under the afflictions which shall befall thee; for this is a duty absolutely incumbent on all men. Distort not thy face out of contempt to men, neither walk in the earth with insolence; for Allah loveth no arrogant, vain-glorious person. (Sura 31, Luqman, vv. 16–18)

The Role of the Muslim Woman

Article 17

The Muslim woman has a no lesser role than that of the Muslim man in the war of liberation; she is the manufacturer of men and plays a major role in guiding and educating the [new] generations. The enemies have realized her role, hence they think that if they can guide her and educate her in the way they wish, away from Islam, they will have won the war. Therefore, you can see them attempting to do this through the mass media and movies, education and culture and using as their intermediaries their craftsmen, who are part of Zionist organizations that assume various names and shapes, such as the [Free] Masons, Rotary Clubs, and espionage gangs, all of which are nests of saboteurs and sabotage. These Zionist organizations have vast material resources, which enable them to play their role amidst societies in an attempt to implement their Zionist goals and to introduce concepts that serve the enemy. These organizations operate [in places] where Islam is absent and is alienated from its people. Thus, Islamists should fulfill their role in confronting the schemes of these saboteurs. When Islam can control the life [of Muslims], it will eliminate those organizations, which are hostile to humanity and Islam.

Article 18
The woman in the fighting (mujahid) house and family, whether she is a mother or a sister, has the most important role in taking care of the home and raising the children according to Islamic concepts and values and educating her sons to observe the religious precepts in preparation for the duty of Jihad awaiting them. Therefore, it is necessary to pay attention to the schools and curricula for Muslim girls so that they will become righteous mothers, [who are] aware of their role in the war of liberation.

[Women] must have the necessary awareness and understanding to manage their household. Economy and avoidance of waste in the household expenditures are prerequisites to [our] ability to continue the struggle in the arduous circumstances surrounding [us]. [Women] should always remember that money is equivalent to blood, which must not flow except in the veins, to ensure the continuity of life of both the young and the old.

> Verily the Muslims of either sex, and the true believers of either
> sex, and the devout men, and the devout women, and the men of
> veracity, and the women of veracity, and the patient men, and the
> patient women, and the humble men, and the humble women, and
> the alms-givers of either sex who remember Allah frequently; for
> them hath Allah prepared forgiveness and a great reward. (Sura 33,
> al-Ahzab, v. 25)

The Role of Islamic Art in the War of Liberation

Article 19
Art has rules and criteria by which one can determine whether it is Islamic or Jahili[18] art. One of the problems of Islamic liberation is that it needs Islamic art that can lift the spirit and does not emphasize one human aspect over the other but, rather, raises all aspects equally and harmoniously.

Man is a strange and miraculous being, [made up] of a handful of clay and a breath of soul. Islamic art addresses man on this basis, whereas Jahili art addresses the body and makes the element of clay paramount.

Hence, those books, articles, bulletins, orations, pamphlets, songs, poetry, hymns, plays, and the like that contain the characteristics of Islamic art are necessary for ideological mobilization, continuous nurturing on the journey, and relaxation of the soul. The road is long and the suffering is great, and the soul will be bored; [but] Islamic art renews the vigor, revives the movement, and arouses lofty concepts and correct conduct. "Nothing corrects the soul if it is deliberating but change from one situation to another."

All this is a serious matter, not a jest, for the Umma fighting its Jihad knows no jest.

Social Solidarity

Article 20

The Muslim society is a society of solidarity. The Messenger—may Allah's prayers and peace be with him—said, "How wonderful people are the Ash'aris. When they were under stress, either [while being] in residence or in travel, they would gather all their possessions and divide it up equally among themselves."

It is this Islamic spirit that should prevail in every Muslim society. A society that confronts a vicious Nazi enemy in its conduct, who does not differentiate between man and woman, elder and young, ought to be the first to adorn itself with this Islamic spirit. Our enemy pursues the method of collective punishment, robbing people of their land and property, and chasing them into their [places in] exile and gathering. It resorted to breaking bones, firing on women, children, and old people, with or without reason, and to throwing thousands and thousands of people into detention camps where they must live in inhuman conditions. This is in addition to destroying homes, making children orphans, and imposing unjust sentences on thousands of young people, who must spend the best years of their life in the darkness of prisons.

The Nazism of the Jews includes [even] women and children; it terrorizes everyone. These Jews ruin people's livelihoods, steal their money, and threaten their honor. In their horrible actions they treat people like the worst war criminals. Deportation from one's homeland is a form of murder.

To oppose such actions, the people must band together in social solidarity and confront the enemy as one body, so that if one of its organs is hurt, the rest of the body will respond with alertness and fervor.

Article 21

Social solidarity means giving aid to the needy, both material or moral, or helping take certain actions. It is incumbent on the members of the Islamic Resistance Movement to look after the interests of the people in the [same] way they look after their own interests, sparing no effort in realizing and maintaining them. They should avoid doing anything that might damage the future or the society of the [younger] generations. The people are part of the movement and for the movement; its power is the [movement members'] power; and its future is their future. The members of the Islamic Resistance Movement should share the people's joys and grief and comply with the demands of the people and anything likely to satisfy both its interests and theirs. With this spirit, [the movement and the people] will become more congenial, cooperation and compassion will prevail, they will become unified, and they will be stronger in the face of their enemy.

The Powers That Support the Enemy

Article 22

The enemy has been planning for a long time in order to achieve what it has [effectively] achieved, taking into account the elements affecting the current of events. It has accumulated huge and influential material wealth, which it devotes to realizing its dream. With this money, it has taken control of the world's media, such as news agencies, the press, publishing houses, and broadcasting. With this money, it has ignited revolutions in various parts of the world with the purpose of fulfilling its interests and benefiting from them. It [the enemy] stood behind the French Revolution, the Communist revolution, and most of the revolutions we have heard and hear about, here and there. It is with this money that it has formed secret organizations throughout the world, in order to destroy societies and achieve the Zionists' interests. Such organizations are the [Free] Masons, Rotary Clubs, Lions Clubs, B'nai B'rith, and others. They all are destructive spying organizations. With this money, it [the enemy] has taken control of the imperialist states and persuaded them to colonize many countries in order to exploit their resources and spread their corruption there.

In regard to local and world wars, it has become common knowledge that [the enemy] was [the trigger] behind the [outbreak of] World War I, in which it realized the abolition of the state of the Islamic Caliphate.[19] The enemy profited financially and took control of many sources of wealth, obtained the Balfour Declaration, and established the League of Nations in order to rule the world through that means. The enemy was also [the trigger] behind the [outbreak of] World War II, in which it made huge profits from trading war matériel and prepared for establishing its state. It inspired the formation of the United Nations and the Security Council instead of the League of Nations, in order to rule the world through them. No war broke out anywhere without its fingerprints on it.

> So often as they shall kindle a fire for war, Allah shall extinguish it; and they shall set their minds to act corruptly in the earth, but Allah loveth not the corrupt doers. (Sura 5, al-Ma'ida, v. 64)

The imperialistic powers in both the capitalist West and the communist East support the enemy with all their might, in material and human terms, alternating their roles. When Islam is on the rise, the forces of unbelief unite to confront it, because the nation of the unbelievers is one.

> O true believers, contract not an intimate friendship with any besides yourselves: they will not fail to corrupt you. They wish for that which may cause you to perish: their hatred hath already appeared from out of their mouths; but what their breasts conceal is yet more inveterate. We have already shown you signs of their ill will towards you, if ye understand. (Sura 3, Al 'Imran, v. 118)

It is not in vain that the [preceding] verse ends with Allah's words "if ye understand."

CHAPTER FOUR

Our Position on [the Following]:

A. The Islamic Movements

Article 23
The Islamic Resistance Movement views the other Islamic movements with respect and appreciation. Even when it disagrees with them on a particular aspect or viewpoint, it agrees with them on other aspects and viewpoints. It considers these movements to be included in the category of Ijtihad[20] as long as they have good intentions and devotion to Allah and as long as their conduct remains within the confines of the Islamic circle. Every Mujtahid has his reward.

The Islamic Resistance Movement considers all these movements as its own and asks Allah for guidance and righteous conduct for all. It shall not fail to continue raising the banner of unity, striving to realize it [based] on the Book and the Prophet's tradition.[21]

> And cleave all of you unto the covenant of Allah, and depart not
> from it, and remember the favour of Allah towards you: since ye
> were enemies, and he reconciled your hearts, and ye became
> companions and brethren by his favour: and ye were on the brink of
> a pit of fire, and he delivered you thence. Allah declareth unto you
> his signs, that ye may be directed. (Sura 3, Al 'Imran, v. 102)

Article 24

The Islamic Resistance Movement does not allow the slandering or condemnation of individuals or groups, because a believer is not a slanderer or profaner. It is necessary, however, to differentiate between that and the positions and modes of conduct of individuals and groups. Thus, when a position or conduct is incorrect, the Islamic Resistance Movement has the right to point to the mistake, to warn against it, to insist on spelling out the truth and applying it to the given issue with impartiality. Wisdom is the object of the believer, and he ought to grasp it wherever he finds it.

> Allah loveth not the speaking ill of anyone in public, unless he who
> is injured call for assistance; and Allah heareth and knoweth:
> whether ye publish a good action, or conceal it, or forgive evil, verily
> Allah is gracious and powerful. (Sura 4, al-Nisa', vv. 147–148)

B. Nationalist Movements in the Palestinian Arena

Article 25

[Hamas] respects them [nationalist movements] and appreciates their conditions and the factors surrounding and affecting them. It supports them as long as they do not give their allegiance to the Communist East or the Crusader West. It reassures all those who have joined them or sympathize with them that the Islamic Resistance Movement is a moral Jihad movement, aware of its view of life and its actions toward others. It abhors opportunism and only has good wishes for people, individuals and groups alike. It does not seek material gain or personal fame, nor does it ask for rewards from the people. It relies on its own resources and what is available to it, [as it is said]:

> Therefore prepare against them what force ye are able . . . (Sura 8,
> al-Anfal, v. 60)

[All that] is for carrying out its duty and winning Allah's favor. It has no ambition other than that.

All nationalist currents operating in the Palestinian arena for the liberation of Palestine may rest assured that [Hamas] is definitely and irrevocably [a source] of support and assistance to them, in both speech and action, at the present and in the future. [It is there to] unite, not to divide; to safeguard, not to squander; to bring together, not to fragment. It values every kind word, [every] devoted effort and commendable endeavor. It closes the door before marginal disagreements and does not listen to rumors and slanders, but at the same time it recognizes the right of self-defense.

Anything that runs contrary to or contradicts these orientations has been fabricated by the enemy or those who support it, with the purpose of sowing confusion, dividing the ranks, and entangling [us] in marginal issues.

> O true believers, if a wicked man come unto you with a tale, inquire
> strictly into the truth thereof; lest ye hurt people through ignorance,
> and afterwards repent of what ye have done. (Sura 49, al-Hujurat, v. 6)

Article 26
Although the Islamic Resistance Movement views favorably those Palestinian nationalist movements that are not loyal to the East or West, it will not refrain from debating events, both local and international, regarding the Palestinian problem. [Such] an objective debate exposes the extent to which such events coincide with, or contradict, the national interest according to the Islamic viewpoint.

C. The Palestine Liberation Organization

Article 27
The Palestine Liberation Organization [PLO] is the movement closest to the Islamic Resistance Movement in that it consists of fathers, brothers, relatives, and friends. Can a Muslim turn away from his father, his brother, his relative, or his friend? Our homeland is one, our plight is one, our destiny is one, and our enemy is common to all of us.

Due to the circumstances that surrounded the formation of the organization [the PLO] and the ideological confusion that prevails in the Arab world as a result of the ideological invasion which has befallen the Arab world since the defeat of the Crusades and that has been intensified by orientalism, the [Christian] mission and imperialism, the organization has adopted the idea of a secular state, and this is how we view it. [But] secular thought[22] is entirely contradictory to religious thought. Thought is the basis for positions, modes of conduct, and decision making.

Therefore, despite our respect for the Palestine Liberation Organization—and what it might become [in the future]—and without underestimating its role in the Arab-Israeli conflict, we cannot use secular thought for the current and future Islamic nature of Palestine. The Islamic nature of Palestine is part of our religion, and everyone who neglects his religion is bound to lose.

> Who will be averse to the religion of Abraham, but he whose mind
> is infatuated? (Sura 2, al-Baqara, v. 130)

When the Palestine Liberation Organization has adopted Islam as its system of life, we will become its soldiers and the fuel of its fires that will burn the enemies. Until this happens—and we pray to Allah that it will be soon—the position of the Islamic Resistance Movement toward the Palestine Liberation Organization is that of a son toward his father, a brother toward his brother, and a relative toward his relative who suffers the other's pain when a thorn hits him, who supports the other in his confrontation with the enemy and wishes him guidance and righteous conduct.

Your brother, your brother! He who has no brother is like one going to battle without a weapon. A cousin for man is like the best wings, and does the falcon take off without wings?

D. The Arab and Islamic States and Governments

Article 28

The Zionist invasion is a vicious one. It does not hesitate to take any road and resort to all despicable and repulsive means to fulfill its desires. In its infiltration and spying activities, it relies to a great extent on the clandestine organizations that it has established, such as the [Free] Masons, the Rotary Club and the Lions Club, and other spying groups. All those organizations, whether secret or open, operate in the interest of Zionism and under its direction. They aim to demolish societies, to destroy values, to violate consciences, to defeat virtues, and to annihilate Islam. It supports the drug and alcohol trade of all kinds in order to facilitate its control and expansion.

The Arab countries surrounding Israel are required to open their borders to the Mujahidin, the sons of the Arab and Islamic peoples, to enable them to fulfill their role and join their efforts with those of their brethren, of the Muslim brothers in Palestine.

The other Arab and Islamic states are required, at the very least, to help the Mujahidin move from and to them.

We must not fail to remind every Muslim that when the Jews conquered Noble Jerusalem in 1967, they stood on the doorstep of the blessed al-Aqsa Mosque and shouted with joy: "Muhammad has died, and left girls behind."

Israel, by virtue of its being Jewish, and its Jews challenge Islam and the Muslims.

"So the eyes of the cowards do not sleep."

E. Nationalist and Religious Associations, Institutions, Intellectuals, and the Arab and Islamic World

Article 29

The Islamic Resistance Movement hopes that the [nationalist and religious] associations will stand by it on all levels, support it, adopt its positions, promote its activities and actions, and solicit support for it, thereby making the Islamic peoples its backers and helpers, and enable it to enter all human and material domains as well as the media, in time and space. [This can be fulfilled] by convening solidarity conferences and issuing clarifying bulletins, supportive articles, and inspirational booklets to make the masses aware of the Palestinian problem, what it faces and what is being plotted against it. [They should] also mobilize the Islamic peoples, ideologically, educationally, and culturally, so that they can fulfill their role in the decisive war of liberation, [just] as they played their role in defeating the Crusades, routing the Tartars, and saving human civilization. And that is not difficult for Allah.

Allah hath written, Verily I will prevail, and my apostles: for Allah is strong and mighty. (Sura 58, al-Mujadila, v. 21)

Article 30

Writers, intellectuals, media people, preachers, teachers and educators, and all the various sectors in the Arab and Islamic world—all are called on to fulfill their role and to carry out their duty in view of the ferocity of the Zionist invasion, its infiltration into many countries, and its control of material and media means, with all the consequences thereof in most countries of the world.

Jihad is not confined to carrying arms and clashing with the enemy. The good word, the excellent article, the useful book, support, and aid—all that, too, is Jihad for the sake of Allah, as long as the intentions are sincere to make Allah's banner paramount.

> Whoever provided equipment to a raider for the sake of Allah, is [considered as if he] raided himself. And whoever effectively reared [such] a raider [by remaining with the] family, in fact raided himself. (Told by al-Bukhari, Muslim, Abu-Dawud, and Al-Tirmidhi)

F. The Members of Other Religions: The Islamic Resistance Movement Is a Humanistic Movement

Article 31
The Islamic Resistance Movement is a humanistic movement. It cares about human rights and is committed to Islam's tolerance of the followers of other religions. It is hostile only to those who are hostile toward it or stand in its way so as to impede its moves or frustrate its efforts.

In the shadow of Islam, it is possible for the followers of the three religions—Islam, Christianity, and Judaism—to coexist in safety and security. Safety and security are possible only in the shadow of Islam, and recent and ancient history is the best witness to that effect.

The followers of other religions must stop struggling with Islam over the domination of this region. Because if they were to dominate, there would be nothing but fighting, torture, and displacement; they would be disgusted with one another, to say nothing of the followers of other religions. The past and the present are full of evidence to that effect.

> They will not fight against you in a body, except in fenced towns, or from behind walls. Their strength in war among themselves is great: thou thinkest them to be united; but their hearts are divided. This, because they are people who do not understand. (Sura 59, al-Hashr, v. 14)

Islam confers on everyone their rights and prevents aggression against the rights of others. The Nazi Zionist practices against our people will not last the lifetime of their invasion. "For the state of oppression [lasts] only one hour, [whereas] the state of justice [lasts] until the hour [of resurrection]."

> As to those who have not borne arms against you on account of religion, nor turned you out of your dwellings, Allah forbiddeth you

not to deal kindly with them, and to behave justly towards them; for Allah loveth those who act justly. (Sura 60, al-Mumtahina, v. 8)

The Attempt to Isolate the Palestinian People

Article 32

World Zionism and the imperialist forces have been attempting, by means of shrewd moves and careful planning, to remove the Arab states, one after the other, from the circle of conflict with Zionism, ultimately in order to have to deal with only the Palestinian people. Egypt has already been removed from the circle of the conflict, to a great extent through the treacherous Camp David accords, and it has been trying to drag other Arab states into similar agreements in order to remove them from the circle of the conflict.

The Islamic Resistance Movement calls on the Arab and Islamic peoples to make a serious and tireless effort to prevent the implementation of that horrible plan and to make the masses aware of the danger of retreating from the circle of conflict with Zionism. Today it is Palestine, and tomorrow it will be another country or other countries. For the Zionist scheme has no limits, and after Palestine it will strive to expand from the Nile to the Euphrates. When it has digested the region it has consumed, it will look to further expansion, and so on. This plan is outlined in the "Protocols of the Elders of Zion," and [Zionism's] present [conduct] is the best witness to what is said there.

Leaving the circle of conflict with Zionism is high treason and [will result in] a curse on its perpetrator.

> For whoso shall turn his back unto them on that day, unless he turneth aside to fight, or retreateth to another party of the faithful, shall draw on himself the indignation of Allah, and his abode shall be hell; an ill journey shall it be thither. (Sura 8, al-Anfal, v. 16)

We must gather together all our forces and capabilities to confront this vicious, Nazi, Tartar invasion. Otherwise, we will lose our homelands, their inhabitants will lose their homes, corruption will spread throughout the earth, and all religious values will be destroyed. Let every person know that he is accountable to Allah.

> And whoever shall have wrought good of the weight of an ant, shall behold the same. And whoever shall have wrought evil of the weight of an ant, shall behold the same. (Sura 99, al-Zalzala, vv. 7–8)

Within the circle of the conflict with Zionism, the Islamic Resistance Movement considers itself the spearhead or avant-garde. It joins all those who are active in the Palestinian arena. What is left to be done is continued action by the Arab and Islamic peoples and Islamic organizations throughout the Arab and Muslim world, for they are [best] prepared for the forthcoming round [of fighting] with the Jews, the traders of wars.

> And we have put enmity and hatred between them, until the day of resurrection. So often as they shall kindle a fire of war, Allah shall extinguish it; and they shall set their minds to act corruptly in the earth, but Allah loveth not the corrupt doers. (Sura 5, al-Ma'ida, v. 64)

Article 33
The Islamic Resistance Movement starts out from these general concepts, which are consistent and in accordance with norms of the universe and flow in the stream of destiny in confronting and fighting the enemy in defense of the Muslim human being, the Islamic civilization, and the Islamic sanctuaries, foremost of which is the blessed Aqsa Mosque. [From this point of departure], it urges the Arab and Islamic peoples as well as their governments and their popular and official associations to fear Allah in their attitude toward and dealing with the Islamic Resistance Movement and to be, in accordance with Allah's will, its supporters and partisans, extending to it assistance and aid until the rule of Allah is secure. [Then] the ranks will follow one another, Jihad fighters will join other Jihad fighters, and the masses will come forward from everywhere in the Islamic world in response to the call of duty, repeating: Come to Jihad! This call will tear apart the clouds in the skies, reverberating until liberation is realized, the invaders are vanquished, and Allah's victory is assured.

> And Allah will certainly assist him who shall be on his side for Allah is strong and mighty. (Sura 22, al-Hajj, v. 40)

CHAPTER FIVE

The Testimony of History

Confronting Aggressors Throughout History

Article 34
Since the dawn of history, Palestine has been the navel of the earth, the center of the continents, and the object of greed for the greedy. The

Messenger—may Allah's prayers and peace be with him—points to that fact in his noble Hadith in which he called on his venerable companion Ma'adh bin Jabal, saying, "O Ma'adh, Allah is going to conquer Syria for you, when I am gone, from al-'Arish[23] to the Euphrates. Its men, women, and slaves will be frontier guards (murabitun) till the day of resurrection. Should any of you choose [to dwell] in one of the Syrian plains or Palestine,[24] will be in [constant] Jihad to the day of resurrection."

The greedy have coveted Palestine more than once, and they have raided it with armies to fulfill their aspirations. It was invaded by hoards of Crusaders carrying their faith and raising their cross. They were able to defeat the Muslims for a while, and for nearly two decades, the Muslims could not recover until they came under the shadow of their religious banner, unified their rule, glorified their Lord, and set out for Jihad under the leadership of Salah al-Din al-Ayyubi. Then came the obvious conquest, the Crusades were vanquished, and Palestine was liberated.

> Say unto those who believe not, Yet shall be overcome, and thrown together into hell; an unhappy couch shall it be. (Sura 3, Al 'Imran, v. 12)

This is the only way to liberation. There is no doubt about the testimony of history. It is one of the rules of the universe and one of the laws of existence. Only iron can break iron, only the true faith of Islam can defeat their falsified and corrupt belief. Faith can be fought only by faith. Ultimately, victory rests with the truth, for truth is certainly victorious.

> Our word hath formerly been given unto our servants the apostles; that they should certainly be assisted against the infidels, and that our armies should surely be the conquerors. (Sura 37, al-Saffat, vv. 171–172)

Article 35

The Islamic Resistance Movement views seriously the defeat of the Crusaders at the hand of Salah al-Din al-Ayyubi and the rescue of Palestine from them, as well as the defeat of the Tartars at 'Ain Jalut, breaking their backs at the hands of Qutuz and al-Dhahir Baybars and regaining the Arab world from the sweep of the Tartar, which destroyed all aspects of human civilization. [The movement] draws lessons and examples from all this. The current Zionist invasion was preceded by Crusader invasions from the West, and others, by Tartar invasions from the East. Just as the

Muslims faced those invasions and planned how to fight and defeat them, they [now] can confront the Zionist invasion and defeat it. This is not difficult for Allah if [our] intentions are pure, if our determination is sincere, if the Muslims draw useful lessons from past experience, if they get rid of the vestiges of the ideological invasion [of the West], and if they heed the experience of their predecessors.

Conclusion

The Islamic Resistance Movement Is Soldiers

Article 36
While it moves forward, the Islamic Resistance Movement repeatedly reminds all the sons of our people and the Arab and Islamic peoples that it does not seek fame for itself, material gain, or social status. [The movement] is not directed against anyone of our people to compete with him or to take his place. Nothing of the sort at all. It will never be against any son of Muslims or [against] non-Muslims who are peaceful toward it, here or elsewhere. It will support only those associations and organizations operating against the Zionist enemy and those in league with it.

The Islamic Resistance Movement accepts Islam as a way of life. It is its faith and its [normative] standard. Whoever takes Islam as a way of life, whether it is here or there, be it a group, an organization, a state, or any other body, the Islamic Resistance Movement is its soldiers, nothing less.

We ask Allah to guide us and to guide [others] through us and to decide between us and our people with truth.

O Lord, do thou judge between us and our nation with truth; for thou art the best judge. (Sura 7, al-A'raf, v. 89)

Our last prayer is praise to Allah, the Lord of the universe.

Notes to Introduction

1. Hamas, Mu'tamar 'Ulama' Filastin, "Fatwa al-Musharaka fi Mu'tamar Madrid wal-Sulh Ma'a Isra'il" [Council of Palestine Islamic Scholars, "Fatwa (learned opinion) on the participation in the Madrid conference and peace with Israel"], Jerusalem, November 1, 1991.

2. Ibid.; Hamas leaflet, "Bayan lil-Tarikh . . . La Limu'tamar Bay' Filastin wa-Bayt al-Maqdis" [Announcement to history . . . no to the conference of sale of Palestine and Jerusalem], September 23, 1991; Hamas charter, article 27.

3. *Islam, Democracy, the State and the West: A Round Table with Dr. Hasan Turabi*, May 19, 1992, World and Islam Studies Enterprise and University of South Florida, Committee for Middle Eastern Studies, pp. 17–18, 24–35.

4. Ira M. Lapidus, "Islam Political Movements: Patterns of Historical Change," in Edmund Burke and Ira M. Lapidus, eds., *Islam, Politics, and Social Movements* (Berkeley and Los Angeles: University of California Press, 1988), p. 5.

5. A conspicuous case is that of Sheikh 'Abdallah 'Azzam, who, by means of a learned Muslim verdict (*fatwa*), tried to validate the priority of holy war (*jihad*) in Afghanistan, volunteered, and was killed there (see chap. 2). For his biography, see *al-Sabil*, December 30, 1989, pp. 4–5.

6. On features of flexible conduct and strategies, see Daniel Druckman and Christopher Mitchell, "Flexibility in Negotiation and Mediation," *Annals* 542 (November 1995): 11.

7. In his extreme challenge to modern state sovereignty, Abu-l-A'la Mawdudi, a

Pakistani Islamic thinker, even coined the term "the sovereignty of God" (*hakimiyyat allah*). Yet Mawdudi also stated that "the power to rule over the earth has been promised to *the whole community of* believers. . . . Every believer is a Caliph of God in his individual capacity." See Abu-l-'Ala' Mawdudi, "Political Theory of Islam," in John Donohue and John I. Esposito, eds., *Islam in Transition* (New York: Oxford University Press, 1982), p. 258.

8. Ibid., p. 254; *Islam, Democracy, the State and the West*, p. 19.

9. *Islam, Democracy, the State and the West*, pp. 27–28; Michael Watts, "Islamic Modernities, Citizenship, Civil Society and Islamism in a Nigerian City," *Public Culture* 8 (1996): 251–289.

10. Yusuf al-Qaradawi, *al-Hall al-Islami Farida wa-Darura* [The Islamic solution, duty and necessity], 5th ed. (Cairo: Maktabat Wahaba, 1993), pp. 155–192; Fathi Yakan, *Nahwa Haraka Islamiyya 'Alamiyya Wahida* [Toward one global Islamic movement], 3d ed. (Beirut: Mu'assasat al-Risala, 1977), pp. 8–21.

11. An example is the Muslim Brotherhood in Egypt, which under the guidance of Hasan al-Banna adopted mainly a reformist approach but also prepared a violent option, by creating its own armed force. Martin Kramer, "Fundamentalist Islam at Large: The Drive for Power," *Middle East Quarterly* (June 1996): 39.

12. See for example, 'Abdallah al-'Akailah, "Tajribat al-haraka al-Islamiyya fi al-Urdun" [The experience of the Islamic movement in Jordan], in 'Azzam al-Tamimi, ed., *Musharakat al-Islamiyyin fi al-Sulta* [The Islamists' sharing in power] (London: Liberty for the Muslim World, 1994), pp. 101–112; *al-Hayat*, September 12, pp. 1, 6.

13. For the Egyptian case, see Sana Abed-Kotob, "The Accommodationists Speak: Goals and Strategies of the Muslim Brotherhood of Egypt," *International Journal of Middle East Studies* 27 (1995): 321–339.

14. See, for example, Hasan al-Turabi's interview in *Qira'at Siyasiyya* [Political readings], (Florida), no. 3, (Summer 1992), p. 20; interview with *Filastin al-Muslima* (November 1992): 34; Olivier Roy, *The Failure of Political Islam* (Cambridge, Mass.: Harvard University Press, 1994), pp. 47, 56–57.

15. *Islam, Democracy, The State and The West*, p. 18; Rashed al-Ghanouchi, *Mahawir Islamiyya* [Islamic pivots] (Cairo: Bait al-Ma'rifa, 1992), pp. 142–144; Yusuf al-Qaradawi, *Awlawiyyat al-Haraka al-Islamiyya fi al-Marhala al-Qadima* [Preferences of the Islamic movement in the coming phase] (Beirut: Mu'assassat al-Risala, 1991], pp. 16–17.

16. *al-Wasat*, November 7, 1994; *Filastin al-Muslima* (November 1992): 34.

17. Taha Nasr Mustafa, "al-Haraka al-Islamiyya al-Yamaniyya: 'Ishruna 'Aaman Min al-Musharaka al-Siyasiyya," in 'Azzam al-Tamimi, *Musharakat al-Islamiyyin fi al-Sulta*, pp. 140–171.

18. On the considerations and vacillations concerning this decision, see *Filastin al-Muslima* (August 1991): 21–23 and (June 1992): 15–17.

19. David Waldner, "Civic Exclusion and Its Discontents," paper presented at the annual meeting of the American Political Science Association, New York, September 1994, p. 1.

20. Dale F. Eickelman and James Piscatori, *Muslim Politics* (Princeton, N.J.: Princeton University Press, 1996), p. 20.

21. Ibid., p. 17; see also Dale F. Eickelman and James Piscatori, "Social Theory in the Study of Muslim Societies," in Dale F. Eickelman and James Piscatori, eds., *Muslim Travelers: Pilgrimage, Migration, and the Religious Imagination* (London: Routledge; and Berkeley and Los Angeles: University of California Press, 1990), pp. 1–25.

22. Steven C. Caton, "Power, Persuasion, and Language: A Critique of the Segmentary Model in the Middle East," *International Journal of Middle East Studies* 19, no. 1 (February 1987): 89.

23. F. G. Bailey, *Stratagems and Spoils: A Social Anthropology of Politics* (New York: Schocken Books, 1969), pp. 174–181.

24. Clifford Geertz, as cited in Avraham Diskin and Saul Mishal, "Coalition Formation in the Arab World: An Analytical Perspective," *International Interactions* 11, no. 1 (1984): 44.

Notes to Chapter One: Social Roots and Institutional Development

1. Eric Hobsbawm, *Nations and Nationalism Since 1780: Programme, Reality* (Cambridge: Cambridge University Press, 1990), pp. 67–73.

2. On the development of the PLO's program from its foundation, see Muhammad Muslih, "A Study of PLO Peace Initiatives, 1974–1988," in A. Sela and M. Ma'oz, eds., *The PLO and Israel: From Armed Conflict to Political Solution, 1964–1994* (New York: St. Martin's Press, 1997), pp. 37–53.

3. On the patterns of action and means in such struggles, see Homi K. Bhabha, "DissemiNation: Time, Narrative and the Margins of the Modern Nation," in Homi K. Bhabha, ed., *Nation and Narration* (London: Routledge, 1994), pp. 290–322.

4. Yehoshua Porath, *The Arab-Palestinian National Movement 1929–1939: From Riots to Revolt* (London: Frank Cass, 1978), pp. 183–189, 233–234; Shay Lahman, "Sheikh 'Izz al-Din al-Qassam," in Elie Kedourie and Silvia Haim, eds., *Zionism and Arabism in Palestine and Israel* (London: Frank Cass, 1982), pp. 54–99.

5. Ziad Abu-Amr, *Islamic Fundamentalism in the West Bank and Gaza* (Bloomington: Indiana University Press, 1994), p. 3; Haim Levenberg, "Ha-Ahim ha-Muslemim be-Eretz Israel, 1945–1948" (master's thesis, Tel Aviv University, 1983), pp. 38–44, 100.

6. Amnon Cohen, *Political Parties in the West Bank Under Jordanian Rule, 1948–1967* (Ithaca, N.Y.: Cornell University Press, 1980), pp. 179, 228. On the origins of the Islamic Liberation Party, see pp. 209–220; Abu-Amr, *Islamic Fundamentalism*, pp. 5–6.

7. On Qutb's thought and influence, see Gilles Kepel, *Muslim Extremism in Egypt: The Prophet and the Pharaoh* (Berkeley and Los Angeles: University of California Press, 1993), pp. 36–69.

8. Abu-Amr, *Islamic Fundamentalism*, p. 9.

9. 'Atif 'Adwan, *al-Sheikh Ahmad Yasin, Hayatuhu wa-Jihaduhu* [Sheikh Ahmad Yasin, his life and struggle] (Gaza: al-Jami'a al-Islamiyya, 1991), pp. 42–43, 81–83. On the development of the Islamic movement among Israel's Arab citizens, see Thomas

Meir, *Hit'orerut ha-Muslemim be-Israel* [The awakening of the Muslims in Israel] (Giv'at Haviva: ha-Makhon le-Limudim 'Arviyim, 1988).

10. Hamas, "al-Haqiqa wal-Wujud" [Truth and existence] (a semiofficial history of Hamas), 1990, part 1, pp. 3–4.

11. Literally, a call (for submission to Allah). Practically, it became a code name for social and cultural activities, primarily Islamic preaching, education and social welfare, conducted by the Muslim Brothers.

12. 'Adwan, *Ahmad Yasin*, pp. 27–28, 33.

13. Besides Yasin, among its leaders were Ibrahim al-Yazuri, 'Abd al-'Aziz Rantisi, and Mahmud al-Zahar: see Abu-Amr, *Islamic Fundamentalism*, p. 16; 'Adwan, *Ahmad Yasin*, pp. 50–52, 57–64; a request for registration, submitted by Jam'iyyat Jawrat al-Shams al-Islamiyya (the official name of the Mujamma') signed by Ya'qub 'Uthman Quwaiq to the Israeli Military Administration, August 4, 1977, ZHL, *Ha-Pe'ilut ha-Islamit be-Hevel 'Aza* [IDF, Islamic activity in the Gaza region] (Gaza: Civil Administration, 1987), pp. 75–77.

14. A. Shabi and R. Shaked, *Hamas: me-Emuna be-Allah le-Derekh ha-Teror* [Hamas: From belief in Allah to the road of terror] (Jerusalem: Keter, 1994), p. 56.

15. ZHL [IDF], *Ha-Pe'ilut ha-Islamit be-Hevel 'Aza*, p. 15; Michael Dumper, "Forty Years Without Slumbering: Waqf Politics and Administration in the Gaza Strip 1948–1987," *British Journal of Middle Eastern Studies* 20, no. 2 (1993): 186, 198; Abu-Amr, *Islamic Fundamentalism*, p. 16, argues that by the early 1990s, the Mujamma' controlled 40 percent of the mosques in the Gaza Strip.

16. Ifrah Zilberman, "Ha-Mishpat ha-Minhagi ke-Ma'arekhet Hevratit be-Merhav Yerushalaim" [Customary law as a social system in the area of Jerusalem], *Ha-Mizrah He-Hadash* 33, nos. 129–132 (1991): 70–93.

17. It is noteworthy that these endowments constituted 10 percent of the real estates in the Strip, including agricultural land, garages, bakeries, residential and commercial buildings, cemeteries, and educational and religious institutions, mostly in the city of Gaza, that provided employment for a few thousand of clergymen, officials, and menial workers. ZHL [IDF], *Ha-Pe'ilut ha-Islamit be-Hevel 'Aza*, pp. 13, 22, 48–49.

18. 'Adwan, *Ahmad Yasin*, pp. 89–91, 137; Jean-François Legrain, "Hamas: Legitimate Heir of Palestinian Nationalism?" in J. L. Esposito, ed., *Political Islam: Revolution, Radicalism or Reform* (Boulder, Colo.: Lynne Rienner, 1997), p. 163.

19. In 1985–1986, there were 4,315 students: ZHL [IDF], *Ha-Pe'ilut ha-Islamit be-Hevel 'Aza*, p. 37.

20. See 'Adwan, *Ahmad Yasin*, pp. 64–78, 87–88; Abu-Amr, *Islamic Fundamentalism*, p. 17; Shabi and Shaked, *Hamas*, pp. 72–75.

21. Glenn E. Robinson, *Building a Palestinian State: The Incomplete Revolution* (Bloomington: Indiana University Press, 1997), p. 35.

22. Shabi and Shaked, *Hamas*, p. 75.

23. ZHL [IDF], *Ha-Pe'ilut ha-Islamit be-Hevel 'Aza*, pp. 82–85, 89; Shabi and Shaked, *Hamas*, pp. 61–63, 99.

24. Shabi and Shaked, *Hamas*, pp. 64–66, 96–97.

Notes to Chapter Two: Dogmas and Dilemmas

1. Aziz al-Azmeh, *Islams and Modernities* (London: Verso, 1993), pp. 64–65.

2. James Piscatori, *Islam in a World of Nation States* (London: Royal Institute of International Affairs, 1983), chap. 4; James Piscatori, "Religion and Realpolitik: Islamic Responses to the Gulf War," in James Piscatori, ed., *Islamic Fundamentalism and the Gulf Crisis* (Chicago: American Academy of Arts and Sciences, 1991), pp. 9, 18. Hassan A. Turabi, "Islam as a Pan-National Movement," *RSE Journal* (August–September 1992): 608–619; and Hassan A. Turabi, "al-Sahwa al-Islamiyya wal-Dawla al-Qutriyya fi al-Watan al-'Arabi" [The Islamic awakening and the territorial state in the Arab homeland], in *al-Sahwa al-Islamiyya: Ru'ya Naqdiyya Min al-Dakhil* [The Islamic awakening: A critical view from within] (Beirut: al-Nashir lil-Tiba'a wal-Nashr, 1990), pp. 86–108.

3. On the characteristics of the two approaches, see Olivier Roy, *The Failure of Political Islam* (Cambridge, Mass.: Harvard University Press, 1994), pp. 24, 77–80; Gilles Kepel, *Muslim Extremism in Egypt: The Prophet and the Pharaoh* (Berkeley and Los Angeles: University of California Press, 1985), pp. 16–20.

4. Ibid., pp. 64–66. On the "enclave" concept in comparative perspective, see Emmanuel Sivan, "Tarbut ha-Muvla'at" [The enclave culture], *Alpayim* 4 (1991): 50–63.

5. Kepel, *Muslim Extremism*, pp. 193–204; *Islam, Democracy, the State and the West: A Round Table with Dr. Hasan Turabi*, May 10, 1992, sponsored by the World and Islam Studies Enterprise and the University of South Florida, Committee for Middle Eastern Studies, p. 19.

6. Kepel, *Muslim Extremism*, pp. 93–94; Iyad Barghuthi, *al-Aslama wal-Siyasa fi al-Aradi al-Filastiniyya al-Muhtalla* [The Islamization and politics of the Palestinian occupied lands] (Jerusalem: Markaz al-Zahra' lil-Dirasat wal-Abhath, 1990), pp. 65–75. One of the organizations inspired by this trend was the Jihad Family (Usrat al-Jihad) of Israeli Arab citizens, which was exposed by the early 1980s. See Thomas Mayer, *Hit'orerut ha-Muslemim be-Israel* [The awakening of the Muslims in Israel] (Giv'at Haviva: ha-Makhon le-Limudim 'Arviyim, 1988), pp. 42–55.

7. Wajih Kawtharany, "Thalathat Azmina fi Mashru' al-Nahda al-'Arabiyya wal-Islamiyya" [Three eras in the Arab and Islamic renaissance project], *al-Mustaqbal al-'Arabi*, no. 120 (February 1989): 4–25.

8. 'Abdallah 'Azzam, *al-Difa' 'An Aradi al-Muslimin Ahamm Furud al-A'yan* [The defense of Muslims' lands, the most important of individuals' duties] (Jidda: Dar al-Mujtama', 1987), pp. 20–21. For a classification of the types of *jihad*, see Mustansir Mir, "Jihad in Islam," in Hadia Dajani-Shakeel and Ronald A. Messier, eds., *The Jihad and Its Times* (Ann Arbor: University of Michigan Press, 1991), pp. 113–126; Muhammad Na'im Yasin, "al-Jihad, Mayadinuhu wa-Asalibuhu" [The Jihad, its arenas and methods], *al-Sirat* (Um al-Fahm, Israel), December 8, 1986, pp. 29–30; Hamas Charter, articles 7, 15 (see app. 2); Emmanuel Sivan, "The Holy War Tradition in Islam," *Orbis* 42, no. 2 (Spring 1998): 173–176.

9. 'Abd al-Sattar Tawila, *al-Sheikh al-Mujahid, 'Izz al-Din al-Qassam* [The holy warrior Sheikh 'Izz al-Din al-Qassam] (Beirut: Dar al-Umma lil-Nashr, 1984); Bayan

Nuwayhid al-Hut, *al-Sheikh al-Mujahid 'Izz al-Din al-Qassam fi Tarikh Filastin* [The holy warrior Sheikh 'Izz al-Din al-Qassam in the history of Palestine] (Acre: Dar al-Aswar, 1988), p. 7.

10. 'Azzam, *al-Difa' 'An Aradi al-Muslimin*, pp. 21–25. 'Azzam's definitions were adopted by Hamas and incorporated in article 12 of its charter.

11. Shmuel Bar: *The Muslim Brotherhood in Jordan* (Tel Aviv: Moshe Dayan Center, Tel Aviv University, 1998), p. 37.

12. 'Azzam, *al-Difa' 'An Aradi al-Muslimin*, pp. 31–32.

13. For the origins and development of the *jihad* concept by Shiqaqi and others, see Tomas Mayer, "Pro-Iranian Fundamentalism in Gaza," in E. Sivan and M. Friedman, eds., *Religious Radicalism & Politics in the Middle East* (Albany: SUNY Press, 1990), pp. 142–155. On the attitude of the Islamic Jihad toward the struggle against Israel, see Barghuthi, *al-Aslama wal-Siyasa*, pp. 72–73; *Minbar October*, no. 20, January 1–15, 1990, pp. 71–72; Hamas (leaflet), "Bayan Yanfi Wuqu' Inshiqaq fi al-Haraka" [Announcement denying the occurrence of a split in the movement], April 15, 1993.

14. Y. Litani, "Militant Islam in the West Bank and Gaza," *New Outlook* 32, nos. 11–12 (November–December 1989): 40–42; and also Y. Litani, "Kakh Baninu et ha-Hamas" [This is how we built Hamas], *Kol Ha'ir* (Jerusalem), December 18, 1992; Housing Minister Ben-Eliezer quoted in *Yediot Aharonot*, June 17, 1994.

15. Leaflet of the "Islamic Bloc" at the Islamic University of Gaza, n.d. (1986).

16. 'Atif 'Adwan, *al-Sheikh Ahmad Yasin, Hayatuhu wa-Jihaduhu* [Sheikh Ahmad Yasin, his life and struggle] (Gaza: al-Jami'a al-Islamiyya, 1991), pp. 109–111; Hisham Ahmad, *Hamas—From Religious Salvation to Political Transformation: The Rise of Hamas in Palestinian Society* (Jerusalem: PASSIA, 1994), p. 26; Emmanuel Sivan, *Radical Islam* (New Haven, Conn.: Yale University Press, 1985), pp. 18–20, 47–49.

17. Z. Schiff and E. Ya'ari, *Intifada: The Palestinian Uprising: Israel's Third Front* (New York: Simon & Schuster, 1989), p. 224.

18. Helena Cobban, "The PLO and the Intifada," *Middle East Journal* 44, no. 3 (Spring 1990): 207–233; Sabri Jiryis, "Hiwar Min Naw' Aakhar Hawl "al-Hiwar" wal-Wahda al-Wataniyya" [A dialogue of another sort over "the dialogue" and national unity], *Shu'un Filastiniyya*, nos. 170–171 (May–June 1987): 21–29.

19. *ZHL, Ha-Pe'ilut ha-Islamit be-Hevel 'Aza* [IDF, Islamic activity in the Gaza region] (Gaza: Civil Administration, 1987), pp. 48–51; 'Adwan, *al-Sheikh Ahmad Yasin*, pp. 120–124.

20. 'Adwan, *al-Sheikh Ahmad Yasin*, pp. 125–128.

21. Namely, the land of the Prophet's night travel, from Mecca to Jerusalem, where he ascended to heaven.

22. "Hamas: al-Haqiqa wal-Wujud," part 1, pp. 1, 5; *Minbar October*, no. 20, January 1–15, 1990, p. 67; 'Adwan, *al-Sheikh Ahmad Yasin*, p. 140; Leaflet distributed in the mosques of Rafah and Khan Yunis, January 8, 1987, signed by "Harakat al-Muqawama al-Islamiyya." This was apparently the first recorded time that this name had been used by al-Mujamma' or possibly by another organization. Schiff and Ya'ari, *Intifada*, p. 258, maintain that this name was first used in March 1987, with Yasin's permission.

23. On the significance of the prisons for the emergence of the new revolutionary leadership, see Glenn E. Robinson, *Building a Palestinian State: The Incomplete Revolution* (Bloomington: Indiana University Press, 1997), p. 22.

24. On the circumstances of the foundation of Hamas, see 'Adwan, *al-Sheikh Ahmad Yasin*, pp. 137–138; *al-Shira'* (Lebanon), January 4, 1993; "Hamas: al-Haqiqa wal-Wujud," part 1, pp. 2–3, 8. This semiofficial history of Hamas refers to Schiff and Ya'ari, *Intifada*, p. 258, to validate the argument that leaflets in the name of the Islamic Resistance Movement had appeared in March and November 1987; article 7 of Hamas Charter (app. 2).

25. Barghuthi, *al-Aslama wal-Siyasa*, pp. 77–79.

26. Robert Satloff, "Islam in the Palestinian Uprising" (*Policy Focus*, The Washington Institute for Near East Policy, no. 7, October 1988), p. 9; Barghuthi, *al-Aslama wal-Siyasa*, pp. 75–76; 'Adwan, *al-Sheikh Ahmad Yasin*, pp. 131–132.

27. See, for example, Ahmad Bin Yusuf, *Harakat al-Muqawama al-Islamiyya* (The Islamic resistance movement] (Worth, Ill.: al-Markaz al-'Aalami lil-Buhuth wal-Dirasat, 1989), pp. 34–35.

28. On the PLO's accusations that Israel had an interest in the establishment of Hamas, see Schiff and Ya'ari, *Intifada*, p. 237; interview with the PLO ambassador in Amman, 'Umar al-Khatib, *al-Nahar* (East Jerusalem), January 18, 1995; Arafat to *al-Nahar* (East Jerusalem), November 29, 1994; *al-Sharq al-Awsat*, July 26, 1995. Hala Mustafa, "al-Tayar al-Islami fi al-Ard al-Muhtalla" [The Islamic current in the occupied land], *al-Mustaqbal al-'Arabi*, no. 113 (August 1988): 86.

29. Among the more conspicuous figures were physicians and pharmacists ('Abd al-'Aziz Rantisi, Mahmud al-Zahar, Isma'il Haniyya, Ibrahim Maqadmah, Ibrahim al-Yazuri, and Musa Abu Marzuq); teachers, university lecturers, and officials (Muhammad Sham'a, 'Abd al-Fattah Dukhan, Sayyid Abu-Musamih, Salah Shihada, Khalid al-Hindi, Muhammad Siyam, and Ahmad Bahr), engineers ('Imad al-'Alami, Isma'il Abu Shanab, and 'Issa al-Nashshar); and clergy ('Imad Faluji and Muhammad Sadr). The founders of Hamas were Ahmad Yasin, Ibrahim al-Yazuri, 'Abd al-'Aziz Rantisi, Muhammad Sham'a, Salah Shihada, and 'Ali al-Nashshar; see "Hamas: al-Haqiqa wal-Wujud," part 1, p. 6; 'Adwan, *al-Sheikh Ahmad Yasin*, p. 139.

30. See, for example, article 14 of the Palestinian National Charter (1968).

31. Yehoshafat Harkabi, *Fatah ba-Istrategia ha-Arvit* [Fatah in the Arab strategy] (Tel Aviv: Ma'arakhot, 1969), pp. 27–47; Ehud Ya'ari, *Strike Terror: The Story of Fatah* (New York: Sabra Books), 1970, pp. 49–55.

32. Yezid Sayigh, "The Armed Struggle and Palestinian Nationalism," in Avraham Sela and Moshe Ma'oz, eds., *The PLO and Israel: From Armed Conflict to Political Solution, 1964–1994* (New York: St. Martin's Press, 1997), pp. 23–35.

33. Wahid 'Abd al-Majid, "al-Intifada al-Filastiniyya: al-Siyaq al-Tarikhi, al-Qiwa al-Fa'ila, al-Masar wal-Mustaqbal" [The Palestinian uprising: The historical context, the acting forces, the course and future], *al-Mustaqbal al-'Arabi* 113 (May 1988): 8–10.

34. Bernard Lewis, "Rethinking the Middle East," *Foreign Affairs* 71, no.4 (Fall 1992): 115.

35. Hillel Frisch, "From Armed Struggle over State Borders to Political

Mobilization and Intifada Within It: The Transformation of the PLO Strategy in the Territories," *Plural Societies* 19 (1989/90): 92–115.

36. 'Adwan, *al-Sheikh Ahmad Yasin*, p. 111; ['Uns 'Abd al-Rahman], *al-Qadiyya al-Filastiniyya Bayn Mithaqain: al-Mithaq al-Watani al-Filastini wa-Mithaq Harakat al-Muqawama al-Islamiyya (Hamas)* [The Palestine question between two charters: The Palestinian national charter and the Islamic resistance movement's charter (Hamas)] (Kuwait: Maktab Dar al-Bayan, 1989), pp. 69–75.

37. 'Abd al-Rahman, *al-Qadiyya al-Filastiniyya bain Mithaqain*, pp. 127–128.

38. Hamas Charter, article 6; Hamas's spokesman, Ibrahim Ghawsha, to *al-Hayat*, January 12, 1993; Jawad al-Hamad and Iyad al-Barghuthi, eds., *Dirasa fi al-Fikr al-Siyasi li-Harkat al-Muqawama al-Islamiyya (Hamas), 1987–1996* [A study of the political thought of the Islamic resistance movement] (Amman: Markaz Dirasat al-Sharq al-Awsat, 1997), p. 121.

39. 'Adwan, *al-Sheikh Ahmad Yasin*, p. 138. The UNC included Fatah, the PFLP, the DFLP, and the Communist Party.

40. Hamas leaflet, August 18, 1988.

41. Hamas leaflet, January 30, 1989; *al-Nahar* (East Jerusalem), October 15, 1992.

42. *al-Quds* (East Jerusalem), November 22, 1988.

43. For a comparison of the two documents, see 'Abd al-Rahman, *al-Qadiyya al-Filastiniyya bain Mithaqain*, pp. 23–65.

44. Hillel Frisch, "The Evolution of Palestinian Nationalist Islamic Doctrine: Territorializing a Universal Religion," *Canadian Review in Nationalism* 21, nos. 1–2 (1994): 51–53.

45. M. I. Kjorlien, "Hamas in Theory and Practice," *Arab Studies Quarterly* 1 and 2 (1993): 4.

46. Barghuthi, *al-Aslama wal-Siyasa*, p. 80.

47. "Idjma'," *The Encyclopedia of Islam*, vol. 3 (Leiden: Brill, 1971), pp. 1023–1025; *Islam, Democracy, the State and the West: A Round Table with Dr. Hasan Turabi*, p. 19; Abu-l-'Ala' Mawdudi, "Political Theory of Islam," in John J. Donohue and John L. Esposito, eds., *Islam in Transition: Muslim Perspectives* (New York: Oxford University Press, 1982), p. 254.

48. Barghuthi, *al-Aslama wal-Siyasa*, p. 66. On Fatah's link to Islam, see Matti Steinberg, "The PLO and Palestinian Islamic Fundamentalism," *Jerusalem Quarterly*, no. 52 (1989): 37–54.

Notes to Chapter Three: Controlled Violence

1. Carl Brockelmann, *History of the Islamic People* (New York: Capricorn, 1960), p. 28.

2. *Filastin al-Muslima* (August 1992): 15.

3. 'Atif 'Adwan, *al-Sheikh Ahmad Yasin, Hayatuhu wa-Jihaduhu* [Sheikh Ahmad Yasin, his life and struggle] (Gaza: al-Jami'a al-Islamiyya, 1991), pp. 129–131, 142–144; A. Shabi and R. Shaked, *Hamas: me-Emuna be-Allah le-Derekh ha-Teror* [Hamas: From belief in Allah to the road of terror] (Jerusalem: Keter, 1994), pp. 103–104.

4. Iyad Barghuthi, *al-Aslama wal-Siyasa fi al-Aradi al-Filastiniyya al-Muhtalla* [The Islamization and politics of the Palestinian occupied lands] (Jerusalem: Markaz al-Zahra' lil-Dirasat wal-Abhath, 1990), pp. 81–82, 88; Shabi and Shaked, *Hamas*, pp. 292–294.

5. 'Adwan, *al-Sheikh Ahmad Yasin*, pp. 140–141; Shabi and Shaked, *Hamas*, p. 105.

6. During the first three years of the Intifada, Hamas committed sixty-six violent actions against Israel: see Shabi and Shaked, *Hamas*, pp. 139–141; 'Adwan, *al-Sheikh Ahmad Yasin*, p. 143.

7. The clash was a result of Palestinian riots triggered by a declared intention of the Israeli "Faithful of the Temple Mount" group to lay the cornerstone for the new Jewish temple in the Muslim compound and by the mass gathering of Jewish pilgrims at the Western Wall's plaza.

8. Shabi and Shaked, *Hamas*, pp. 288–290.

9. Shmuel Bar: *The Muslim Brotherhood in Jordan* (Tel Aviv: Moshe Dayan Center, Tel Aviv University, 1998), pp. 46–47.

10. Shabi and Shaked, *Hamas*, pp. 150–154.

11. Special leaflet, November 10, 1988.

12. Shabi and Shaked, *Hamas*, pp. 244–245; Shaul Mishal and Reuben Aharoni, *Speaking Stones, Communiqués from the Intifada Underground* (Syracuse, N.Y.: Syracuse University Press, 1994), p. 40.

13. *Sabr* is closely related to *sumud* (steadfastness), a term that had been used by the PLO to legitimize the normal life of Palestinian inhabitants in the occupied territories under the Israeli government—that is, by exempting them from the duty of armed struggle—by relating to it the virtue of preserving the Palestinian national land.

14. Shabi and Shaked, *Hamas*, pp. 14–19, 161, 298–299, 310.

15. Ibid., pp. 302–307.

16. The instructions were issued to a military activist in the Nablus district by a written message carried by an emissary (ibid., p. 313).

17. On Hizballah's influence on Hamas in this respect, see, for example, *Ha'aretz*, April 21, 1994; *Nida' al-Watan* (Lebanon), November 15, 1996.

18. *Ha'aretz*, August 25, 1995.

19. Shabi and Shaked, p. 326.

20. See, for example, Hamas, "Tajannub al-Iqtital wa-Hudud al-Difa' 'an al-Nafs" [Avoidance of mutual fighting and the boundaries of self-defense], October 1993, internal circular; and Hamas, "Barnamaj Muqtarah lil-Muwajaha al-Jamahiriyya wal-Siyasiyya fi al-Dakhil fi Muwajahat Ittifaq Ghazza wa-Ariha" [Proposed plan for popular and political resistance from within in confrontation with the Gaza-Jericho agreement], October 9, 1993, internal circular. These documents are further discussed in chap. 4.

21. *Filastin al-Muslima* (June 1994).

22. By the end of September 1993, 73 percent of the Palestinians in the occupied territories supported the Oslo accord and the peace process. See Beverly Milton-Edwards, *Islamic Politics in Palestine* (London: Tauris Academic Studies, 1996), p. 163.

23. Hamas, "Tajannub al-Iqtital wa-Hudud al-Difaʿ ʿan al-Nafs," October 1993; Mahmud al-Zahar to *al-Nahar* (East Jerusalem), October 25, 1995; Hamas, *al-Tahlil al-Siyasi* [Political analysis], no. 35, May 7, 1994 (internal periodical), 6. See also chap. 4.

24. On such an agreement in the Hebron area, see the preceding note; joint leaflet, April 22, 1994; *al-Quds* (East Jerusalem), March 16, 1993, and June 10, 1994.

25. Quoted from an internal document reproduced in *al-Wasat*, December 1995, p. 18. Hamas, "Barnamaj Muqtarah lil-Muwajaha al-Jamahiriyya wal-Siyasiyya fi al-Dakhil fi Muwajahat Ittifaq Ghazza-Ariha," October 9, 1993.

26. Hamas, *al-Risala* (internal periodical), October 13, 1993; *al-Tahlil al-Siyasi* [Political analysis] (internal periodical), no. 31, June 25, 1994.

27. Y. M. Ibrahim, "Palestinian Religious Militants: Why Their Ranks Are Growing," *The New York Times*, November 8, 1994; Y. Melman, "War and Peace Process," *The Washington Post*, January 29, 1995.

28. *Sawt al-Haqq wal-Hurriyya* (ʾUmm al-Fahm, Israel), May 13, 1994; *al-Muharrir* (Jordan), December 4, 1994.

29. According to a survey by the Center for Palestinian Studies and Research in Nablus, conducted in early February 1995, 46 percent of the Palestinians in the West Bank and Gaza Strip supported continued violence against Israeli targets, and 81 percent were opposed to negotiations with Israel if the policy of settlement continued (*Haʾaretz*, February 12, 1995).

30. PA Ministry of Information, "al-ʿAlaqat Bayn al-Sulta al-Wataniyya al-Filastiniyya wa-ʿAnasir al-Muʿarada" [Relations between the Palestinian National Authority and elements of the opposition], April 12, 1995.

31. *al-Hayat al-Jadida* (Ramallah), October 11, 1995.

32. *al-Quds* (East Jerusalem), December 22, 1995; *al-Nahar* (East Jerusalem), December 23, 1995.

33. *al-Quds* (East Jerusalem), December 24, 1995; *al-Wasat*, January 1, 1996, p. 30; *al-Bilad*, January 2, 1996. The violation of this understanding by Hamas activists who carried out the two suicide bombings in Jerusalem in August and September 1997 from area B (under joint administration of Israel and the PA) explains the harsh measures taken against Hamas. In addition to arrests, the PA for the first time closed down sixteen Hamas charitable and educational institutions (*Haʾaretz*, September 28, 1997).

34. *al-Quds* (East Jerusalem), October 12, 1995.

35. *al-Watan al-ʿArabi* (Lebanon), November 4, 1994, p. 27; *al-Wasat*, September 28, 1995, pp. 23–24; *Kol Ha-ʿir* (Jerusalem), March 8, 1996, pp. 68–71.

36. Muhammad Subhi al-Suwairky, "al-Haraka al-Islamiyya wa-Tahaddiyat al-Mustaqbal" [The Islamic Movement and the future challenges], *al-Watan*, March 30, 1995; Mahmud al-Zahar to *al-Quds* (East Jerusalem), October 10, 1994; Ahmad Bahr and Musa Abu Marzuq to *al-Quds* (East Jerusalem) April 20, 1994; *Haʾaretz*, January 8, 1996; *Haʾaretz*, October 8, 9, 1997; *Kol Ha-ʿIr* (Jerusalem), March 8, 29, 1996; *The New Yorker*, August 19, 1996, p. 26.

37. *Haʾaretz*, October 9, 1997.

38. Khalid al-Kharub, "Harakat Hamas Bayn al-Sulta al-Filastiniyya wa-Israʾil:

Min Muthallath al-Qiwa Ila al-Mitraqa wal-Sandan" [Hamas movement between the Palestinian Authority and Israel: From the triangle of forces to the hammer and anvil], *Majallat al-Dirasat al-Filastiniyya,* no. 18 (1994): 28–29.

39. *al-Wasat,* March 4, 1996, p. 21; *Ha'aretz,* January 8, 1996.

40. Hillel Cohen, "ha-Heskem 'Im Hamas," *Kol Ha'ir* (Jerusalem), April 19, 1996, including a photocopy of the draft agreement, dated February 1, 1996.

41. *al-Hayat al-Jadida,* October 11, 1995.

42. *News from Within* (Jerusalem) (November 1997): 18.

43. *al-Hayat al-Jadida, al-Quds,* and *al-Nahar* (East Jerusalem), January 7, 1996; *Ha'aretz,* January 8, 1996.

44. Ronen Bergman, "Lama Ein Piggu'im?" [Why there are no (terrorist) strikes], *Ha'aretz* weekly suppl., June 5, 1998, pp. 32, 34; *Ha'aretz,* February 25, 1996. Following the capture and interrogation of Hasan Salama by Israel's internal security service (Shabak), it emerged that a claim made by Israel's director of military intelligence that the bombings were instigated by Iran in order to bring about the downfall of the Labor Party in the 1996 Israeli general elections was problematic. The suicide terrorist attacks were most probably a direct reaction to the assassination of 'Ayyash and had no far-reaching political goal (interview with an Israeli official involved in Salama's interrogation). Indeed, even as a speculation, this argument was peculiar, given the fact that the elections had just been advanced to late May 1996, so that an attempt to unseat Prime Minister Peres would more logically be made as close as possible to election day, not two or three months earlier.

45. It was revealed that the suicide bombing carried out in Tel Aviv in early March 1996 had been planned and launched from the Gaza Strip with the support of an Israeli Arab citizen.

46. Early religious opinions (*fatawa*), justifying the suicide bombings as a manifestation of self-sacrifice in the course of legitimate *jihad* were published in *al-Sabil* (Jordan), March 12, 1996, and *al-Safir* (Lebanon), March 26, 1996. Conversely, Sheikh Muhammad al-Sayyid al-Tantawi, the rector of al-Azhar University, defined the suicide attacks and the killing of innocent and unarmed civilians as "evil," differentiating them from fighting a terrorist enemy (*al-Safir,* April 1, 1996).

47. Nawaf Ha'il al-Takruri, *al-'Amaliyyat al-Istishhadiyya fi al-Mizan al-Fiqhi* [The suicide operations in the balance of jurisprudence] (Damascus: Maktabat al-Asad, 1997). On the background of this book and its editor, a member of the Palestinian Islamic movement and one of the deportees to Lebanon in December 1992, see pp. 9–10, 12. The book includes a review and reproductions of the Islamic scholarly opinions (*fatawa*) published in the Arab press immediately after the bombings (pp. 83–101), including that of Tantawi (see above, note 46).

48. Ibid., p. 14.

49. In April 1977, the Palestinians' support of the peace process dropped to 60 percent, compared with 79 percent in late 1996, according to Rami Khouri's article in the *Jordan Times,* reproduced in *Ha'aretz,* May 1, 1997.

50. *Ha'aretz,* August 20, 22 and September 28, 1998.

51. ʿAmos Harʾel, "Kashe Legayyes Mitʾabdim" [Difficult to mobilize suiciders], *Haʾaretz*, February 6, 1998; Danny Rubinstein, "be-Hamas ʿAsakim Karagil" [Business as usual in Hamas], *Haʾaretz*, January 21, 1998. On the ambiguity regarding military decision making in Hamas, see Zeʾev Schiff, "Maduaʿ Ein Terror?" [Why is there no terror?], *Haʾaretz*, July 1, 1998; Ronen Bergman, "James Bond Lo Haya Sham" [James Bond was not there], *Haʾaretz*, September 25, 1998. *Haʾaretz*, July 24, 1998, p. 4.

52. *Haʾaretz*, July 24, 1998, p. 4.

53. Hamas leaflet, April 17, 1998; *Haʾaretz*, March 23 and April 14, 15, 20–21, 1998.

54. *al-Quds*, *al-Hayat al-Jadida*, September 12, 1998; *Haʾaretz*, September 25, 1998; Yasin in *al-Quds*, October 2, 1998.

55. In early October, a member of Hams was killed in Ramallah while preparing a car bomb; two Hamas members were arrested at the Erez checkpoint while trying to smuggle a large quantity of explosives from Gaza into Israel, and a laboratory and hundreds of kilograms of explosives were found in Hebron (*al-Quds*, October 2, 1998; *Haʾaretz*, October 1–2, 4, 9, 1998).

56. *Haʾaretz*, November 1–2, 1998.

57. Ibid.

58. Bassam Jarrar to *al-Quds*, February 5, 1994; Jamil Hamamiʾs statement in *al-Nahar* (East Jerusalem), February 9, 1994; Hamas, "Siyasat al-Tawjih fil Marhala al-Qadima (Baʿd Ittifaqiyyat Ghazza-Ariha)" [The indoctrination policy in the next phase (following the Gaza-Jericho agreement)], internal circular, October 28, 1993.

Notes to Chapter Four: Coexistence Within Conflict

1. As suggested by J. F. Legrain, "Mobilisation islamiste et soulevement palestinien 1987–1988," in G. Kepel and Y. Richard, eds., *Intellectuels et militants de l'Islam contemporain* (Paris: Seuil, 1990), p. 153.

2. Hamasʾs charter, article 27; "Hadha Huwa Raʾyuna fi Munazamat al-Tahrir al-Filastiniyya" [This is our view of the PLO], *Filastin al-Muslima* (May 1990): 8; "Hamas, Hadath ʿAbir Am Badil Daʾim?" [Hamas, a passing episode or a permanent alternative?], *al-Sawaʾid al-Ramiya: Sawt al-Haraka al-Islamiyya fil-Watan al-Muhtal*, March 1990, p. 9.

3. UNC leaflets, September 6 and November 27, 1988.

4. Hamas charter, article 27; Ziyad Abu-Amr, *Islamic Fundamentalism in the West Bank and Gaza* (Bloomington: Indiana University Press, 1994), p. 31.

5. This session declared the establishment of a Palestinian state on the basis of UN General Assembly resolution 181 of November 1947, which called for the partition of Palestine into two states, one Jewish and one Arab.

6. Hamas leaflet, November 10, 1988; see also Hamas leaflet, November 11, 1991.

7. See, for example, Mahmud al-Zahar to *al-Quds*, November 28, 1994; Abu-Amr, *Islamic Fundamentalism*, p. 78.

8. Mahmud al-Zahar to *al-Watan* (Gaza), May 5, 1995.

9. "Wahdat al-Saff . . . Matlab Islami Thamin" [Unity of rank . . . a precious Islamic demand], *Sawt al-Aqsa*, January 1, 1990 (reproduced in *al-Sabil*, January 31, 1990); "Naʿam lil-Wahda al-Wataniyya . . . wa-Lakin" [Yes to national unity . . . but],

Filastin al-Muslima (July 1990): 25–26; Hamas leaflet, October 24, 1991; Ibrahim Ghawsha in *Filastinn al-Muslima* (October 1992): 11; Hamas, *Waraqa Awwaliyya Hawl Tajannub al-Iqtital wa-Hudud al-Difa' 'an al-Nafs*, September–October 1993, internal circular; Sheikh Hasan Abu Kuwaik to *al-Quds*, August 30, 1994. For a theological explanation of the prohibition of internal bloodshed, see *al-Quds*, May 8, 1994.

10. *Yedioth Aharonoth* (Tel Aviv), September 16, 1988; Sheikh Ahmad Yasin to *al-Sirat* (publication of the Islamic movement in Israel), April 10, 1989.

11. Mu'tamar 'Ulama' Filastin, "Fatwa al-Musharaka fi Mu'tamar Madrid wal-Sulh Ma'a Isra'il," Jerusalem, November 1, 1991; 'Abdallah 'Azzam, *al-Difa' 'An Aradi al-Muslimin Aham Furud al-A'yan* (Jidda: Dar al-Mujtama', 1987), pp. 59–60. Hamas leaflet, "Bayan lil-Tarikh . . . La Limu'tamar Bay' Filastin wa-Bayt al-Maqdis," September 23, 1991.

12. For details on Hamas's activity in Europe and the United States and on the beginning of contacts with Iran,, see A. Shabi and R. Shaked, *Hamas: me-Emuna be-Allah le-Derekh ha-Teror* [Hamas: From belief in Allah to the road of terror] (Jerusalem: Keter, 1994), pp. 168–172, 240–241; *al-Wasat*, November 30, 1992.

13. *Ha'aretz*, November 20, 1989; The Ten Front leaflet, "Fali-Tasqut Mu'amarat al-Tasfiya wali-Tastamirr al-Intifada al-Mubaraka" [Down with the conference of liquidation, let the blessed Intifada go on] (Hamas appears first on the list), October 24, 1991, *Filastin al-Muslima* (November 1991): 31. Apparently, the Front was passive until it renewed its activity a year later. See "Bayan Siyasi Ham" [An important political announcement], a leaflet signed by Hamas and eight other Palestinian factions, September 15, 1992.

14. On Iran's support for the Islamic Palestinian movements, see Fathi Shiqaqi to *al-Diyar* (Lebanon), August 30, 1994, p. 17; on military training in Iran and Syria undertaken by Hasan Salama, the head of 'Izz al-Din al-Qassam in Hebron who commanded the mass suicide attacks of February–March 1996 in Jerusalem, Tel Aviv and Ashkelon, see *Ha'aretz*, August 15, 1996.

15. *al-Watan al-'Arabi* (Paris), November 7, 1994; Y. Melman, "War and Peace Process," *The Washington Post*, January 29, 1995; see also Arafat's allegations that Hamas received $30 million from Iran, *al-Wafd* (Egypt), December 19, 1992, p. 6, FBIS, NESA, *Daily Report*, December 22, p. 5; *al-Wasat*, February 22 and November 30, 1993; *al-Shira'*, January 4, 1993; *al-Manar* (Jerusalem), March 29, 1993.

16. *The New Yorker*, August 19, 1996; *al-Watan al-'Arabi*, November 4, 1994.

17. Hamas leaflet, "al-Tayar al-Islami fi al-Jami'at wal-Ma'ahid al-Filastiniyya fi al-Watan al-Muhtall" [The Islamic current in the universities and institutions in the occupied homeland], March 1992; for the financial difficulties of the Palestinian universities, see *al-Quds*, July 15, 1992, p. 4; *Ha'aretz*, May 17, 1992, quoting Na'if Hawatima's interview with *al-Haqa'iq* (Tunisia); *Kol Yerushalayim*, July 26, 1991.

18. Hisham Ahmad, *Hamas* (Jerusalem: PASSIA, 1994): 66; Y. Torpstein, "Nadvanim le-Allah" [Super philanthropists] *Ha'aretz*, January 13, 1993; "She'atam ha-Yaffa Shel ha-Gizbarim ha'Islamiyim" [The great moment of the Islamist treasurers], *Ha'aretz*, March 15, 1992.

19. Iyad al-Barghuthi, *al-Haraka al-Islamiyya al-Filastiniyya wal-Nizam al-'Alami*

al-Jadid [The Palestinian-Islamic movement and the new world order] (Jerusalem: al-Jam'iyya al-Filastiniyya al-Acadimiyya lil-Shu'un al-Dawliyya, 1992), pp. 30–31; Guy Bekhor, "Yamim Kashim Le'Ashaf" [Difficult days for the PLO], *Ha'aretz*, November 13, 1992; Report by Y. Torpstein, *Ha'aretz*, January 1, 1993; leaflet by "al-Haraka al-Tashihiyya fi Munazzamat al-Tahrir al-Filastiniyya" [The reformist movement in the PLO], Jerusalem, September 4, 1992.

20. On Hamas's political penetration into popular institutions, see Mahmud al-Zahar, "al-Haraka al-Islamiyya, Haqa'iq wa-Arqam" [The Islamic movement; facts and figures], *al-Quds*, November 10, 1992; and Dani Rubinstein's report, *Ha'aretz*, November 27, 1992.

21. *al-Quds*, June 15 and August 5, 1992.

22. *al-Bayadir al-Siyasi*, May 30, 1992; Y. Torpstein, "She'urei Dat le'Ashaf" [Religion classes for the PLO], *Ha'aretz*, June 3, 1992.

23. Husam 'Abd al-Hadi, "Nahwa Haraka Wataniyya Islamiyya" [Toward a national Islamic movement], *al-Quds*, August 9, 1992. See also Arafat's comment on Hamas's alignment with the Marxist factions in the framework of the Ten Front, proceedings of the Fatah-Hamas talks in Khartoum, January 1–4, 1993, *al-Manar* (Jerusalem), March 29, 1993.

24. 'Abd al-Sattar Qasim, *Ayyam fi Mu'taqal al-Naqab* [Days in the Negev prison] (Jerusalem: Lajnat al-Difa' 'An al-Thaqafa al-Wataniyya al-Filastiniyya, 1989): 98.

25. A joint Fatah-Hamas leaflet (n.d.), reproduced in *Filastin al-Muslima* (October 1990): 4; Ziyad Abu Ghanima, "Mithaq al-Sharaf Bayn Hamas wa-Fatah, Bariqat Amal li-Sha'bina . . . wa-Saf'a li-'Aduwwina" [The pact of honor between Hamas and Fatah, a gleam of hope to our people . . . and a blow to our enemies], *al-Dustur* (Jordan), September 24, 1990.

26. Hamas leaflet, July 22, 1990; *Ha'aretz*, November 11, 1992.

27. On the PLO-Hamas dispute, see "Hadha Ra'yuna fi Munazamat al-Tahrir al-Filastiniyya," *Filastin al-Muslima* (May 1990): 8; "Likay la Tadi' al-Haqiqa: Radduna 'Ala al-Hamasiyyin" [So that truth is not missed: Our response to Hamas people], *Filastin al-Thawra*, July 8, 1990; "Qira'a fi Radd Hamas 'Ala al-Musharaka fi al-Majlis al-Watani" [Reading in Hamas's response regarding participation in the National Council], *Filastin al-Muslima* (July 1990). See also Sheikh Ahmad Yasin's interview with *al-Mukhtar al-Islami* (Egypt), May 1989.

28. Hamas leaflet, no. 77, August 3, 1992, according to *Filastin al-Muslima*, September 1992, p. 5.

29. Hamas leaflets nos. 77, 81, 85, 87, 88, 89, August 3, 1991–July 5, 1992; Mahmud al-Zahar to *al-Sharq al-Awsat*, July 17, 1992, p. 8.

30. Hamas leaflets, December 27, 1991, April 26, 1992, July 31, 1992.

31. Hamas leaflet, "Awlawiyyat al-Jihad al-Filastini fi al-Marhala al-Rahina," June 21, 1992; Hamas leaflets, December 1, 1991, and April 7, 1992, reproduced in *Filastin al-Muslima*, May, June 3, and August 3, 1992; leaflet of the Islamic Jihad, "Nida' Ila al-Sha'b wal-Mu'assasat wal-Wujaha: 'Uwqifu al-Majazir Qabl Wuqu'iha" [A call to the people, the institutions and leaders: Stop the massacres before they occur], April 8, 1992.

32. Faraj Shalhub, "Hamas wa-M. T. F.: Wahda Min Ajl Bina' al-Mashru' al-Jihadi" [Hamas and the PLO: Unity for the sake of building a jihadist program], *Filastin al-Muslima* (October 1990): 2; Marwan al-Barghuthi to *al-Liwa'*, July 15, 1992, p. 13; *Keyhan* (Iran), October 31, 1992, p. 16, FBIS, NESA, *Daily Report*, November 30, 1992, pp. 9–11; Hamas leaflet, "Awlawiyyat al-Jihad al-Filastini fi al-Marhala al-Rahina" [The priority of *jihad* in Palestine in the current phase], June 21, 1992.

33. *Ha'aretz*, November 11, 1992.

34. Faisal al-Husaini's call to Hamas to join the PLO in convening the PNC to strengthen the national unity, *al-Quds*, May 4, 1992; *Ha'aretz*, July 2, 8, 1992; Hamas leaflets, "al-I'tida'at al-Mutakarrira 'Ala Buyut Allah . . . Man Yaqif Wara'aha!? wali-Maslahat Man Yatim Tanfidhuha!?" [The repeated aggression against Allah's homes . . . who is behind it and in whose interest it is carried out?], December 27, 1991, April 7, 1992, reproduced in *Filastin al-Muslima*, May and June 3, 1992; battalions of 'Izz al-Din al-Qassam leaflet, September 29, 1992.

35. "Wathiqat Sharaf" [A document of honor], a joint Fatah-Hamas leaflet, June 7, 1992; Hamas leaflet, "Bayan Hawl Wathiqat al-Sharaf" [An announcement about the document of honor], June 8, 1992.

36. *Ha'aretz*, July 10, 14, 1992; among the members in these committees were Haidar 'Abd al-Shafi and Faisal al-Husaini, as well as Israeli Arab figures, including Haj Ra'id Salah, interview with 'Abd al-'Aziz al-Rantisi, *al-Quds*, July 15, 1992, p. 2.

37. Arafat to *Algiers Voice of Palestine*, January 14, 1993, FBIS, NESA, *Daily Report*, January 15, 1993, p. 9; and interview with *al-Ra'i* (Jordan), November 30, 1992, p. 12, FBIS, NESA, *Daily Report*, November 30, p. 6; see Muhammad Nazzal's response, *al-Sharq al-Awsat*, December 30, 1992, p. 5, FBIS, NESA, *Daily Report*, January 5, 1993, p. 4; *Ha'aretz*, November 11, 1992.

38. *al-Hayat*, December 24, 1992; *Ha'aretz*, December 21, 1992; January 21, 1993; *al-Watan al-'Arabi*, January 1, 1993, pp. 16–21.

39. Hamas, "Miswaddat Ittifaq Bayn al-Hukm al-Irani wa-Harakat Hamas" [A draft agreement between the Iranian regime and the Hamas movement] (internal document, n.d., faxed on November 16, 1992); *al-Watan al-'Arabi*, January 1, 1993, pp. 20–21.

40. *al-Watan al-'Arabi*, January 1, 1993; PLO memorandum: "al-Hiwar Ma'a Hamas" [The dialogue with Hamas], summarizing the PLO-Hamas talks in Tunis, December 24, 1992.

41. Hamas's delegation was composed of the head of the Political Bureau, Musa Abu Marzuq; Hamas spokesman Ibrahim Ghawsha; the official representatives in Iran and Jordan, 'Imad al-'Alami and Muhammad Nazzal, respectively; and two senior members of the Islamic movement in Jordan.

42. PLO memorandum: "al-Hiwar Ma'a Hamas," summarizing the PLO-Hamas talks in Tunis, December 24, 1992. See also *al-Watan al-'Arabi*, January 1, 1993.

43. The proceedings of the Khartoum talks were published by *al-Manar* (Jerusalem), March 29, 1993. See also *Ha'aretz*, January 24, 1993; *al-Quds*, January 12 and February 2, 1993.

44. *al-Manar*, March 29, 1993; *al-Quds*, January 12, 1993.

45. *al-Manar*, March 29, 1993; *al-Quds*, February 2, 1993; *Ha'aretz*, January 20, 1993.

46. *al-Quds*, February 2, 1993; *al-Sharq al-Awsat*, December 30, 1992, p. 5, FBIS, NESA, *Daily Report*, January 5, 1993, p. 4.

47. *al-Quds*, March 16, 1993.

48. Hamas, Annual Political Report, August 1, 1992, to September 20, 1993, quoted in *al-Wasat*, December 18, 1995, pp. 17–18.

49. *al-Risala* (Hamas internal periodical), October 13, 1993.

50. *al-Quds* (Jerusalem), September 13, 1993.

51. Ali al Jarbawi, "The Position of Palestinian Islamists on the Palestine-Israel Accord." *Muslim World* 83, nos. 1–2 (January–April 1994): 144–153, analyzes the way Hamas coped with the challenge of the Declaration of Principles.

52. On Hamas's instructions to the movement's followers to prevent internecine Palestinian violence (*iqtital*) in the name of Palestinian national unity and a joint front against the Jews, see, for example, Ahmad, *Hamas*, p. 71. This was also the line adopted by the Islamic Jihad: see Fathi Shiqaqi's statement, *al-Diyar* (Lebanon), August 30, 1994, p. 17; FBIS, NESA, *Daily Report*, September 13, 1994, p. 10.

53. The pattern of a clash of interests between the local Palestinian factor and the PLO—tacitly assisted by Israel—is not unfamiliar in the history of the occupied territories since 1967. A previous occurrence was in early 1982 between the National Guidance Committee and the PLO, eventuating in the dismantling of the former. The same pattern was repeated in the way Israel and the PLO tackled the local grassroots leadership of the uprising.

54. *al-Risala* (Hamas internal periodical), April 21, 1994.

55. *al-Quds*, June 10, 1994; joint leaflet, April 22, 1994; Khalid al-Kharub, "Harakat Hamas Bayn al-Sulta al-Filastiniyya wa-Isra'il: Min Muthallath al-Qiwa Ila al-Mitraqa wal-Sandan" [Hamas movement between the Palestinian Authority and Israel: From the triangle of forces to the hammer and anvil], *Majallat al-Dirasat al-Filastiniyya*, no. 18 (1994): 28–29.

56. *al-Wasat*, November 14, 1994, June 28, 1995, p. 22.

57. *al-Wasat*, June 12, 1995, pp. 22–23, 33–34.

58. *Time*, November 21, 1994, p. 63.

59. *Time*, November 28, 1994.

60. *al-Quds*, November 20 and December 17, 1994; *al-Nahar* (East Jerusalem), October 12, 1995; Mahmud al-Zahar to *al-Watan*, December 8, 1994, p. 1; 'Imad Faluji's interview with *Sawt al-Haqq wal-Hurriyya*, January 27, 1995, p. 13.

61. *al-Quds*, December 22, 1995; *al-Nahar* (East Jerusalem), December 23, 1995.

62. *al-Nahar* (East Jerusalem), October 11, 1995; *al-Wasat*, January 1, 1996, p. 30.

63. For more on this distinction, see Milton Rokeach, "Attitude Change and Behavioral Change," *Public Opinion Quarterly* 30 (1966/67): 529–550.

64. Referring to the July 1993 unofficial understanding between Israel and Hizballah, following Operation Din ve-Heshbon (Accountability) in southern Lebanon.

65. *al-Wasat*, November 14, 1994, p. 16.

66. Statement by the Political Bureau of Hamas, March 16, 1994; Ibrahim Ghawsha to *al-Sabil* (London), quoted by Reuters, April 19, 1994; *al-Nahar* (East Jerusalem), May 15, 1995.

67. 'Azzam, *al-Difa' 'An Aradi al-Muslimin*, pp. 59–63; leaflet, signed by "Mu'tamar 'Ulama' Filastin," November 1, 1991; Rabitat al-Tullab al-Islamiyyin fi Filastin, "Hukm al-Sulh Ma'a al-Yahud" [Islamic Students Association in Palestine, "The law of peace with the Jews"] (n.d.).

68. On the polemic over the legitimacy of the agreement with Israel and the religious judgment of Ibn Baz, see *al-Watan* (Gaza), January 11, p. 6, January 19, p. 13; February 28, 1995, p. 8.

69. *Voice of Palestine Radio*, March 24 and November 11, 1995; *al-Jumhuriyya* (Egypt), September 17, 1993; his speech in Johannesburg on May 24, 1994.

70. For the text of the decision, see *Filastin al-Thawra*, June 12, 1974.

71. Interview with Mahmud al-Zahar for *al-Watan* (Gaza), January 19, 1995, p. 8; interview with Ibrahim Ghawsha for *al-Watan*, February 2, p. 8; interview with Musa Abu Marzuq for *Filastin al-Muslima* (June 1994): 16; Majdi Ahmad Husain, "al-Hisad al-Murr li-Ittifaq Ghazza-Ariha" [The bitter harvest of the Gaza-Jericho agreement], *Sawt al-Haqq wal-Hurriyya*, December 2, 1994, p. 11.

72. Typical of that was a Hamas leaflet issued on June 4, 1994, several days after the withdrawal of the IDF from Gaza, which threatened the Palestinian police over their persecution of Islamic activists. See also the interview with Mahmud al-Zahar for *Filastin al-Muslima*, June 1995, pp. 13–15.

73. Ahmad Yusuf, "al-Islamiyyun wa-Marhalat Ma Ba'd al-Ittifaq" [The Islamists and the postagreement phase], *Filastin al-Muslima*, June 1994, p. 19.

74. Ahmad Yasin to *al-Wasat*, November 1, 1992.

75. See the report on the meeting of representatives from Hamas and the National Islamic Salvation Party with representatives of Fatah and the PA to start a "national dialogue," following the incidents of the Hashmonean Tunnel in October 1996, *al-Quds* (East Jerusalem), February 28, 1997; Danny Rubinstein, "Be-Hamas 'Asakim ka-Ragil" [Business as usual in Hamas], *Ha'aretz*, January 21, 1998.

76. *al-Hayat* (London), April 19, 1998; Ronen Bergman, "Lama Ein Piggu'im?" [Why are there no (terrorist) attacks?], *Ha'aretz* (weekly suppl.), June 5, 1998, p. 34.

Notes to Chapter Five: Calculated Participation

1. Yusuf al-Qaradawi, *al-Hall al-Islami: Farida wa-Darura* [The Islamic solution: Duty and necessity], 5th ed. (Cairo: Maktabat Wahaba, 1993), pp. 155–192; Fathi Yakan, *Nahwa Haraka Islamiyya 'Alamiyya Wahida* [Toward one global Islamic movement], 3d ed. (Beirut: Mu'assassat al-Risala, 1977), pp. 8–21.

2. Martin Kramer, "Fundamentalist Islam at Large: The Drive for Power," *Middle East Quarterly* (June 1996): 39.

3. Sana Abed-Kotob, "The Accommodationists Speak: Goals and Strategies of the Muslim Brotherhood of Egypt," *International Journal of Middle East Studies* 27 (1995): 321–339.

4. See for example, the interview with Ibrahim Kharisat, spokesman for the Islamic movement in the Jordanian parliament, explaining the irrationality of using force to pass legislation in the parliament, for *Filastin al-Muslima* (November 1992): 29; 'Abdallah al-'Akailah, "Tajribat al-haraka al-Islamiyya fi al-Urdun," in 'Azzam al-Tamimi, *Musharakat al-Islamiyyin fi al-Sulta* [The Islamists' participation in power] (London: Liberty for the Muslim World, 1994), pp. 101–112; *al-Hayat*, September 12, 1994, pp. 1, 6.

5. Tim Niblock, "Islamic Movements and Sudan's Political Coherence," in H. L. Beuchot, C. Delmet, and D. Hopewood, eds., *Sudan: History, Identity, Ideology* (Reading, Pa.: Ithaca Press, 1991); Hasan al-Turabi, *al-Haraka al-Islamiyya fi al-Sudan* [The Islamic movement in Sudan] (n.p., n.d.), pp. 34–35. The book was published by Muhammad Hashimi, an activist member of the Islamic Renaissance (al-Nahda) Movement in Tunisia.

6. Tah Nasr Mustafa, "al-Haraka al-Islamiyya al-Yamaniyya: 'Ishruna 'Aaman min al-Musharaka al-Siyasiyya" [The Islamic movement in Yemen: Twenty years of political participation], in 'Azzam al-Tamimi, *Musharakat al-Islamiyyin fil al-Sulta*, pp. 140–171.

7. Gideon Gera, "ha-Tnu'a ha-Islamit be-Algeria" [The Islamic movement in Algeria], in Meir Litvak, ed., *Islam ve-Demokratiya ba-'Olam ha-'Arvi* [Islam and democracy in the Arab world] (Tel Aviv: Ha-Kibbutz ha-Me'uhad, 1998), pp. 224–230.

8. For a positive summary of Hizballah's parliamentary experience, see the interview with the deputy secretary-general, Na'im al-Qasim, for *Filastin al-Muslima* (October 1994): 25.

9. See, for example, John L. Esposito and James P. Piscatori, "Democratization and Islam," *Middle East Journal* 45, no. 3 (Summer 1991): 427–440; Emmanuel Sivan, "Eavesdropping on Radical Islam," *Middle East Quarterly* 2, no. 1 (1995): 13–24; Glenn E. Robinson, "Can Islamists Be Democrats?" *Middle East Journal* 51, no. 3 (Summer 1997): 373–388.

10. See, for example, the interview with Turabi in *Qira'at Siyasiyya* (Florida), no. 3 (Summer 1992): 20; his interview with *Filastin al-Muslima* (November 1992): 34; Olivier Roy, *The Failure of Political Islam* (Cambridge, Mass.: Harvard University Press, 1994), pp. 47, 56–57; Rivka Yadlin, "ha-Yelkhu Shnayim Yahdav Bilti 'Im No'adu?" [Would the two go together unless they had agreed?], in Meir Litvak, ed., *Islam ve-Democratya ba-'Olam ha-'Arvi*, pp. 76–79.

11. *Islam, Democracy, the State and the West: A Round Table with Dr. Hasan Turabi*, May 19, 1992, World and Islam Studies Enterprise and University of South Florida, Committee for Middle Eastern Studies, p. 18; Rashed al-Ghanouchi, *Mahawir Islamiyya* [Islamic pivots] (Cairo: Bait al-Ma'rifa, 1992), pp. 142–144; Qaradawi, *Awlawiyyat al-Haraka al-Islamiyya*, pp. 16–17.

12. Amir Weissbrod, "ha-Islam ha-Radicali be-Sudan: Hagut 'u-Ma'ase—Mishnato ha-Datit veha-Politit shel Hasan al-Turabi" [Radical Islam in Sudan: Thought and practice—The religious and political doctrine of Hasan al-Turabi] (master's thesis, Hebrew University of Jerusalem, 1997), p. 154; *al-Wasat*, November 7, 1994; *Filastin al-Muslima* (November 1992): 34.

13. Rashed al-Ghannouchi, "Hukm Musharakat al-Islam fi Nizam Ghair Islami" [The rule of Islamic participation in a non-Islamic regime], in 'Azzam al-Tamimi, *Musharakat al-Islamiyyin fi al-Sulta*, pp. 13–24, Kotob, "The Accommodationists Speak," pp. 328–329.

14. Leaflet signed by ten organizations (Hamas is first on the list), "Fali-Tasqut Mu'amarat al-Tasfiya fali-Tastamirr al-Intifada al-Mubaraka" (Down with the conspiracies of elimination, let the blessed Intifada go on), October 24, 1991, *Filastin al-Muslima* (November 1991): 31.

15. Samuel P. Huntington, *The Third Wave: Democratization in the Late Twentieth Century* (Norman: University of Oklahoma Press, 1991), p. 186.

16. G. Kramer, "The Integration of the Integrist: A Comparative Study of Egypt, Jordan and Tunisia," in Ghassan Salame, ed., *Democracy Without Democrats? The Renewal of Politics in the Muslim World* (London: Tauris, 1994), pp. 204–205; R. Meijer, *From al-Da'wa to al-Hizbiyya: Mainstream Islamic Movements in Egypt, Jordan and Palestine in the 1990s* (Amsterdam: Research Center for International Political Economy, 1997), p. 4.

17. Emmanuel Sivan, "Eavesdropping on Radical Islam," *Middle East Quarterly* 2, no. 1(1995): 21.

18. On the debate in this respect by the Islamic movements in Egypt, see 'Isam al-'Iryan, "'Awa'iq al-Musharaka al-Siyasiyya fi Misr" [The obstacles for political participation in Egypt], in 'Azzam al-Tamimi, *Musharakat al-Islamiyyin fi al-Sulta*, pp. 217–219; Meijer, *From al-Da'wa to al-Hizbiyya*, p. 6. For Jordan, see A. Ghara'ibah, *Jama'at al-Ikhwan al-Muslimin fi al-Urdun, 1946–1996* [The Society of Muslim Brotherhood in Jordan 1946–1996] (Amman: Markaz al-Urdun al-Jadid lil-Dirasat, 1997), pp. 137–138.

19. A. Benningsen, "The National Front in Communist Strategy in the Middle East," in Walter Laqueur, ed., *The Middle East in Transition* (London: Routledge & Kegan Paul, 1958), pp. 351–360. The impact of this concept on Turabi in Sudan is reflected in the name he gave to his movement in 1985: The National Islamic Front (al-Jabha al-islamiyya al-qawmiyya), as well as in his approach to other issues. Weissbrod, *Ha-Islam ha-Radicali be-Sudan*, pp. 167–168.

20. On the foundation of the Front, see A. J. Azem, "The Islamic Action Front," in J. Schwedler, ed., *Islamic Movements in Jordan* (Amman: al-Urdun al-Jadid Research Center, 1977), p. 115.

21. 'Abdallah al-'Akailah, "Aina Nahnu wa-Matha Nurid" [Where are we and what do we want], *al-'Amal al-Islami* (Jordan) (September–November 1996): 19–23; *al-Hayat*, September 12, 1996, pp. 1, 6; *al-Ra'i*, November 25, 1996, p. 39. For the conservative attitude, see *al-Ra'i*, November 4, 6, 1996, p. 32 (for both).

22. On the Palestinization and radicalization of the movement in the 1990s, see Shmuel Bar, *The Muslim Brotherhood in Jordan* (Tel Aviv: Moshe Dayan Center, Tel Aviv University, 1998), pp. 44–49; On the MB's decision to boycott the elections and its differences with the Islamic Action Front, see *al-Hayat*, July 10, 1997, and *al-Dustur* (Jordan), July 13, 1997.

23. Taha Nasr Mustafa, "al-Haraka al-Islamiyya al-Yamaniyya," pp. 140–171.

24. On the considerations and vacillations concerning this decision, see *Filastin al-Muslima* (August 1991): 21–23, and (June 1992): 15–17.

25. Interviews with Hamas's "outside" leaders: Ibrahim Ghawash for *Filastin al-Muslima* (May 1991): 24–25, and (October 1992): 10–11; 'Imad al-'Alami for *Filastin al-Muslima* (April 1992): 33; Muhammad Nazzal for *Filastin al-Muslima* (March 1992): 19, and (September 1992): 13.

26. The expression appeared in a Hamas leaflet criticizing the PA's director of security, June 4, 1994.

27. Hamas, *al-Rasid* (a noncirculating internal bulletin), no. 2 (April 15, 1992): 1.

28. An internal Hamas document, faxed on July 27, 1992.

29. State of Israel, Ministry of Foreign Affairs, *Israeli-Palestinian Agreement on the West Bank and the Gaza Strip* (Jerusalem: Ministry of Foreign Affairs, 1995).

30. On Arafat's efforts to convince Hamas and other movements to take part in the elections or join Fatah's list of candidates, see Lamis Andoni, "The Palestinian Elections: Moving Toward Democracy or One-Party Rule?" *Journal of Palestine Studies* 25, no. 3 (Spring 1996): 6–9; *Al-Nas wal-Intikhabat*, a special weekly on the elections, financed by the German Friedrich Ebert Foundation and distributed as a supplement to the *al-Quds* daily of East Jerusalem. It was issued on six consecutive Sundays before the election and on the election day itself, December 12, 1995.

31. Interview with Ibrahim Ghawsha for *Filastin al-Muslima* (October 1992), 10–11; his announcement, *al-Ra'i*, November 11, 1993.

32. Interview with the deputy chairman of the Association of the [Islamic] Scholars of Palestine, Sheikh Taysir al-Tamimi, for *Filastin al-Muslima* (October 1994): 40; interview with Ahmad Yasin for *Filastin al-Muslima* (November 1993): 5; Ibrahim Ghawsha to *Voice of Palestine from Jericho*, September 25, 1995, FBIS, NESA, *Daily Report*, September 26, 1995.

33. *al-Quds* (East Jerusalem), November 1, 1993, p. 11. *Filastin al-Muslima* (November 1993): 7. See also Muhammad Nazzal's statement in *Shihan* (Amman), April 22, 1994; FBIS, NESA, *Daily Report*, April 14, 1994.

34. *al-Dustur* (Jordan), April 11, 1995, p. 29; Muhammad Nazzal to *Voice of the Islamic Republic of Iran* (Arabic), August 8, 1995, FBIS-NESA, *Daily Report*, August 9, 1995; Ali al Jarbawi, "The Position of Palestinian Islamists on the Palestine-Israel Accord," *Muslim World* 83, nos. 1–2 (January–April 1994): 152–153.

35. Graham Usher, "Arafat's Opening," *New Statement and Society* 8, no. 82 (December 1, 1995): 25; Sami Aboudi, "Palestinian Militants Rail Against False Democracy," *Reuters*, January 19, 1996.

36. For a report on the pall (the sample included 1,271 people), see *Ha'aretz*, June 2, 1995.

37. *Biladi—Jerusalem Times*, October 27, 1995, pp. 17–19; *News from Within* (Jerusalem) (November 1995): 10.

38. Interviews with Ibrahim Ghawsha for *Radio Monte Carlo* (Arabic), October 12, 1995, FBIS-NESA, *Daily Report*, October 13, 1995; *al-Ra'i* (Jordan), October 25, 1995. Mahmud al-Zahar affirmed Hamas's response to the PA's request, *al-Dustur* (Jordan), February 19, 1996, p. 25.

39. Quoted from *al-Watan (Gaza), Biladi—Jerusalem Times,* October 27, 1995.

40. *News from Within* (Jerusalem) (November 1995): 17.

41. *Biladi—Jerusalem Times,* November 17, 1995, p. 2.

42. On Arafat's efforts to convince Hamas and other Palestinian groups to take part in the elections or join Fatah's lists of candidates, see Andoni, "The Palestinian Elections"; *al-Nas wal-Intikhabat,* December 12, 1995.

43. As'ad Ghanem, "Founding Elections in Transitional Period: The First Palestinian General Elections," *Middle East Journal* 50, no. 4 (1996): 4–8.

44. *Biladi—Jerusalem Times,* January 26, 1996. In an interview with *al-Hayat* (London), February 6, 1996, pp. 1, 6, Arafat argued that five of Hamas's members had been elected; Khalil Shikaki, "The Palestinian Elections: An Assessment," *Journal of Palestine Studies* 25, no. 3 (Spring 1996): 18; Andoni, "The Palestinian Elections," p. 5. For slightly different data, see As'ad Ghanem, *Ha-Behirot ha-Falastiniot ha-Klaliyot ha-Rishonot, January 1996—Mivhan ha-Demokratya* [The first general Palestinian elections, January 1996—the test of democracy] (Giv'at Haviva: ha-Makhon le-Heker ha-Shalom, 1996), pp. 16, 18. The general voter turnout was 75.86 percent—73.5 percent in the West Bank and 86.77 in the Gaza Strip.

45. Huntington, *The Third Wave,* pp. 182–186.

46. Our description of Arafat's manipulative strategies in the elections is partly based on Adir Waldman, "Democratic Opposition in Palestine," seminar paper, Department of Political Science, Yale University, 1996.

47. "Peace Monitor," *Journal of Palestine Studies* 25, no. 1 (Autumn 1995): 106.

48. *Al-Nas wal-Intikhabat,* January 20, 1996, p. 5; Andoni, "The Palestinian Elections," pp. 9–10.

49. Graham Usher, "Arafat's Opening," *New Statesman and Society* 8, no. 82 (December 1, 1995): 25.

50. Arend Lijphart, *Election Systems and Party Systems* (Oxford: Oxford University Press, 1994), p. 20.

51. Martin Peretz, "Global Vision," *The New Republic,* January 22, 1996, p. 12; Ethan Eisenberg, "Democracy in Gaza: An Election Diary," *Congress Monthly* 63, no. 2 (March–April 1996): 9.

52. Shyam Bhatia, "Vote Arafat for Dictator, *"The Observer,* January 14, 1996, p. 21.

53. *al-Watan* (Gaza), January 19, 1995, pp. 8–9.

54. Sheikh Jamal Salim, "al-Hizb al-Siyasi al-Islami: Min Mutatallabat al-Marhala" (The Islamic political party: A necessity of the [current] stage), *al-Quds* (East Jerusalem), June 10, 1994; Muhammad al-Hindi, "al-Islamiyyun wal-Taswiya" (The Islamists and the settlement), *al-Quds* (East Jerusalem), July 1, 1994; interview with Mahmud al-Zahar for *al-Quds* (East Jerusalem), November 28, 1994; interview with Muhammad Nazzal for *al-Urdun* (Jordan), February 5, 1996, FBIS, NESA, *Daily Report,* February 6, 1996.

55. Interview with Musa Abu Marzuq for *Filastin al-Muslima* (June 1994): 16; Interview with 'Abdallah al-Shami, leader of the Islamic Jihad in Gaza, for *al-Quds* (East Jerusalem), December 17, 1994; interview with Ibrahim Ghawsha for *Voice of*

the Islamic Republic of Iran (Arabic), August 17, 1995, FBIS-NESA, *Daily Report*, August 18, 1995.

56. *Time*, November 21, 1994; *Ha'aretz*, May 30, 1995.

57. Hamas (internal circular), "Siyasat wa-Madamin al-Khitab al-I'lami lil-Marhala al-Qadima Ithra Ittifaq Ghazza-Ariha" [Policies and contents of the propaganda speech in the next stage, following the Gaza-Jericho agreement], October 28, 1993.

58. Mahmud al-Zahar, "al-Qiwa al-Filastiniyya . . . wa-Intikhabat al-Hukm al-Dhati" [The Palestinian forces . . . and the elections of self-government], *Filastin al-Muslima* (October 1994): 30; Ibrahim Ghawsha to *Radio Monte Carlo* (Arabic), October 12, 1995, FBIS, NESA, *Daily Report*, October 13, 1995.

59. Interview with Rabi' 'Aql, a senior activist in Hamas, for *Sawt al-Haq wal-Hurriyya*, December 3, 1993.

60. Interview with Fakhri 'Abd al-Latif for *Ha'aretz*, December 17, 1995.

61. Interview with Mahmud al-Zahar for *Filastin al-Muslima* (June 1995): 14–15.

62. Isma'il Haniyya, *Filastin* (Gaza), September 30, 1994, FBIS, NESA, *Daily Report*, October 21, 1994; Muhammad H. Hamid, "al-Islamiyyun wal-Hizb al-Siyasi" [The Islamists and the political party], *al-Quds* (East Jerusalem), June 11, 1994.

63. There are five documents, each discussing a separate aspect of the party's foundation. The most important document was entitled "Mashru' Ta'sis Hizb Siyasi Islami" [Plan for establishing an Islamic party] (n.d.), which summarized the other documents. See also 'Imad Faluji's proposal for a party similar to the Islamic Action Front in *al-Quds* (East Jerusalem), June 22, 1994.

64. Interview with Ibrahim Ghawsha for *al-Mujtama'* (Kuwait), October 31, 1995, FBIS, NESA, *Daily Report*, December 7, 1995.

65. Hamas (internal document), "Al-Nizam al-Asasi lil-Hizb" [The party's basic law] (n.d.).

66. *Ha'aretz*, December 20, 1995.

67. Hamas, "Al-Nizam al-Asasi lil-Hizb."

68. Hamas, "Ta'rif al-Hizb wa-Ahdafuhu" [Definition of the party and its goals] (n.d.).

69. *al-Nahar* (East Jerusalem), November 24 and December 17, 1995.

70. *al-Quds* (East Jerusalem), December 17, 20, 1995.

71. *al-Quds* (East Jerusalam), March 22, 1996. Isma'il Abu Shanab was still in an Israeli prison, and Ahmad Bahr was in a Palestinian prison.

72. See for example, *Ha'aretz*, July 24, 1998.

Notes to Chapter Six: Patterns of Adjustment

1. UPI release, January 17, 1982; for more details, see Anis F. Kassim, "The Palestine Liberation Organization's Claim to Status: A Juridical Analysis Under International Law," *Denver Journal of International Law and Policy* 9, no. 1 (1980): 19–22, 29, 30.

2. For more details, see Aaron David Miller, *The PLO and the Politics of Survival* (Washington, D.C.: Georgetown University Center for Strategic and International Studies, 1983), pp. 97–98.

3. On the "enclave" concept and its social and symbolic dimensions in a comparative context, see Emmanuel Sivan, "Tartbut ha-Muvla'at" [The enclave culture], *Alpayim* 4 (1991): 94–95.

4. For additional structural features of social movements, see David Knoke, *Political Networks, the Structural Perspective* (Cambridge: Cambridge University Press, 1990), p. 490.

5. On the Sufi influence on Hasan al-Banna, see Richard P. Mitchell, *The Society of the Muslim Brothers* (Oxford: Oxford University Press, 1969), pp. 1–6.

6. David Farhi, "ha-Mo'atza ha-Muslemit be-Mizrah Yerushalayim 'ube-Yehuda ve-Shomron me-'Az Milhemet Sheshet ha-Yamim" [The Muslim Council in East Jerusalem and Judea and Samaria since the six-day war], *Ha-Mizrah He-Hadash* 28 (1979): 3–21.

7. Ifrah Zilberman, "Hitpathut ha-Islam ha-Kitzoni ba-Shtahim me-'Az 1967" [The development of radical Islam in the territories since 1967], in M. Ma'oz and B. Z. Kedar, eds., *Ha-Tnu'a ha-Le'umit ha-Falastinit: Me-'Immut le-Hashlama?* [The Palestinian national movement: From confrontation to acquiescence?] (Tel Aviv: Ma'arachot, 1996), pp. 321–347.

8. On the features of formal organizations and social movements, see Knoke, *Political Networks*, pp. 75–76, 91–98.

9. A. Shabi and R. Shaked, *Hamas: me-Emuna be-Allah le-Derekh ha-Teror* [Hamas: From belief in Allah to the road of terror] (Jerusalem: Keter, 1994), p. 81.

10. *Ha'aretz*, December 16, 1990.

11. Shabi and Shaked, *Hamas*, pp. 119–121.

12. "A Guide to the Muslim Student," cited in Udi Levi, "Hashivut ha-Da'wa 'u-Missuda ba-Tnu'ot ha-Islamiyot" [The Importance of *da'wa* and its institutionalization in the Muslim movements], seminar paper, Department of International Relations, Hebrew University of Jerusalem, 1997.

13. Shabi and Shaked, *Hamas*, pp. 282–284.

14. Ibid., pp. 118, 124.

15. Ibid., p. 119.

16. See for instance, the statements by Ibrahim al-Yazuri, AFP (Paris), October 13, 1994, FBIS, NESA, *Daily Report*, October 14, 1994; interviews with Mahmud al-Zahar, *al-Hayat* (London), October 17, 1994, *al-Hayat al-Jadida* (Gaza), April 24, 1995, p. 5, FBIS, NESA, *Daily Report*, April 27, 1995.

17. T. Burns and G. Stalker, *The Management of Innovations* (London: Tavistock, 1961), cited in Dennis A. Rodinelli, *Development Projects as Policy Experiments*, 2d ed. (London: Routledge, 1993), p. 163.

18. Interview with a senior Israeli official in charge of antiterrorist warfare, May 27, 1998.

19. According to another version, the Advisory Council has twenty-four members. See *al-Wasat*, November 30, 1992.

20. *al-Shira'*, January 4, 1993.

21. Shabi and Shaked, *Hamas*, p. 154.

22. *al-Wasat*, November 30, 1992, and February 22, 1993.

23. For details, see Shabi and Shaked, *Hamas,* p. 154.

24. Ibid., p. 152.

25. *al-Mujtama'* (Kuwait), October 31, 1995, pp. 32–33; FBIS-NESA, *Daily Report,* December 7, 1995, p. 11.

26. *Radio Monte Carlo* (Paris), November 20, 1994; FBIS-NESA, *Daily Report,* November 22, 1994, p. 16.

27. *Voice of Palestine* (Jericho), October 10, 1995; FBIS-NESA, *Daily Report,* October 11, 1995, pp. 23–24.

28. FBIS-NESA, *Daily Report,* October 12, and October 13, 1995, p. 5.

29. T. E. Lawrence, *Seven Pillars of Wisdom: A Triumph* (Garden City, N.Y.: Doubleday, 1938), p. 38.

30. Ira Sharkansky, "The Potential of Ambiguity: The Case of Jerusalem," in Efraim Karsh, ed., *From Rabin to Netanyahu* (London: Frank Cass, 1997), p. 191.

Notes to Appendix One: Hamas's Internal Structure

1. For a comparison with another Islamic movement with a similar structure, such as the Islamic Tendency Movement of Tunisia, see François Burgat and William Dowell, *The Islamic Movement in North Africa* (Austin: University of Texas Press, 1993), p. 189.

2. The Hamas leadership outside the West Bank and the Gaza Strip—the full list of members and functions is officially unknown. Its prominent members include Khalid Mash'al (chairman since 1995), Musa Abu Marzuq (chairman, 1989–1995), 'Imad al-'Alami (representative in Syria since 1998), Muhammad Nazzal (representative in Jordan), Ibrahim Ghawsha (spokesman), Mustafa Liddawi (representative in Lebanon), Mustafa Qanu' (representative in Iran since 1998), and 'Usama Hamdan (representative in Sudan).

3. A group of influential figures in the West Bank and Gaza operating informally and in a decentralized manner.

4. A title for all operational military units, informally based on geographic district.

5. Five are in the West Bank (Jenin, Tulkarm, Nablus, Ramallah, and Hebron), and seven are in the Gaza Strip (Gaza, Rafah, Dair al-Balah, Jabaliyya, Khan Yunis, Shati', and Nusairat), with functions similar to those of the Political Bureau.

6. Between 1996 and 1998, military activities in the West Bank were carried out by units from Hebron, Jerusalem, and the northern region of the West Bank. They were nominally controlled by Hamas's Political Bureau in Amman. Since the establishment of the Palestinian Authority in the Gaza Strip, the military units of 'Izz al-Din al-Qassam have had difficulty operating in the Gaza Strip, raising doubts about their ability to operate as district apparatuses.

Notes to Appendix Two: The Charter of the Islamic Resistance Movement

1. There is no official English version of Hamas charter. A translation by Muhammad Maqdsi in 1990 for the Islamic Association for Palestine, in Dallas, Texas, has since been considered a semiofficial one. For the full text of this version, see the

Journal of Palestine Studies 22, 4 (Summer 1993): 122–134. We, however, have revised it, for the sake of clarity, fluidness, and precision. For another translated version of the charter, see Raphael Israeli, "The Charter of Allah: The Platform of the Islamic Resistance Movement (Hamas)," in Y. Alexander, A. H. Foxman, and E. Mastrangelo (contibuting ed.), *The 1988–1989 Annual on Terrorism* (The Hague: Nijhoff, 1990), pp. 109–132. Unless otherwise mentioned, translations of quotations from the Qur'an (Koran) are from George Sale, *The Koran*, trans. into English from the original Arabic (London: Warne, n.d.). The only departure is the word God, which we have replaced with the word Allah.

2. Hamas means "force and bravery": see *al-Mu'jam al-Wasit*, vol. 1 (original reference).

3. A prominent Indian-Muslim thinker and theologian.

4.'Izz al-Din al-Qassam was killed in November 1935 in a battle with British soldiers in northern Samaria. His disciples, however, adopted al-Qassam's concept of jihad. They came to be known as Ikhwan al-Qassam, or Qassamiyyun and some of them played a leading role during the 1936–1939 Arab revolt in Palestine. History has been rewritten here, appropriating the heroic image of al-Qassam and his followers by referring to them as "Muslim Brothers", a movement that did not yet officially exist in Palestine.

5. Members of the Muslim Brotherhood from Egypt, Syria, Sudan, and Libya who volunteered to fight against the Jews in support of the Palestinian Arabs, constituted the largest contingent of a single ideological movement that operated in the Palestine war of 1948.

6. Imam Muslim, *Sahih Muslim*, vol. 4, trans. Hamid Siddiki (Lahore: Sh. Muhammad Ashraf, 1976), p. 1510, hadith no. 6985 (according to Maqdsi's translation of the charter, *Journal of Palestine Studies* 22 (4) (Summer 1993): 124.

7. Originally (*Hadith*) *Marfu'*.

8. Originally (*Hadith*) *Mawquf*.

9. *Qibla* is the direction in which Muslims face during prayer. The Muslims were first instructed to face Jerusalem in their prayers, apparently in an attempt to attract the Jews of Hijaz to the new faith. However, when this expectation was frustrated, the Prophet Muhammad ordered his followers to face Mecca in their prayers, reflecting the political and symbolic significance of this city to the peoples of Arabia.

10. Islam's two holiest sanctuaries are located in Mecca and Medina.

11. Umma is the community of Muslim believers.

12. General Allenby was the chief commander of the Allied forces that conquered Palestine and Syria. For his alleged statement, see the next note.

13. General Gouraud was the first French high commissioner in Syria. Such arguments, relating the same statements to the British and French generals, had, until the 1960s, been repeatedly made by Arab nationalist spokesmen in their attacks on Western imperialism.

14. Referring to the verse in the Qur'an, cited in article 14 of the charter, about the

Prophet's night journey (Isra') from the Holy Mosque in Mecca to the al-Aqsa Mosque and his ascension (Mi'raj) from it to heaven.

15. Imam al-Bukhari, *Sahih al-Bukhari*, vol. 4, trans. M. M. Khan (Istanbul: Hilaal yayinlari), p. 91, hadith no. 142. The Hadith and reference are quoted in Maqdsi's translation of the charter, *Journal of Palestine* 22 (4) (Summer 1993): 127.

16. Abdul Hamid Siddique, trans., *Selections from Hadith* (Kuwait: Islamic Book Publishers), p. 160. The hadith and reference are quoted in Maqdsi's translation of the charter, ibid..

17. Sunna is the Prophet Muhammad's sayings and doings.

18. Jahiliyya is the term for the pre-Islamic era, which is usually depicted as one of idolatry, ignorance, darkness, lawlessness, and oppression, in diametric contrast to the revelation of Islam to the Prophet Muhammad.

19. Namely, the Ottoman Empire, which was carved up after its defeat in the war, followed by the abolition of the Islamic caliphate in 1924 by the Republican Turkish government headed by Kemal Pasha.

20. Ijtihad is either creative self-exertion to derive legislation from the *shari'a* (Islamic law)—a practice that ended in the thirteenth century—or, more likely, an effort for the sake of Allah and in dedication to him.

21. Namely, the Qur'an and the Sunna.

22. *Al-'ilmaniyya*—means no religiosity (*la diniyya*), secularism (original reference). The article refers to the acceptance by the PNC in 1969 of a decision supporting the establishment of a "secular and democratic state" over the whole territory of Palestine.

23. A town at the northeastern corner of the Sinai peninsula.

24. Originally, Bait al-Maqdis (Holy House). The term was used to denote Jerusalem and then Palestine as a whole.

Books and Articles in Arabic and Hebrew

'Abd al-Majid, Wahid, ed. "al-Intifada al-Filastiniyya: al-Siyaq al-Tarikhi, al-Qiwa al-Fa'ila, al-Masar wal-Mustaqbal" [The Palestinian uprising: The historical context, the acting forces, the course and future] (a symposium). *al-Mustaqbal al-'Arabi* 11 (May 1988): 6–33.

'Abd al-Rahman, 'Uns. *al-Qadiyya al-Filastiniyya Bayn Mithaqain: al-Mithaq al-Watani al-Filastini wa-Mithaq Harakat al-Muqawama al-Islamiyya (Hamas)* [The Palestinian question between two charters: The Palestinian national charter and the charter of the Islamic resistance movement (Hamas)]. Kuwait: Maktab Dar al-Bayan, 1989.

'Adwan, 'Atif. *al-Sheikh Ahmad Yasin, hayatuhu wa-jihaduhu* [Sheikh Ahmad Yasin, his life and jihad]. Gaza: al-Jami'a al-Islamiyya, 1991.

'Azzam, 'Abdallah. *al-Difa' 'An Aradi al-Muslimin Ahamm Furud al-A'yan* [The defense of Muslims' lands, the most important of individuals' duties]. Jidda: Dar al-Mujtama', 1987.

al-Barghuthi, Iyad. *al-Aslama wal-Siyasa fi al-Aradi al-Filastiniyya al-Muhtalla* [Islamization and politics in the Palestinian occupied lands]. Jerusalem: Markaz al-Zahra lil-Dirasat wal-Abhath, 1990.

———. *al-Haraka al-Islamiyya al-Filastiniyya wal-Nizam al-'Aalami al-Jadid* [The Palestinian Islamic movement and the new world order]. Jerusalem: al-Jam'iyya al-Filastiniyya al-Akadimiyya lil-Shu'un al-Dawliyya, 1992.

Bin Yusuf, Ahmad. *Harakat al-Muqawama al-Islamiyya Hamas, Khalfiyyat al-Nash'a wa-Aafaq al-Masir* [The Islamic resistance movement Hamas, its emergence and horizons of action]. Worth, Ill.: al-Markaz al-'Aalami lil-Buhuth wal-Dirasat, 1989.

Farhi, David. "Ha-Mo'atza ha-Muslemit be-Mizrah Yerushalayim 'ube-Yehuda ve-Shomron Me'az Milhemet Sheshet ha-Yamim" [The Muslim Council in East Jerusalem and Judea and Samaria since the six-day war]. *Ha-Mizrah he-Hadash* 28 (1979): 3–21.

Frisch, Hillel. "Mi-Ma'avak Mezuyan le-Giyus Polity: Tmurot ba-Astrategia shel Ashaf ba-Shtahim" [From armed struggle to political mobilization: Changes in the PLO's strategy in the territories]. In G. Gilbar and A. Susser, eds., *Be-'Ein ha-Sikhsukh: ha-Intifada* [In the eye of the conflict: The uprising], pp. 40–67. Tel Aviv: ha-Kibutz ha-Me'uhad, 1992.

Ghanem, As'ad. *ha-Behirot ha-Falastiniyot ha-Klaliyot ha-Rishonot, January 1996— Mivhan ha-Demokratya* [The first general Palestinian elections, January 1996—The test of democracy]. Giv'at Haviva: ha-Makhon le-Heker ha-Shalom, June 1996.

al-Ghanouchi, Rashed. *Mahawir Islamiyya* [Islamic poles]. Cairo: Bait al-Ma'rifa, 1992.

Ghara'ibah, A. *Jama'at al-Ikhwan al-Muslimin fi al-Urdun 1946–1996*. Amman: Markaz al-Urdun al-Jadid lil-Dirasat, 1997.

Hala, Mustafa. "al-Tayar al-Islami fi al-Ard al-Muhtalla" [The Islamic current in the occupied land]. *al-Mustaqbal al-'Arabi* 113 (August 1988): 75–89.

al-Hamad, Jawad, and Iyad al-Barghuthi, eds. *Dirasa fi al-Fikr al-Siyasi li-Harakat al-Muqawama al-Islamiyya (Hamas), 1987–1996* [A study of the political thought of the Islamic resistance movement (Hamas), 1987–1996]. Amman: Markaz Dirasat al-Sharq al-Awsat, 1997.

Hamas. "al-Haqiqa wal-Wujud" [The truth and the existence] (a semiofficial history of Hamas), 1990.

Harkabi, Yehoshafat. *Fatah ba-Astrategia ha-'Arvit* [Fatah in the Arab strategy]. Tel Aviv: Ma'arakhot, 1969.

al-Hut, Bayan Nuwaihid. *al-Sheikh al-Mujahid 'Izz al-Din al-Qassam Fi Tarikh Filastin* [The holy warrior Sheikh 'Izz al-Din al-Qassam in the history of Palestine]. Acre: Dar al-Aswar, 1988.

al-Kharub, Khalid. "Harakat Hamas Bayn al-Sulta al-Filastiniyya wa-Isra'il: Min Muthallath al-Qiwa Ila al-Matraqa wal-Sandan" [The Hamas movement between the Palestinian Authority and Israel: From the triangle of forces to the hammer and anvil]. *Majallat al-Dirasat al-Filastiniyya*, no. 18 (1994): 24–37.

Levenberg, Hayim. " 'ha-Akhim ha-Muslemim' be-Eretz Israel 1945–1948" ['The Muslim Brothers' in Palestine 1945–1948]. Master's thesis, Tel Aviv University, 1983.

Litvak, Meir, ed. *Islam ve-Demokratya ba-'Olam ha-'Arvi* [Islam and democracy in the Arab world]. Tel-Aviv: Dayan Center, Tel Aviv University, ha-Kibutz ha-Me'uhad, 1998.

Ma'oz, M., and B. Z. Kedar, eds. *Ha-Tenu'a ha-Le'umit ha-Falastinit: me-'Imut le-Hashlama?* [The Palestinian national movement: From confrontation to acquiescence]. Tel Aviv: Ma'arakhot, 1996.

Mayer, Thomas. *Hit'orerut ha-Muslemim be-Israel* [The Muslims' awakening in Israel]. Giv'at Haviva: ha-Makhon le-Limudim 'Arviyim, 1988.

Qasim, 'Abd al-Sattar. *Ayyam fi Mu'taqal al-Naqab* [Days in the Negev prison]. Jerusalem: Lajnat al-Difa' 'an al-Thaqafa al-Wataniyya al-Filastiniyya, 1989.

al-Qaradawi, Yusuf. *al-Hall al-Islami, Farida wa-Darura* [The Islamic solution, a duty and necessity]. 5th ed. Cairo: Maktabat Wahaba, 1993.

———. *Awlawiyyat al-Haraka al-Islamiyya fi al-Marhala al-Qadima* [The Islamic movement's preferences in the coming phase]. Beirut: Mu'assassat al-Risala, 1991.

Shabi, A., and R. Shaked. *Hamas: me-Emuna be-Allah le-Derekh ha-Teror* [Hamas: From belief in Allah to the road of terror]. Jerusalem: Keter, 1994.

Sivan, Emmanuel. "Jihad, Mitos ve-Historia" [Jihad, myth and history]. *Alpayim* 11 (1995): 9–21.

———. "Tarbut ha-Muvla'at" [The enclave culture]. *Alpayim* 4 (1991): 45–98.

Takruri, N. Ha'il. *al-'Amaliyyat al-Istishhadiyya fi al-Mizan al-Fiqhi* [The suicide operations in jurisprudence view]. Damascus: Maktabat al-Asad, 1997.

al-Tamimi, 'Azzam. *Musharakat al-Islamiyyin fi al-sulta* [The Islamists' sharing in power]. London: Liberty for the Muslim World, 1994.

Tawila, 'Abd al-Sattar. *al-Sheikh al-Mujahid 'Izz al-Din al-Qassam* [The holy warrior Sheikh 'Izz al-Din al-Qassam]. Beirut: Dar al-Umma lil-Nashr, 1984.

al-Turabi, Hasan. "al-Haraka al-Islamiyya fi al-Sudan" [The Islamic movement in Sudan]. n.p., n.d.

———. "al-Sahwa al-Islamiyya wal-Dawla al-Qutriyya fi al-Watan al-'Arabi" [The Islamic awakening and the territorial state in the Arab homeland]. In *al-Sahwa al-Islamiyya: Ru'ya Naqdiyya min al-Dakhil* [The Islamic awakening: A critical view from within], pp. 86–108. Beirut: al-Nashir lil-Tiba'a wal-Nashr wal-Tawzi' wal-I'lan, 1990.

Tzahal, Ha-Minhal ha-Ezrahi. *Ha-Pe'ilut ha-Islamit be-Hevel 'Aza* [IDF, the civil administration, the Islamic activity in the Gaza region]. Gaza: IDF, 1987.

Weissbrod, Amir. "ha-Islam ha-Radikali be-Sudan: Hagut u-Ma'ase—Mishnato ha-Datit veha-Politit Shel Hasan al-Turabi" [Radical Islam in Sudan: Thought and practice—The religious and political doctrine of Hasan al-Turabi]. Master's thesis, Hebrew University of Jerusalem, January 1997.

Yakan, Fathi. *Nahwa Haraka Islamiyya 'Aalamiyya Wahida* [Toward one global Islamic movement]. 3d ed. Beirut: Mu'assassat al-Risala, 1977.

Zilberman, Ifrah. "ha-Mishpat ha-Minhagi ke-Ma'arekhet Hevratit be-Merhav Yerushalayim" [Customary law as a social system in the area of Jerusalem]. *Ha-Mizrah he-Hadash* 33 (1991): 70–93.

Books and Articles in English

Abed-Qotob, Sana. "The Accommodationists Speak: Goals and Strategies of the Muslim Brotherhood of Egypt." *International Journal of Middle East Studies* 27 (1995): 321–339.

Abu-Amr, Ziad. *Islamic Fundamentalism in the West Bank and Gaza Strip.* Bloomington: Indiana University Press, 1994.

Ahmad, Hisham. *Hamas.* Jerusalem: PASSIA, 1994.

Andoni, Lamis. "The Palestinian Elections: Moving Toward Democracy or One-Party Rule?" *Journal of Palestine Studies* 25, no. 3 (Spring 1996): 5–16.

Azem, A. J. "The Islamic Action Front." In J. Schwedler, ed., *Islamic Movements in Jordan,* pp. 95–144. Amman: al-Urdun al-Jadid Research Center, 1977.

al-Azmeh, Aziz. *Islams and Modernities.* London: Verso, 1993.

Bailey, F. G. *Strategems and Spoils: A Social Anthropology of Politics.* New York: Schocken Books, 1969.

Bar, Shmuel. *The Muslim Brotherhood in Jordan.* Tel Aviv: Moshe Dayan Center, Tel Aviv University, 1998.

Benningsen, A. "The National Front in Communist Strategy in the Middle East." In Walter Laqueur, ed., *The Middle East in Transition,* pp. 351–360. London: Routledge & Kegan Paul, 1958.

Bhabha, Homi K. "DissemiNation: Time, Narrative and the Margins of the Modern Nation." In Homi K. Bhabha, ed., *Nation and Narration,* pp. 290–322. London: Routledge, 1994.

Brockelmann, Carl. *History of the Islamic People.* New York: Capricorn, 1960.

Burgat, François, and William Dowell. *The Islamic Movement in North Africa.* Austin Center for Middle Eastern Studies, University of Texas, 1993.

Burns, T., and G. Stalker. *The Management of Innovations.* London: Tavistock, 1961.

Caton, Steven C. "Power, Persuasion, and Language: A Critique of the Segmentary Model in the Middle East." *International Journal of Middle East Studies* 1 (February 1987): 77–102.

Cohen, Amnon. *Political Parties in the West Bank Under Jordanian Rule 1948–1967.* Ithaca, N.Y.: Cornell University Press, 1980.

Druckman, Daniel, and Christopher Mitchell. "Flexibility in Negotiation and Mediation." *Annals,* no. 542 (November 1995).

Eisenberg, Ethan. "Democracy in Gaza: An Election Diary." *Congress Monthly* 63, no. 2 (March–April 1996): 9–13.

Eickelman, Dale F., and James Piscatori. *Muslim Politics.* Princeton, N.J.: Princeton University Press, 1996.

———. "Social Theory in the Study of Muslim Societies." In Dale F. Eickelman and James Piscatori, eds., *Muslim Travelers: Pilgrimage, Migration, and the Religious Imagination,* pp. 1–25. London: Routledge, 1990.

Esposito, John L., and James P. Piscatori. "Democratization and Islam." *Middle East Journal* 45, no. 3 (Summer 1991): 427–440.

Fricsh, Hillel. "The Evolution of Palestinian Nationalist Islamic Doctrine: Territorializing a Universal Religion." *Canadian Review in Nationalism* 21, nos. 1–2 (1994): 45–55.

Gelner, Ernest. *Nations and Nationalism.* Ithaca, N.Y.: Cornell University Press, 1983.

Ghanem, As'ad. "Founding Elections in Transitional Period: The First Palestinian General Elections." *Middle East Journal* 50, no. 4 (1996): 513–528.

Hobsbawm, Eric. *Nations and Nationalism Since 1780: Programme, Reality.* Cambridge: Cambridge University Press, 1990.

Huntington, Samuel P. *The Third Wave.* Norman: University of Oklahoma Press, 1991.

Islam, Democracy, the State and the West: A Round Table with Dr. Hasan Turabi, May 19, 1992. World and Islam Studies Enterprise and the University of South Florida, Committee for Middle East Studies.

Israeli, Raphael. "The Charter of Allah: The Platform of the Islamic Resistance Movement (Hamas)." In Y. Alexander and A.H. Foxman (eds.), E. Mastragelo (contributing ed.), *The 1988–1989 Annual on Terrorism* (The Hague: Martinus Nijhoff Publishers, 1990), pp. 109–132.

al Jarbawi, Ali. "The Position of Palestinian Islamists on the Palestine-Israel Accord." *The Muslim World* 83, nos. 1–2 (January–April 1994): 127–154.

Kassim, Anis F. "The Palestine Liberation Organization's Claim to Status: A Juridical Analysis Under International Law." *Denver Journal of International Law and Policy* 9, no. 1 (1980): 19–30.

Kepel, Gilles. *Muslim Extremism in Egypt: The Prophet and the Pharaoh.* Berkeley and Los Angeles: University of California Press, 1985.

Kjorlien, M. L. "Hamas in Theory and Practice." *Arab Studies Journal* 1, no. 2 (1993): 4–7.

Knoke, David. *Political Networks: The Structural Perspective.* Cambridge: Cambridge University Press, 1990.

Kramer, G. "The Integration of the Integrist: A Comparative Study of Egypt, Jordan and Tunisia." In Ghassan Salame, ed., *Democracy Without Democrats? The Renewal of Politics in the Muslim World*, pp. 200–226. London: Tauris, 1994.

Kramer, Martin. "Fundamentalist Islam at Large: The Drive for Power." *Middle East Quarterly* 3, no. 2 (June 1996): 37–49.

Lahman, Shay. "Sheikh 'Izz al-Din al-Qassam." In Elie Kedourie and Silvia Haim, eds., *Zionism and Arabism in Palestine and Israel*, pp. 54–99. London: Frank Cass, 1982.

Lapidus, Ira M. "Islam Political Movements: Patterns of Historical Change." In Edmund Burke and Ira M. Lapidus, eds., *Islam, Politics, and Social Movements*, pp. 3–35. Berkeley and Los Angeles: University of California Press, 1988.

Lawrence, T. E. *Seven Pillars of Wisdom: A Triumph.* Garden City, N.Y.: Doubleday, 1938.

Legrain, J. F. "Hamas: Legitimate Heir of Palestinian Nationalism?" In John L. Esposito, ed., *Political Islam: Revolution, Radicalism or Reform*, pp. 159–178.
Boulder, Colo.: Lynne Rienner, 1997.

———. "Mobilisation islamiste et soulevement palestinien 1987–1988." In G. Kepel
and Y. Richard, eds., *Intellectuels et militants de l'Islam contemporain*, pp.
131–166. Paris: Seuil, 1990.

Lewis, Bernard. "Rethinking the Middle East." *Foreign Affairs* 71, no. 4 (Fall 1992):
99–119.

Lijphart, Arend. *Election Systems and Party Systems*. Oxford: Oxford University
Press, 1994.

Litani, Y. "The Militant Islam in the West Bank and Gaza Strip." *New Outlook* 32,
nos. 11–12 (November–December 1989): 40–42.

(Maqdsi, Muhammad). "The Charter of the Islamic Resistance Movement
(Hamas)," *Journal of Palestine Studies*, XXII, no. 4 (Summer 1993), pp.
122–134.

Mawdudi, Abu-l-'Ala'. "Political Theory of Islam." In John J. Donohue and John J.
Esposito, eds., *Islam in Transition*, pp. 252–271. New York: Oxford University Press, 1982.

Mayer, Tomas. "Pro-Iranian Fundamentalism in Gaza." In E. Sivan and M. Friedman, eds., *Religious Radicalism and Politics in the Middle East*, pp. 142–155.
Albany: State University of New York Press, 1990.

Meijer, R. *From al-Da'wa to al-Hizbiyya: Mainstream Islamic Movements in Egypt,
Jordan and Palestine in the 1990s*. Amsterdam: Research Center for International Political Economy, 1997.

Miller, Aaron David. *The PLO and the Politics of Survival*. Washington, D.C.:
Georgetown University Center for Strategic and International Studies, 1983.

Mir, Mustansir. "Jihad in Islam." In Hadia Dajani-Shakeel and Ronald A. Messier,
eds., *The Jihad and Its Times*, pp. 113–126. Ann Arbor: University of Michigan Press, 1991.

Mishal, Shaul, and Reuven Aharoni. *Speaking Stones, Communiqués from the Intifada
Underground*. Syracuse, N.Y.: Syracuse University Press, 1994.

Mitchell, Richard P. *The Society of the Muslim Brothers*. Oxford: Oxford University
Press, 1969.

Niblock, Tim. "Islamic Movements and Sudan's Political Coherence." In H. Bleu-
chot, C. Delmet, and D. Hopewood, eds., *Sudan: History, Identity, Ideology*,
pp. 253–268. Reading, Pa.: Ithaca Press, 1991.

Olivier, Roy. *The Failure of Political Islam*. Cambridge, Mass.: Harvard University
Press, 1995.

Piscatori, James. *Islam in a World of Nation-States*. London: Royal Institute of International Affairs, 1983.

Porath, Yehoshua. *From Riots to Revolt: The Arab-Palestinian National Movement
1929–1939*. London: Frank Cass, 1974.

Robinson, Glenn E. *Building a Palestinian State, the Unfinished Revolution.* Bloomington: Indiana University Press, 1997.

———. "Can Islamists Be Democrats? The Case of Jordan." *Middle East Journal* 51, no. 3 (Summer 1997): 373–388.

Rodinelli, Dennis A. *Development Projects as Policy Experiments.* 2d ed. London: Routledge, 1993.

Rokeach, Milton. "Attitude Change and Behavioral Change." *Public Opinion Quarterly* 30 (1966–1967): 529–550.

Sale, George. *The Koran.* Translated into English from the original Arabic (London: Warne, n.d.).

Satloff, Robert. "Islam in the Palestinian Uprising." *Orbis* 33, no. 3 (Summer 1989): 389–401.

Schiff, Z., and E. Ya'ari. *Intifada, the Palestinian Uprising, Israel's Third Front.* New York: Simon & Schuster, 1989.

Sela, Avraham, and Moshe Ma'oz, eds. *The PLO and Israel: From Armed Conflict to Political Solution, 1964–1994.* New York: St. Martin's Press, 1997.

Sivan, Emmanuel. "Eavesdropping on Radical Islam." *Middle East Quarterly* 2, no. 1 (1995): 13–24.

———. *Radical Islam.* New Haven, Conn.: Yale University Press, 1985.

Sharkanski, Ira. "The Potential of Ambiguity: The Case of Jerusalem." In Efraim Karsh, ed., *From Rabin to Netanyahu*, pp. 187–200. London: Frank Cass, 1997.

Shikaki, Khalil. "The Palestinian Elections: An Assessment." *Journal of Palestine Studies* 25, no. 3 (Spring 1996): 17–22.

State of Israel, Ministry of Foreign Affairs. *Israeli-Palestinian Agreement on the West Bank and the Gaza Strip.* Jerusalem: Ministry of Foreign Affairs, 1995.

Steinberg, Matti. "The PLO and Palestinian Islamic Fundamentalism." *Jerusalem Quarterly*, no. 52 (1989): 37–54.

Turabi, Hasan. "Islam as a Pan-National Movement." *RSE Journal* (August–September 1992): 608–619.

Usher, Graham. "Arafat's Opening." *New Statement and Society* 8, no. 381 (December 1, 1995): 25.

Voll, O. John. "Fundamentalism in the Sunni Arab World: Egypt and Sudan." In Martin E. Marti and Scott R. Appleby, eds., *Fundamentalism Observed*, pp. 345–395. Chicago: University of Chicago Press, 1991.

Waldner, David. "Civic Exclusion and Its Discontents." Paper presented at the annual meeting of the American Political Science Association, New York City, September 1994.

Watts, Michael. "Islamic Modernities? Citizenship, Civil Society and Islamism in a Nigerian City." *Public Culture* 8 (1996): 251–289.

Ya'ari, Ehud. *Strike Terror: The Story of Fatah.* New York: Sabra Books, 1970.

Primary Sources, Periodicals, and Newspapers

PALESTINIAN

al-Bayadir al-Siyasi (East Jerusalem)
Biladi—Jerusalem Times (East Jerusalem)
Filastin (Gaza)
Filastin al-Muslima (London)
Filastin al-Thawra
al-Hayat al-Jadida (Gaza)
al-Istiqlal (Gaza)
Majallat al-Dirasat al-Filastiniyya
al-Manar (East Jerusalem)
al-Nahar (East Jerusalem)
al-Quds (East Jerusalem)
al-Rasid (noncirculating internal Hamas report)
al-Risala (circulating internal Hamas report)
Shu'un Filastiniyya (Nicosia)
al-Tahlil al-Siyasi (circulating internal Hamas report)
al-Watan (Gaza)

JORDAN

al-'Amal al-Islami
al-Dustur
Jordan Times
al-Muharrir
al-Ra'i
al-Sabil
al-Urdun

LEBANON

al-Diyar (Lebanon)
al-Mustaqbal al-'Arabi (London)
al-Shira' (Lebanon)

ISRAEL

Ha'aretz (Tel Aviv)
Ha-Mizrah he-Hadash (Jerusalem)
Kol Ha'ir (Jerusalem)
Kol Yerushalayim (Jerusalem)
Ma'ariv (Tel Aviv)
News from Within (Jerusalem)
Sawt al-Haqq wal-Hurriyya (Umm al-Fahm)
Yediot Aharonot (Tel Aviv)

OTHER ARAB AND FOREIGN NEWSPAPERS

al-Hayat (London)
FBIS-NESA, *Daily Report*
al-Mujtama' (Kuwait)
The New Republic (Washington, D.C.)
The Observer (London)
Qira'at Siyasiyya (Florida)
al-Sharq al-Awsat (Paris)
al-Wasat (London)
al-Watan al-'Arabi (Paris)

Jordan, 58, 65, 78, 87, 104, 112, 114, 117–118, 128; Hamas, policy toward, 162; Islamic Action Front of, 117–118; Islamic movement of, 8, 16, 18, 21–22, 24–25, 29, 31, 40–41, 43–44, 91, 105, 169, 218n4, 219n22; Jerusalem and the West Bank, 16–17, 43, 155

Khaybar, 52–53
Khalid Ibn al-Walid, 52
Khalidi, Isma'il al-, 19
Khalifa, 'Abd al-Rahman, 55
Khamena'i, 'Ali, 81, 97
Khan Yunis, 153
Khartoum, 99–100, 134
Knesset (Israel's parliament), 118
Kuwait, 88, 99, 112, 114, 164

Lawrence, T. E., 168
League of Nations, 189–190
Lebanon, 5, 14, 24, 30, 33, 39, 41, 78, 87, 89, 97, 108, 114, 118, 128, 149, 162
Lijphart, Arend, 137
Lions Clubs, 189, 193

Madina, al-, 108
Madrid Peace Conference, 65, 83, 86–87, 89–95, 97–98, 115, 119–120, 129
Majd, 34, 156, 173
Majlis Shura. See Advisory Council
Malta, 32
Mandela, Nelson, 96
Maqadma, Ibrahim, 76
Mash'al, Khalid, 72, 111, 162
Maslaha (interest, a theological principle), 86, 109, 115
Mawdudi Abu-l-A'la, 201–202n7
Mecca, 10, 89, 115, 185
Morocco, 114
Mosad, 72, 111, 162

Muhammad, 52
Mujahidun, 53. *See also Jihad*
Mujamma', al-Islami al-, 16, 18–24, 32–36, 40–41, 46, 49, 57, 87, 152–154, 156, 161, 173; attitude to and relations with Hamas, 35–36; control of Mosques by, 21–22, 204n15; Intifada, 35; *jihad* against Israel, 33–35, 42
Murabitun. See Frontier Guards
Muslim Brotherhood Society, viii, 5, 8, 16, 25, 28–29, 113, 115, 117–118, 128, 143–144, 153, 155, 177, 180, 202n7; political participation and principle of National Front of, 113–118, 202n11, 219n19; role of in Palestine War of 1948, 225n5
Muslim Brothers in Palestine. *See* Islamic movement in Palestine
Muslim World League (*Rabitat al-'aalam al-islami*), 24
Mu'ta (battle), 52
Mutual fighting (Palestinian) (*Taqtil, Iqtital*), Hamas's prohibition of, 85, 216n52

Nabhani, Taqi al-Din al-, 17
Nablus (including *al-Najah* University), 25, 36, 65, 71, 78, 90–91, 140, 166
Nahda, al- (Tunisia), 8, 115
Najah University, al-. *See* Nablus
Nasrallah, Hasan, 81
Nasser, Jamal 'Abdel (*also* Nasserism), 17, 29, 37–38, 42, 50, 115, 117
National Islamic Salvation Party (*Hizb al-khalas al-watani al-islami*), 144–145, 173
Nazzal, Muhammad, 162
Netanyahu, Benjamin, 72, 77, 145
Nusairat (refugee camp), 153

Organization of Jihad and Da'wa (*Majd*), 34